DON DUNPHY
at Ringside

DON DUNPHY

AT RINGSIDE

HENRY HOLT AND COMPANY
NEW YORK

To my wife, Muriel,
for her patience, her sense of humor,
and, of course, her help

And to Don Jr., Bob, Elsie, and Muz

Copyright © 1988 by Don Dunphy
Published by Henry Holt and Company, Inc.,
115 West 18th Street, New York, New York 10011.
Published in Canada by Fitzhenry & Whiteside Limited,
195 Allstate Parkway, Markham, Ontario L3R 4T8.

Library of Congress Cataloging-in-Publication Data
Dunphy, Don.
Don Dunphy at ringside / by Don Dunphy.—1st ed.
p.   cm.
Includes index.
ISBN 0-8050-0530-7
1. Dunphy, Don.   2. Sportscasters—United States—Biography.
3. Boxing—United States—History.   I. Title.
GV742.42.D86A3   1988
070.4'49796'0942—dc19
[B]   87-28098
                                                                    CIP

First Edition

Designed by Jeffrey L. Ward
Printed in the United States of America
1 3 5 7 9 10 8 6 4 2

ISBN 0-8050-0530-7

Contents

v

Contents

Sixteen pages of photographs begin on page 147.

Acknowledgments

Some who helped along the way: Herb Gluck, Rudy Riska, Harry Markson, Ralph Branca, Irwin Rosee, Alvin Cooperman, Murray Goodman, Spencer Drayton, LeRoy Neiman, Art Rust, Jr., Walter Kaner, Mike Cohen, Phil Ruggiero, Julie Weintraub, Barney Corrigan, Walter Kaner, Jack Butler, Ernie Braca, Bill Stynes, Don Freeman, Stan and Kay Maas, and my editor David Stanford.

Preface

Good evening, everyone—I'm Don Dunphy, your ringside commentator. With the many thousands who are here in the parking lot of Caesar's Palace in Las Vegas, I'm awaiting with eager anticipation the welterweight championship bout between Sugar Ray Leonard and Thomas Hearns."

The date was September 16, 1981. Forty years earlier, I had waited with equally eager anticipation for the start of another great championship bout, the one between the great Joe Louis and his famous challenger for the heavyweight championship of the world, Billy Conn.

Forty years! Little did I think that night of June 18, 1941, when I was about to do the blow-by-blow description of the greatest fight of its time, that forty years later I would be the ringside commentator for the greatest fight of yet another era.

Louis, Conn, Leonard, Hearns: only four of the great fighters who come flashing through my mind. Rocky Marciano, Sugar Ray Robinson, Willie Pep, Muhammad Ali, Joe Frazier, Carlos Monzon, Marvelous Marvin Hagler, Carmen Basilio, Rocky Graziano—I could go on and on, there have been hundreds. I don't have the space to mention all of them but I want to talk about the greatest and most interesting of them as we go along.

And I want to talk about the great fights—besides those I just mentioned, how about the Ali–Frazier bouts, Pep–Saddler, Marciano–Walcott, Robinson–Basilio. In forty years, I must have broadcast in the neighborhood of two thousand bouts, two hundred of which were title affairs, at least fifty in the heavyweight division alone. I wouldn't want you to get the impression that I thought they were all great. Even apples and eggs have an occasional stinker, and boxing has had its share. Great fights are often followed by terrible return bouts. Let us not forget such lemons as the second Louis–Conn, second Marciano–Walcott, second Ali–Liston, second Leonard–Duran, and so on. However, not all return bouts were duds. Robinson–Basilio and Graziano–Zale were as good as the originals.

Yes, there were nights when I sat there happy that the Good Lord had permitted me to be part of such a thrilling event. But there were others, believe me, when I said to myself, "What am I doing here?" and wished I were somewhere else. On the other hand, I didn't have to pay to get in. The famous fights come quickly to mind, but I also remember infamous ones—the two occasions when irate fans started to throw things at the ring, and I ended up under it saying, "This is Don Dunphy saying good night from under the ring at Madison Square Garden."

It wasn't all glamour and excitement. There were tragedies too, like the night that Benny "Kid" Paret was carried out of the Garden ring on a stretcher to die ten days later from the punches he took in a title bout with Emile Griffith. And there were lesser but also poignant tragedies, as when Joe Louis's ill-fated comeback took him into a bout with Rocky Marciano, and his career ended on the ring floor, or Muhammad Ali's futile effort to regain long-gone greatness which led him to a beating by Larry Holmes and then on to "The Trauma in the Bahamas" and his final bout, a disastrous defeat by Trevor Berbick. With Cardinal Wolsey, he could indeed have said, "Farewell! A long farewell, to all my greatness!"

But I didn't start out to be a boxing announcer. In the beginning, I wanted to do football and baseball, and along the way I did. I announced professional and college football, including the Cotton Bowl game; Yankees and Giants baseball and the 1944 World Series between the two St. Louis teams, the Cardinals and the Browns; the track meets at the Garden and the Drake Relays and the Penn Relays; the Garden basketball games and harness racing and professional bowling. But I guess, just as water seeks its own level, I ultimately settled in with boxing. That's how I became known as "The Voice of Boxing."

Many times during the last year I've asked myself, "Why am I writing this book?"

There are several reasons.

One is that so many people have said to me over the years, "Don, you should write a book." Young men and women who weren't even born when I was regularly at the ringside microphones have asked about my experiences, and are interested in my thoughts and ideas. For that reason I decided to write this, to invite them to go back with me through the years to see the sports scene as I saw it, and possibly feel it as I felt it.

And I know that there is a feeling of nostalgia in the air, an interest in earlier times. I've always reminisced, and that's what I'm going to do in these pages. It's not intended to be a history of boxing or of sports broadcasting on radio and television, but it is about those things.

Broadcasting has always had a certain fascination for me, and so have sports. When I was a youngster I was a good all-around athlete. I played baseball by the hour and at one time thought I might make the big leagues. What happened? "Good field, no hit," as the saying goes. I played a lot of football and a lot of basketball too. And I was on the track team at Manhattan College. But box? I never boxed. But when it came to broadcasting, guess what sport I found easiest to do? Boxing. It should have been baseball, which I knew inside out, but somehow, of them all, boxing just came easiest to me. Don't ask me why, it just did.

Here's another contradiction: I always knew sports, loved them, played them, then wrote about them, but I was never much on speaking. As a kid, I was shy and I lisped. But when I heard Ted Husing and Graham McNamee, in the early days of radio, I became fascinated with sports broadcasting. I used to walk down the street imitating Ted doing the Army–Notre Dame game. And if I went to a baseball game or a fight, I'd broadcast it to myself. My mother helped me get rid of the lisp by sending me for voice lessons.

I started out as a writer, and I'm ending up as one. But it's the in-between I want to tell you about. I want to tell you about the great fights (and the terrible ones), the great fighters, the sports announcers, and share some observations. I'll tell you who I think were the best fighters, and why. I'll tell you how we used to do things in the old days. Those of you who weren't around may be surprised. Those who were there with me will enjoy remembering. I hope you have as much pleasure reading as I have had writing.

PART ONE

Early Times

I was born on 39th Street in Manhattan. When I was about two, my father died and my mother moved to 103rd Street on the West Side between Columbus and Amsterdam avenues, and that's where I grew up. It was an ideal location. There was an entrance to Central Park, where we played baseball, and also an entrance to Riverside Drive. There was a subway station at 103rd and Broadway, and an elevated station for the Sixth and Ninth avenue trains at 104th and Columbus. The Polo Grounds, where the Giants and Yankees played baseball, was at 155th Street and Eighth Avenue. I could leave my house, grab an el train, and be at the Polo Grounds in twenty minutes. The Ascension School, where I went for eight years, was minutes away at 108th Street.

The Hudson River, a clean body of water in those days, was just off Riverside Park, and in the summer many of the neighborhood kids went swimming there. The New York Central freight trains ran on the tracks near Riverside Drive; they're covered over now for the West Side Highway, but then they were in full view. To go swimming, the kids would go down a slope to the tracks, climb up on an idle freight train, climb down the ladder on the other side, and run across to the river to swim at what became known as Bare Ass Beach. I never went in, but I did hop the freights.

My street was a mixture of apartment houses and brownstones. There must have been at least fifteen fellows in my age group, and we had great times, a lot of our attention going into sports. There was little automobile traffic in those days, which made the street great for stickball. Occasionally we'd play stoopball off one of the brownstones. This irritated some of the owners, and sometimes they'd call the police. I remember one day we were playing stoopball when Jack Mason came flying up the street on a pusho, which was a scooter made of a couple of boards and old roller skates. Jack had spotted a cop who had commandeered a cab and was crouched on the running board, coming after us. Jack was trying to warn us about the cop on the cab, but the cop was on us in no time at all. Most of the kids sped in the same direction, toward Columbus Avenue, as the cop ran brandishing his nightstick. Buster Finnerty and I figured that the law would chase the fleeing group, so we started in the opposite direction. This was a mistake. The cop made for us. I caught up quickly, stopped on a dime, and ran toward Columbus Avenue. Poor Buster practically ran into the cop's arms. He was hauled down to the police station on 100th Street and had to be bailed out by Rohr's ice cream store, where he worked after school. All this for a stoopball game.

We made up for our annoying stoopball games, though. Sometime during each winter, the kids on 103rd Street would hold their annual raffle. A book of ten chances would cost a dollar, and the winner of the drawing would receive five dollars. Don't snicker; that was good money in the twenties. The people on the street who enjoyed our stickball games from their windows were very good to us, and the raffle paid for the uniforms that our team, the Blue Sox, wore during the spring and summer. There were White Sox and Red Sox in the big leagues so we called ourselves the Blue Sox. (Get it? Red, White, and Blue.)

Our team, with its varied forebears, could have represented the League of Nations. By position, with ancestry and some nicknames, the team roster was as follows:

1B	Frank Holzer	Hungarian	Yankee
2B	Abie Fleischer	Jewish	Porky
S.S.	Don Dunphy	Irish	Donnie
3B	Joey Geller	Jewish	Yussel
LF	Tony DeMatteo	Italian	Tony
CF	Jack Devereaux	French	Jack
RF	Mike Kiely	Irish	Mike
C	Erwin McCrosky	?	Missouri
P	Eric Braun	Swedish	Swede
P	Carlos Lemmey	English	Carly
Mgr.	Edwin Finnerty	Irish	Buster

I had a routine for Saturdays in the spring and summer. Stickball in the morning until lunch, then to Van Cortlandt Park for baseball in the afternoon. After dinner, I played stickball until dark. My team put on quite a show, and the neighbors loved it as they watched the games from their stoops or windows. When it got dark I bought a sports magazine, a half-pint of ice cream, and a box of pound cake, and devoured them until bedtime. It was quite a day in quite an era in a wonderful neighborhood.

I always wanted to be connected with sports when I grew up. As a kid, in my neighborhood, you had to know sports. All of us did.

Baseball was big in those days, and most of us could quote the batting averages. The Giants and the Yankees both played in the Polo Grounds; Yankee Stadium was built later. Loyalties were divided equally between the two teams. Nobody cared for the Dodgers, over in Brooklyn, who were then known as the Brooklyn Robins in honor of their manager, Wilbert Robinson.

Pro football was practically a nonentity in New York, the National Football League consisting of such undefined teams as the Portsmouth Spartans, the Frankford Yellowjackets, and the Green Bay Packers. New York didn't have a team until 1924, and its star was Wally Koppisch, the former Columbia University back.

College football was fairly big in our thoughts, with the Big Three—Harvard, Yale, and Princeton—getting most of our attention. Notre Dame, with George Gipp as its star and Knute Rockne as its coach, was becoming prominent and soon would be our favorite as we joined the "Subway Alumni."

Basketball was about as big as pro football, which meant pygmy-size, although we knew about the Celtics. Parish houses had good local teams, and we went to many games at the Ascension Parish House on 108th Street, and at the West End Church on 105th. There was some interest in the local colleges, Columbia, Fordham, Manhattan, NYU, St. John's, and CCNY. It was a big thing to root for or against those teams.

Hockey was something they played in Canada, which we knew was up north somewhere.

There were a lot of newspapers in New York when I was a kid, practically no radio—maybe a few crystal sets around—and television hadn't even been invented. It's hard to believe that the great city of New York is now reduced to four papers, the *News*, the *Times*, and the *Post* in the city, and *Newsday* on Long Island. We used to have so many. The morning papers included the *World*, the *Times*, the *Tribune*, the *Herald* (which became the *Herald-Tribune*), the *News*, the *Mirror*, and the *New York American*. The evening papers were the *Globe*, the *Telegram*, the *Evening World*, the *Post*, the *Sun*, the *Mail*, and the *Journal*. Brooklyn had the famous *Brooklyn Eagle* and the *Citizen*, among others, and there was the *Bronx Home News*.

I was a Yankee fan, and it warmed my heart to walk past a newsstand and see a headline such as GIANTS LOSE. YANKS WIN. RUTH HITS TWO.

All the saloons had General News tickers that gave not only the stock quotations but also sports results, mainly baseball scores. The saloon had a big scoreboard on which the scores were posted with some kind of white chalky paste. I remember sneaking under the swinging doors and catching the 1919 and 1920 World Series at Guilfoyle's saloon at 103rd Street and Amsterdam Avenue, also the Dempsey–Willard slaughter for the heavyweight championship and the match race between the great Man o' War and the Kentucky Derby winner Sir Barton. It was fun but Prohibition put an end to the corner saloons, and with them the scores.

In those days, before TV and before most people had radios, you could see a sort of animated version of a World Series game on the Hearst Building at Columbus Circle in New York. There was a huge baseball diamond on the outside of the second floor. It had three bases and home plate and a larger space for the outfield. The foul lines extended way out on the board and the lineups of the contending teams were posted on either side. It operated like this. The name of the batter was inserted beside home plate. A light moved from the pitching mound to home plate. If the pitch was taken, a light went on next to BALL or STRIKE or FOUL. If it was batted, a tracer light would show where it went with a sign flashing HIT or OUT. For instance, if the batter was out short to first, a light would move from the plate to short and over to first. If the batter hit a triple, the light would move around the bases and stop at third. It may sound ridiculous in light of today's comprehensive TV coverage, but back then it was the only show in town, and as many as fifteen or twenty thousand people would jam Columbus Circle to "see" a Series game that way.

I remember the 1921 World Series, the first of three consecutive "subway series" between the Giants and the Yankees. I scraped together a dollar ten and bought a bleacher seat for Saturday's game, but it was rained out and postponed until Sunday. Of course, my rain check was good for Sunday's game, but Sunday morning I was playing shortstop for the Blue Sox in Central Park. When I told the other players that I would have to leave the game early to get to the Polo Grounds with my rain check, a man standing nearby overheard, and offered me two dollars for the ticket. "But," I said naïvely, "I only paid a dollar ten for it." He insisted that he would give me two dollars. I took it and raced the three blocks home to get the rain check. I was back at the field in fifteen minutes, in time to lead off the next inning, elated that I'd made ninety cents on the deal. It doesn't sound like much now, does it? But in those times it was quite a sum.

I was at the Polo Grounds the day Ray Chapman, the Cleveland shortstop, was beaned by Carl Mays, the Yankee pitcher. Mays threw underhanded, or what was known as a "submarine ball." He was a big, burly fellow who was generally disliked around the league, which made what happened all the more sensational.

There have been several versions of the incident but this is what I saw from a seat above home plate in the upper stand. The Yankees and the Indians were battling for the pennant, and Chapman faced Mays in a very close game. The big pitcher was a controversial figure whose sale by the Boston Red Sox to the Yankees almost broke up the league. Ban Johnson, the American League president, tried to nullify the sale, accusing the Yankee owners, Colonel Jacob Ruppert and Captain Til Huston, of buying the pennant (which is exactly what they were doing). The Yankees threatened to go to court, and they were backed by the Chicago White Sox and the St. Louis Browns. Johnson was forced to let the sale go through.

This background situation added fuel to an already torrid situation and made it worse when Mays beaned Chapman. I don't believe it, but people at the time said he did it deliberately.

The ball hit Chapman on the skull with a crack that sounded as though Chapman had hit a line drive. The ball rolled halfway back to the pitcher's mound. Mays and Muddy Ruel, the Yankee catcher, thought it had hit the bat and was in play. Mays picked up the ball and threw it to first baseman Wally Pipp, and Ruel, using standard procedure for an alert catcher, ran down to back up first. Only Tommy Connolly, the plate umpire, seemed to sense what had happened. He grabbed the now reeling Chapman and kept him from falling. Aided by a couple of teammates, Chapman was walked— yes, *walked*—to the clubhouse in deep center field. (There is now a rule that an injured player must be taken out on a stretcher.) We didn't think much about it at the time and concentrated on the ball game, which the Indians won. But as we left the ballpark and came out on Eighth Avenue we saw an ambulance. Only then did we kids get a sinking feeling of impending doom. Chapman died the next day. I have wondered many times how it might have turned out if Chapman had been taken off on a stretcher.

One game was postponed in memory of the Cleveland shortstop but two days later I was back in the Polo Grounds to see the Yankees and the Indians again.

How did I, with practically no money at all, get to see so many games? I'll let you in on the secret. The ball clubs weren't so commercial-minded in those days, and the gatekeepers were very lenient. The kids from 103rd Street found out that you could pull a two-on-one and they'd let you do it. We'd wait outside on Eighth Avenue for a kindly-looking man headed for the game, and this conversation might ensue.

"Mister, can I go in on your ticket?"

Startled, he'd say, "What?"

I would explain. "Look, I'd like to go in on your ticket. The gatekeeper will let us."

The way the turnstiles operated was that each revolution of the stile, caused by a spectator going through, registered an admission, and these were tallied at the end of the day to get the attendance. If two people went through together, it still registered as just one admission. As I said, the gatekeepers were lenient, and if the kids didn't become nuisances they'd let them through if they could come up with a good prospect. How we 103rd-ers found out about it I don't remember, and apparently we were the only ones in the whole city who knew about this bonanza. We didn't advertise it. We didn't want to kill a good thing.

So we'd wait for a man headed for the game. Sometimes I'd approach one who was too dumb to understand and he'd chase me away, but most would shrug their shoulders and let us go in with them. Sometimes we'd get into the grandstand and sometimes the bleachers.

One memorable day in 1922, I had an experience with the man many consider the greatest player of all time, Tyrus Raymond Cobb, the Georgia Peach. Cobb, a great hitter and superb base stealer (he held the record for stolen bases for many, many years), had often been accused of using his spikes to intimidate basemen. He had a nasty reputation in some quarters. There are those who said he would spike his mother in order to gain a base. Once in Philadelphia, he had gone into the stands after a fan who was heckling him unmercifully. I was a rabid Yankee fan and saw Cobb play against my favorites many times. I must say he was a hard player, but in the years that I saw him, I never saw him spike anyone, never saw him in a fight with an opposing player, never saw him do anything but try to win fairly.

Recently, when Pete Rose was on his way to breaking Cobb's record for most hits in a career, all the mean things that were said about Cobb surfaced again, which is why it pleases me to recall this story.

In 1922 in New York, the Giants of the National League and the Yankees of the American League shared the Polo Grounds. When one team was at home, the other was on the road. Yankee Stadium was not opened until 1923. The Polo Grounds, before it was remodeled, had wooden bleachers that encircled the entire outfield. Later, the clubhouse, for both home and visiting teams, was in deep center field and was reached by steps on both sides of it. The clubhouse was in full view of all the fans. But back in 1922 the clubhouse was behind the bleachers, out of view of the spectators, and was reached by the players walking under the center-field bleachers. The Yankee bull pen was in deep right field and actually on the playing surface. As a staunch Yankee rooter, I usually sat in the right-field bleachers behind my hero, Babe Ruth. I might add that in those days you could walk down from the bleachers and see the players as they went in and out of the clubhouse. On this particular day the Yankees were playing the Detroit Tigers, featuring, of course, Ty Cobb.

After batting practice, the players usually walked from their dugouts across the field and to the clubhouse to change uniforms. I'd been looking at the Yankee bull pen for a couple of years, and had a yen to sit in it. I suddenly got a brainstorm. When batting practice was over, I waited for Cobb. Sure enough, he headed for the visiting part of the clubhouse. I ran up to him. "Mr. Cobb," I said hopefully, "could I sit in the Yankee bull pen?" He looked down at me and laughed. "Of course," he said. "Come on."

He walked me over to the Yankee bull pen and sat me down and went into the visiting team's clubhouse. I was in my glory. The only Yankee ballplayer on the bench whom I recognized was Chick Fewster, a reserve infielder. One or two Tiger players were there also, and I recall one of them saying that Doc Ayres was pitching for Detroit that day, so the Babe ought to get one or two. I knew he meant homers. Soon the Babe himself came along and said hello to me. It was a great moment for me, but nothing lasts forever. Soon it was time for the game to begin, and the attendant came over to me. He said, "Sonny, the game's gonna start, now you'll have to sit up in the bleachers."

"Oh no," I said. "Mr. Cobb said I could sit here."

Needless to say, I sat upstairs. But what beautiful memories I had. I didn't tell the other kids about it. I knew they wouldn't believe me.

The Six-Day Bicycle Race was held at the Garden twice a year. It was a big event in those days. There was a tremendous amount of interest, and it received big coverage from the papers. It was very popular and ran twenty-four hours a day for six straight days. The event ended on a Saturday night and the winning team was the one that was ahead in laps. The riders competed as two-man teams. One man of each team had to be on the track at all times. The men on the track would circle leisurely in single file until someone broke from the pack in an attempt to steal a lap. This was when the excitement started. The aspiring stealer would go flying around the track with the others in wild pursuit. When he tired, his partner would replace him, and the other teams did the same. It was a wild spectacle, with the teams interchanging, and riders and bikes all over the place. Sometimes the team would succeed in its purloining and sometimes it wouldn't, but it always brought down the house. Very often when things were quiet, a Hollywood star such as Al Jolson, for instance, would offer a hundred dollars to any team that could steal a lap. A cloak and suiter (a clothing store) might offer two suits, or a restaurateur a dinner for four. It was all very exciting, especially when there was a jam on the track.

The Garden track was an oval and inside it pup tents were pitched, so the team members who went off duty could rest or sleep if they could when things were quiet. There seemed to be a gentlemen's agreement that no one would try to steal a lap in the wee hours of the morning. But there had to be riders on the track at all times. Inside the track, there were stairs leading down to the washrooms and to a commissary where the riders and the sportswriters could eat.

My Uncle Joe, who lived with us, was an avid fan who never missed the race. He'd leave the house Sunday afternoon and we wouldn't see him all week. Early the next Sunday morning there would be a knock on the door, and my uncle would be standing there, fast asleep.

The Six-Day Bicycle Race lasted through the thirties, but then, with the emerging popularity of college basketball, followed by the pro game and hockey, it became difficult for the big arenas to give up a whole week to the race and it faded out.

In 1925, Harold "Red" Grange, of the University of Illinois, was considered the greatest college football player of all time. Many have starred on the gridiron since those days, but there are still those who consider him the all-time best. He had several nicknames, all of which fitted him perfectly. "Galloping Ghost" was one of them, and that's just what he was. The finest broken-field runner of his time, maybe of any time, the Illinois halfback was almost impossible to bring down when he was in one of his broken-field canters. He was known as the Wheaton Illinois Iceman because during summer vacations he would work at delivering ice in his hometown of Wheaton, Illinois. (Delivering ice? You youngsters might not know that there were few refrigerators in those days. People had ice boxes then, insulated cabinets that were cooled by big blocks of ice that had to be delivered to their homes. That's what the redhead did on summer vacation.)

Grange played in a tough conference, the Big Ten. They were

really the powers of college football, teams such as Michigan, Minnesota, Ohio State, and Illinois. Against them, Grange usually had a romp. As he scored touchdown after touchdown, he was rarely brought down by any tackler in front of him. With his hips swiveling and his body pirouetting, he could avoid any tacklers he could see. When he was brought down, it was usually from behind.

I mention Grange now for two reasons: I saw him play in a game in 1925, and I feel that the impact he had on professional football is worth noting.

At that time, the Galloping Ghost was a national hero and as such was a marketable commodity. As the 1925 college season ended, with Grange tearing a fine University of Pennsylvania team apart on a muddy field, he startled the nation by announcing that he was going to turn pro and sign a contract with the Chicago Bears of the National Football League. As I said earlier, pro football at this time was no big deal. College football was getting all the headlines and all the interest of football fans, with the Big Ten in the Midwest, such as Southern California, Stanford, and California in the Far West, and, in the East, Pennsylvania, the Big Three—Harvard, Yale, and Princeton—plus Navy and Army. And let's not forget Notre Dame, with the famed Knute Rockne as its coach. It probably had more fans than any of the others.

No, indeed, pro football was not the big attraction that it is today. It was struggling. But George Halas, who owned and coached the Chicago Bears, was a forward-looking man. He foresaw the impact of having Red Grange in the Bears backfield. And he was right. Although the regular 1925 season of the league was practically over, he booked the Bears, who would now have the great Galloping Ghost with them, in an exhibition series with the other teams in the league. One of these games was at the Polo Grounds against the New York Giants. I wanted to see it, but it was an immediate sellout. However, I found a way to get in that Sunday afternoon—another special technique. If you had two dollars and were lucky, you might be able to do it. You looked for a man standing out in the crowd who had people coming up to him. That was the tipoff. I went up to him and told him I wanted to get in. The deal was that I gave him one dollar and got on the line going through the turnstiles. He would wave to the ticket taker and point to me. Making believe I was handing in a ticket, I would give the gateman the other dollar and I was in. After that I was on my own. My day was complete when the redhead intercepted a Giant pass late in the game and ran it back for the winning score.

Grange caught on immediately in pro football. He didn't dominate it the way he had the college game, but he was good. And he brought out the crowds. From city to city, the Bears and Grange were sellouts, and the pro game was on its way.

They say you can't compare athletes and teams of one era against those of another. I don't quite agree. Grange was part of the glorious Golden Age of Sport. It was the time of Jack Dempsey in boxing, Babe Ruth in baseball, Bobby Jones in golf, Bill Tilden in tennis, Man o' War in horse racing, and great teams such as the 1927 New York Yankees and the Four Horsemen of Notre Dame.

I don't know that these were the best in their sports, but the records show that when new football stars came along, they were always compared with Grange; new baseball stars were compared with Ruth; golfers and tennis players were compared with Jones and Tilden, and other baseball teams with the '27 Yankees. But new stars do come along. In boxing, for instance, there was no one to compare with John L. Sullivan until Dempsey, no one to compare with Dempsey until Joe Louis. And finally there was Muhammad Ali, who reached the top of popularity in his prime.

College Correspondent

In 1926 I went to Manhattan College with the intention of becoming a lawyer, but I got over the idea in a hurry. Times and customs have changed a lot since the late twenties, but the feeling then was that if you wanted to be a lawyer you had to learn Latin in college. It was supposedly necessary as a vocabulary builder. So I dutifully registered for the Latin course. In high school, at Manhattan Prep, I had done very well in the two language courses I carried, French and Spanish. Other courses may have bothered me—and some did a great deal—but not French and Spanish, both of which I breezed through. So I figured Latin would be no big deal as I entered the freshman class. After all, everyone said it was easier than either French or Spanish. But for me it wasn't easy at all, and I quickly developed a mental block against it. Possessing as I did a very practical nature, I reasoned that if you knew French, Spanish, Italian, or German, you could converse in those languages—but whom would you talk to in Latin? The more I thought about this, the harder the class became, so I threw in the towel and dropped the course. In the light of what happened in later years, I think it was a good idea. I don't think the profession of sports announcing could tolerate two ex-lawyers. (Other party's name issued on request.)

So I forgot about law, took general courses, and started to think of other things—mainly sports. As a youngster I was a good all-around athlete, and was exceptionally fast. I still had the feeling that perhaps I could make the big leagues in baseball. At Manhattan I played freshman baseball, but my baseball dreams disappeared when I tried out for the varsity. "Good field, no hit" was an oft-used expression in those days, and it applied to me. I won my letter as a quarter-miler on the track team that won three Penn Relays watches. But my best sports were nonvarsity ones, touch football and stickball.

There were about 170 of us who graduated from Manhattan. Of course, there was the usual class poll in which we voted for "the best looking," "the best dressed," "the most likely to succeed," and so forth. In the category of "best all-around athlete," six of my classmates voted for me. I didn't come close to winning, but it was heart-warming and made me feel awfully good. My friend Mike Mazurki, a future movie star and great athlete who won varsity letters in football, basketball, and track, won in a landslide.

As a sophomore I made the mile relay team. The big event we looked forward to was the annual Penn Relays at Franklin Field of the University of Pennsylvania in Philadelphia. I remember our first jaunt to Philly as though it were yesterday. We got there on Friday and were quartered at the Penn Athletic Club on Rittenhouse Square. Our race was on Saturday afternoon, but we went out to the relays on Friday with the intention of loosening up and perfecting our passing of the baton. But the weather intervened. It poured rain, so we didn't practice, but just sat up in the stands, watching the races. Pete Waters, our coach, had told me that I would run the starting leg of the relay on Saturday. This surprised me because I was the youngest and most inexperienced runner on the team. And I was probably the most nervous. In those days Franklin Field, like most outdoor tracks, was a cinder path, and as we watched, it got muddier and muddier. To make matters worse, the start of the race was about twenty yards from the first turn, which meant that if you were starting you had to get out in a hurry or get pinched off. Our seats in the grandstand were just above the first turn, which didn't do me any good. With the muddying track and the scramble for the turn at the start of each race, one runner or more would invariably go down. Looking on, I almost became nauseated. I could visualize that happening to me the next day.

And the next day it rained even harder. This was the last weekend in April and things were cold and clammy and the track was becoming wetter and wetter. I was to start the relay; Jack Geoghegan, a senior, would own the second leg; and Louie Mancz and Tom Philbin, juniors, would run third and fourth. As we neared our starting time I got more nervous. I just hoped I wouldn't drop the baton or go down in a heap with other runners.

And then fate intervened. A few minutes before the start, Mancz developed a nosebleed. They tried to stop it but couldn't. Then Pete Waters put his thinking cap on. He reasoned that if Mancz ran the third leg of the relay he would have lost more blood by that time than if he ran the first leg, so Mancz started and I ran third. This may seem silly stuff now, but it's what happened. Louie came out flying at the start and gave Geoghegan a five-yard lead. Jack increased it to ten and I made it fifteen. Philbin finished in a breeze, and we won handily. It so happened that if you got out in front on the muddy track it was awfully hard to pass you. Maybe the nosebleed won the race for us.

My modest accomplishments as an athlete gave me some good times in college, but my activities as a college journalist ultimately showed me my true calling. While I was at Manhattan College, I became sports editor of *The Quadrangle*, the school paper. This is what led me to a sports career. In those days the local papers used student correspondents to cover the athletic activities at their particular college. In the fall of my senior year I became the Manhattan College sports correspondent for several New York papers, one of which was the famed *New York World*. I remember the first football game I covered for the paper. It was a Saturday afternoon, and Manhattan was playing St. Francis of Loretto, Pennsylvania. It was my baptism by fire as a sportswriter. I was covering the game for the *Telegram*, the *Journal*, and the *Evening World*, all evening papers, and for the Sunday edition of the *Morning World*. A Western Union telegrapher would send my coverage to the various papers—with different leads of the same story to each one. I got through the evening papers all right, and then decided I would bring the *Sunday World* story to the paper myself. Manhattan College was located near Van Cortlandt Park, I lived on 103rd Street on the West Side, and the *World* was located at Park Row near the Brooklyn Bridge. Since this was my first coverage and no one had told me otherwise, I assumed that an evening paper came out in the evening, and a morning paper came out in the morning. So, with the *World* story in my pocket, I stopped off at home and had dinner before going down to the paper. When I got to the Pulitzer Building, which housed the *World*, I met a classmate and we spent about fifteen minutes discussing the game, which Manhattan had lost. Finally I made my way to the sports department. They raised hell with me for being late—by about three hours. The first editions were already on the streets, without the Manhattan College story! I'm surprised they didn't can me immediately. Fortunately, they accepted my claim that I hadn't known any better, gave me a rewrite man, and my coverage made the final edition. I was never late with an assignment again.

As a college correspondent, I wasn't given a regular salary but was paid on the basis of space—about a dollar an inch. Since I was covering Manhattan College for several New York papers, I did pretty well that fall. I did most of my work for the *Morning* and *Evening World*s, and I think if things had not gone awry I might have been assigned as a regular sportswriter. But just when things were going great, the *Evening World*, the *Morning World*, and the *Sunday World* all went out of business on March 1, 1931. It was a sad day for many people, including me. The *World* was one of the nation's great newspapers and prided itself on many notable achievements. Among the most important of these was its having taken on the Ku Klux Klan in the mid-1920s. It sent its reporters and great columnists to the South and, through a series of devastating daily articles, practically destroyed the Klan. In 1931 I was proud to say I was covering events for the *World*. But the Depression did the *World* in. One of its main sources of revenue was the classified section for jobs, and in the Depression there were no jobs, so the paper's funds dried up and it went downhill. Finally, the Pulitzers closed it by selling its name to the *Telegram*, which then became the *World Telegram*.

For me, the bottom had dropped out of everything. I still covered Manhattan events for the *Evening Journal*, the *New York American*, and a couple of other papers, but I didn't make much money doing it.

Sometimes the *New York American* used me to cover hockey games at the New York Coliseum, which was located at Starlight Park in the Bronx. At one of those games I got an introduction to sports broadcasting at its most creative. The Coliseum featured amateur hockey, with teams from the New York Athletic Club, the Crescent Club in Brooklyn, and several other local clubs. They also had a team in a minor professional league that actually consisted of farm clubs for the National Hockey League. In the same building with the arena was the Bronx radio station WBNX—it was natural for the station to air the Coliseum events and try to sell them. They had a very enterprising radio time salesman, who sold the professional league games to a sponsor with himself as the play-by-play announcer. One night when I was a spectator in the press box within earshot of him, he got in a jam. He had sold these games to start at eight o'clock, which was when he went on the air. But the game didn't start on time. At eight the players were just skating leisurely around. Undaunted, and to the amazement of everyone in the press box, he started announcing his own game on the air. He was a good hockey announcer, and had the teams flying up and down the ice, executing well-planned plays, taking great shots that in turn had the respective goalies making unbelievable saves. All was going well with the imaginary game until the real one was finally ready to start. As usual, they struck up the national anthem, which went over the public address system and, of course, was carried out on the airwaves. Without missing a beat, this unflappable fellow announced, "Ladies and gentlemen, we must pause. The District Attorney has just arrived and they're playing 'The Star-Spangled Banner' in his honor."

In the next year or so, I covered quite a few games at the Coliseum for local papers. I didn't make much on the deal, but at least I was working. Going there often and being seen by the Coliseum's establishment paid off, for in 1933 they hired me as Publicity Director for hockey and wrestling. The pay was thirty dollars per week, which to me, in those Depression days, was a lot of dough. In the long run, it turned out to be a great move. The fact that WBNX was in the building gave me an idea: Why couldn't I broadcast the hockey games and the wrestling matches? This I did once a week for each. I must have had terrific gall, guts, or *chutzpah*. I had never done a broadcast in my life, and now I was going to take on two of the toughest sports to describe—hockey, the fastest, and wrestling, the slowest. Wrestling descriptions on radio were really something to hear. Wrestling televises very well—but radio? Sometimes a guy would get a wrist lock or something similar on his opponent and hold it for as long as five minutes, and I had to keep talking. It didn't seem to bother me. I just did it. I wish I had recordings of those shows.

I don't remember the hockey players, but the top wrestlers of the circuit played the Coliseum. Jim Londos, the Gorgeous Greek, was the champion and he defended on WBNX several times. I can recall other wrestling stars—Gus Sonnenberg of Dartmouth, Sammy Stein, the New York Giants football star, good-looking Paul Boesch, and Mike Mazurki, my classmate at Manhattan.

The promoter was Jeff Pfeffer, a dapper little fellow who always appeared in a tuxedo and a black homburg. There may have been a reason for his distinctive dress. He was easily spotted by the wrestlers from the ring when they were in action. I could spot him, too, at ringside. The bout might be on for quite a while, with the promoter nowhere in sight. All of a sudden he would circle the ring. You got the idea the match would be over in minutes. The excitement would mount. There were dull moments with the grapplers, but the end was always exciting—particularly when Londos was defending. It was the day of the flying tackle, and the underdog would come flying across the ring, throwing himself at the champion and knocking him down. Again and again he did this, and the crowd was on its feet. Slowly and more slowly the champ would get back to his feet, sometimes seeming to be groggy. Would the title change hands? It seemed likely. And then came the end. Stein had Londos in real trouble and was apparently on his way to the title. With victory in his grasp, he set himself for one more flying tackle. From across the ring he rushed at the dazed Londos. But the champ had just enough left to step aside as Stein came at him. Stein missed and his momentum took him flying out of the ring and into the press section. Now it was Sammy who was dazed, and when he got back into the ring the champ had enough left to pin him and regain the title. It was a wow of an ending.

Also ending, but not with a wow, was my tenure at the New York Coliseum. There was a "policy difference" between Captain E. W. Whitwell, the managing director of the Coliseum, and me. In such situations the manager stays and the inkstained wretch goes, so I went out into the Depression of 1934. The situation was so bad there weren't even jobs to apply for. I thought many times that I'd been foolhardy not to get along with Captain Whitwell. I could have stayed on the job if I had been more pliant. Days ran into weeks and weeks ran into months. Fortunately my mother was employed, and I was able to pick up a few bucks covering Manhattan College events for the papers, but it was a tough time and I was sorry I had lost that job.

But how often have we found that a bad break is often a good one in disguise. I look back now and think how fortunate it was that I was cut off from the Coliseum job. Had I remained, chances are I would not have gone much further in life than turning out publicity copy about wrestling and hockey. You probably would never have heard of me and certainly you wouldn't be reading this book. So how about a couple of good loud cheers for getting fired?

WHOM

One cold day in the winter of 1934, before I knew I was lucky to have been fired, I dropped into WHOM on West 48th Street. WHOM was a New Jersey station with New York studios. The HOM part stood for Harry O'Melia, the owner, who was at the time one of the Jersey City commissioners of Mayor Frank Hague. Through a fortunate coincidence, I met Lennie Ohl there. Lennie had been my engineer when I'd been broadcasting hockey and wrestling the previous year on WBNX. Lennie introduced me around, and the people were very friendly.

Having nothing else to do those days except cover an occasional Manhattan game for the New York papers, I decided to hang around the place. Eventually I persuaded Carleton Alsop, the program director, to let me do a fifteen-minute sports talk every evening. I received no salary, but it gave me something to do and was a step toward my getting more recognition. I applied for and got press passes for games of New York's three baseball teams, and was added to Madison Square Garden's press list, which meant admission to games and fights there. Naturally, I would have liked to be paid, but I realized that economic conditions being what they were in 1934, I had to be patient.

During the summer vacation I was asked to substitute for the station's three staff announcers, for which I received fifteen dollars per week. The money helped, but the much-needed mike experience was even more important. About this time an Italian group headed by Commendatore Clemente Giglio took over WHOM, and the station went foreign-language. There were programs in Italian, Polish, Greek, German, and perhaps others. The new owners were nice people and allowed me to continue my evening sports talks, in English of course, and for the same fee I was getting before: nothing. But I was glad that I could keep my spot on the air because I knew I was making some progress.

Then, in September of 1934, something good happened. One of the staff announcers left and I was asked to take his place. I was to sign on the station at the Jersey City studios in Journal Square seven days a week from 7:00 A.M. until 10:00 A.M. and sign it off at the New York studio every night at 10:00 P.M. The pay was seven dollars a week, and I didn't argue. I looked on it as a break, and I grabbed it. Fortunately my mother went to business and by this time we lived in Greenwich Village, so I could grab the Hudson Tubes to Jersey City and be there in no time at all. As for the seven dollars a week, I remind myself that a dollar bought a lot in those days. A phone call was a nickel, and so were the subway and bus fare. You could get a good chicken potpie for a quarter, and a hot roast beef sandwich at Jack Delaney's on Sheridan Square in the Village was sixty cents. Beer was a nickel a glass, and drinks were about thirty-five cents. The morning paper was two cents, and the evening paper was three. Then there were the Woolworth five-and-ten-cent stores where you could get really good things for a nickel or a dime.

In my spare time I went around the city trying to get a sponsor for my WHOM sports talk. On lower Broadway I passed a clothing auction store—Brown and Schiff, Clothiers. I met both owners and tried to interest them in buying a spot in my sports talk. They weren't interested in taking a spot, which cost eighteen dollars a week, but they were interested in talking sports with me, particularly boxing. They were avid fight fans and said they went to the Garden often. Now I got another brainstorm. I used to get two ringside seats for each Garden fight, and they were marked sixteen dollars each. I got them free, but had to pay the service charge if I went. I made a deal with Brown and Schiff. They would take a one-minute spot in my sports talk, and I would give them two ringside seats to each Garden fight. They went for it and threw in a couple of suits and a topcoat. My commission for selling the spot was three dollars and sixty cents a week. I felt pretty good about it, and felt even better when I got back to the station. There they told me that they had just raised my salary as staff announcer to fifteen dollars a week. Figuring in the three-sixty commission on the spot I'd just sold, that meant my weekly salary had jumped from seven bucks to eighteen-sixty, all in one day. Boy, did I feel good!

In the early fall of 1935, I saw an item in the paper that gave me another idea. Huey Long, the "Kingfish," the governor of Louisiana, was staying at the New Yorker Hotel, which was located near Penn Station. Long had built Louisiana State University into a great center of learning. He had also built its football team into one of the best in the country and traveled to all its games. I knew that Louisiana State would be playing my alma mater, Manhattan College, at Ebbets Field in about a month and that Governor Long would be back for the game. I decided to take a chance. Why not try to get him as a guest on my sports show the day before the game? Knowing that I had nothing to lose by trying, I called the New Yorker and asked for Governor Long. A voice with a fine New Orleans drawl answered the phone. It wasn't a secretary or a hanger-on, but the Kingfish himself. He listened patiently as I told him who I was, that I thought he'd be back in New York for the LSU–Manhattan game, and that I wondered if he would be kind enough to be a guest on my program. He thanked me for the invitation and said he'd be happy to be my guest. He said he'd be at the New Yorker for the game and that I should call him there. To me, this was a real scoop. Aside from President Roosevelt, Huey Long was probably the best-known officeholder in the country. There were those who felt that Long was a real threat to Roosevelt for the Democratic nomination at the 1936 presidential convention.

I was elated.

But between that exciting phone conversation and the football game, Huey Long was assassinated on the steps of the state capitol in Baton Rouge, Louisiana.

So things didn't always work out, but I was always getting ideas, looking ahead, trying. One day in 1934, while I was struggling along without pay at WHOM, I noticed in the paper that WINS, a pretty good New York station (pretty good, that is, compared to WHOM), was going to broadcast the Manhattan College football games that year. (I might note that at the time Manhattan College was located in the Bronx and played its football games at Ebbets Field in Brooklyn.) Earl Harper was the sports director at WINS and was to be the announcer of the games. It occurred to me that I might be able to help out on the games. I rarely missed a Manhattan College sports event, and knew its teams inside out. I called Harper. He was very friendly and asked me to drop over to see him, which I did. After chatting with me, he said he would like me to help him but there wouldn't be any money in it for me. I didn't argue about it. After all, I was doing sports talks for nothing at WHOM. I had the free time and looked upon it as an opportunity to become better known. Why not? So Earl added me to the crew for the Manhattan football broadcasts.

Thinking back to 1934, I'm reminded of one of the most remembered professional football games of all time, the famous "sneakers game" between the Giants and the Chicago Bears at the old Polo Grounds in New York. WINS got the radio rights to the game, which was for the league championship. Earl and his crew, including me, were on the fifty-yard line in the upper stands.

Then as now, the Chicago Bears were the Monsters of the Midway. They had two great stars who shone brightly in the Bears' firmament: one was Bronko Nagurski, who carried the ball on offense and played tackle on defense. The men played both offense and defense in those days. Platooning was to come later. At either position he was an all-time All-American. The other great star was Jack Manders, who was called "Automatic Jack" because he never missed a field goal from any reasonable distance. This team had other capable stars and was heavily favored over the Giants.

The Giants' attack was built around Ken Strong, the All-American from New York University—a great runner and a superb punter. Another all-time great was in the center of the Giants' line—Mel Hein, a man who will never be forgotten by those who saw him play. Like Strong, he was also good on defense. That Sunday was bitterly cold and the Polo Grounds field was frozen. It was hard to get your feet to grip the ground. This favored the offense, which naturally had the momentum. Nagurski was virtually impossible to stop. Tackling him did little good, for he would carry the tacklers another five or six yards before they could bring him down. I remember Rud Rennie writing of him in the *New York Herald-Tribune*: "Tackling Nagurski," he said, "is like getting the brass ring on the merry-go-around. You get a free ride."

With Bronko eating up the yardage and Manders adding points, the Bears ran up a substantial first-half lead. To use the old cliché, the Giants seemed to have two chances: slim and none.

Then someone got an idea. Since the football cleats could not grip the frozen turf and the defense was constantly giving way, why not use sneakers? It so happened that Gus Mauch, the Giants' trainer, and Doc Sweeney, their team doctor, both operated in the same capacity at Manhattan College. One of them may have gotten the idea. While the first half was still under way, a car was dispatched to Manhattan College, about seven miles from the Polo Grounds. The gym was opened and every basketball sneaker in the place was rushed down to the Polo Grounds. The Giants put them on between halves, and the result was unbelievable. The team that was foundering and slipping through the first half suddenly was like a stone wall on defense and mobile on offense. Now it was the Bears who were giving ground. The Giants gained momentum because their sneakers could get traction on the frozen turf. Instead of tackling Nagurski and being carried along by him, they now threw their bodies at his legs, which definitely brought him down. The now former Monsters of the Midway were held almost helpless by the aroused New Yorkers. George Halas's Bears failed to score in the second half, while Steve Owens's Giants ran up 27 points for a 30–13 win. It was an amazing upset. WINS probably had an audience of millions listening to Earl Harper's play-by-play that day. It was a big moment for me, too, because while I didn't get on the air vocally, I got a lot of publicity from the broadcast. I remember that all through the second half, I kept passing notes to Harper about the flow of the action and so forth. Invariably he used my stuff and gave me credit. I was getting known. There are two other things I remember about that game. Ned Irish, then a sportswriter for the *New York World Telegram*, handled publicity for the Giants and Arthur Daley, who wrote for *The New York Times*, was the public-address announcer. Ultimately, both reached great heights. Irish went on to become President of Madison Square Garden and Daley, who soon became a sports columnist for the *Times*, went on to win a Pulitzer Prize for his writing.

Harper apparently had a lot to say at WINS, for shortly after that he augmented the WINS schedule by adding the Brooklyn Dodgers football games. The Dodgers, who also played their home games at Ebbets Field, were, with the New York Giants, a vital part of the National Football League. I did so well at helping Harper as the offensive spotter for the Manhattan games that he asked me to work on the pro games as well. For the same fee. Nothing. Heck, I didn't mind. I felt I was making progress, and I was. The next year, 1935, I worked in the same capacity on the Manhattan and pro games and it paid off. In January of 1936, Harper got me added to WINS as a staff announcer and sports assistant to him. The salary was twenty-five dollars a week, which I thought was great for those times.

At WHOM in 1935, I had come up with the idea of supplementing my meager income by putting Irish programs on the air. I had

heard some Irish programs on local New York stations and they
sounded pretty good. I took the idea to the station management
and they consented. They gave me two fifteen-minute spots twice
a week to see how it would work out. I must say that although I
was of Irish descent, I wasn't too knowledgeable about the Irish
and their customs. Still, as the Irish will readily admit, you can't
blame a man for trying, especially during a depression. And try I
did. Wholeheartedly! I became an avid reader of both New York
Irish newspapers, the *Irish Echo* and the *Irish World*. That was where
I noticed that Friday night was Irish dance night on the East Side
of New York City, and one night I decided to look in on them. I
went from one to another and still another. They were all crowded
and everyone seemed to be having a good time. Another idea suddenly struck me: If those dances were so successful in New York
City, why shouldn't they be equally successful in Jersey City? After
all, they were similar people, separated only by the Hudson River.
WHOM, of course, was a Jersey City station and I reasoned that
with my Irish programs I could get the dances a lot of publicity
and make a lot of money.

I started looking into it, and learned something discouraging. In
Jersey City there was an ordinance against public dancing. This
was a disastrous shot on the jaw. I went down, but got up off the
floor. I checked out the situation. No dancing in Jersey City. Well,
how about Union City, which was next door to Jersey City? They
had no law prohibiting public dancing in Union City, so my mind
continued to churn. Where to hold the dance? Would you believe
it—the only place in Union City that fit the bill was the Union City
Hofbrauhaus, which, as the name implies, was a German establishment. It so happened that the Hofbrauhaus bought daily time
on WHOM's German hour. Otto Feller was the announcer and
Carl Strobel was the salesman. I went to them with my idea, and
they thought it had possibilities. "Sure," they said, "let's go up to
Union City and talk to Max Damas." Max owned the Hofbrauhaus
and was a genial gentleman, very easy to talk with. At first he was
skeptical of the idea of an Irish dance in a German beer stube, but
the conversation over a few of his beers eased his reticence and

convinced him he could make some money on the dances. I think we agreed he could keep all the money from drinks and that he and I would share equally in the admission charges. We would also share the expenses.

We set up a date for the first dance, and I went to work publicizing the affair. The Irish papers were very nice and carried optimistic notices of the dances. I mentioned them frequently on my own programs. Beyond that, I bought about three hundred penny postcards (yes, they were only a penny in those days, and that included the stamp). I went through the Jersey City phone book and indiscriminately picked out Irish names and sent them postcards that in effect said. "This card will admit you and a friend free of charge to the first of a series of Irish dances to be held at the Union City Hofbrauhaus," and gave the date. I also invited several friends, and I'm glad I did. They were the only ones in the hall. The whole thing was a big bomb, a first-class fiasco. A few potential dancers showed up, took one look at the almost empty hall, and quickly left. We lost sixty dollars, and I never ran another Irish dance.

My discouragement over the flop of my dance promotion was big but only temporary. I was down for the count but I came up swinging. I tried again but with a new tack. This was the heyday of Major Bowes's "Amateur Hour," one of the most popular of the coast-to-coast radio programs. If you had been listening in those days, you would have heard the Major praise and give prizes to capable contestants. Now, in those days of vaudeville there were amateur hours where, if a contestant failed to please the audience, a giant hook would come out from the wings and drag him off. Major Bowes was more kind. He would merely tap a gong with a hammer and the performer would be off the air. My new brainstorm was to do an Irish amateur hour on the radio. WHOM, somewhat to my surprise, was receptive to the idea and I was in business again. I plugged the show on my own programs, and the Irish papers were again cooperative with notices.

I got the show on the air, although I know now that I never should have gone ahead with the idea. Although I know a lot about sports and about worldly news too, I know little about music in any language, and while at that point I had a passable speaking voice, as a singer I couldn't carry a tune across the street. I also found it difficult to recognize talent—or the lack of it. But hope springs eternal, and "The Irish Amateur Hour" went on the air. It's been about fifty years since then, and two memories have stayed with me. One night a contestant was singing a sad old Irish song that was very touching. If I remember correctly, that type of Irish song was called a "comalye" or "come all ye." When he finished, I thanked him and introduced the next warrior. "And now here's James McNally, who will sing for us." But no Mr. McNally came to the microphone. A long pause. "Mr. McNally, you're on." Still no Mr. McNally. Frantically I looked around. There was Mr. McNally in a corner, crying bitter tears and unable to compose himself. The previous song had reminded him of his departed mother and completely done him in.

That didn't kill the program, but I'll tell you what did. After about the third program, I began to feel pretty good about it. Maybe it was going well. At the end of this particular show, the switchboard operator called me and said, "Mr. Dunphy, there's a call for you." I felt fine as I picked up the phone. "Mr. Dunphy?" the voice on the other end asked. It was a beautifully cultured University of Dublin–type voice, of which I believe there is no purer speech.

"Yes," I said, "this is Don Dunphy."

"Mr. Dunphy," he continued quietly, "I've been listening to your 'Irish Amateur Hour.' "

"Oh good," I replied.

The voice continued, "I notice that you don't interrupt the contestants with a gong as Major Bowes does."

"That's right, I don't."

"Then," said he, "may I make a suggestion?"

"Of course."

He said, "Why don't you try a machine gun?"

That was it for the program.

While working at WHOM in 1935, I continued to help Earl Harper with the Manhattan games on Saturdays and the Brooklyn Dodgers

contests on Sundays. More and more during the season, he gave
me spots on the air, until eventually I was a commentator too. Once
in a while, when a special game came up somewhere, we would do
a ticker broadcast from the studio. This consisted of having a telegrapher come to the studio, who would feed us the game by way
of Morse code over a Western Union wire. Earl would have his
WINS crew furnish sound effects such as varying crowd noises plus
the opening national anthem. Doing a ticker broadcast those days
wasn't as difficult as it would be today. In the first place, there was
no platooning then, since both teams used the same men for offense
and defense. Second, as a rule the teams used a single-wing offense,
which meant that if it was "single wing right," the right halfback
would line up to the right and just a bit behind the right end. The
quarterback, believe it or not, was usually the blocking back. He'd
line up a little behind the center and to the right. The fullback
would be about four steps behind the center, and the left halfback
would be back a little more. The left halfback invariably was a triple
threat and carried the offense work load since he could run, pass,
and kick. Judging from the information received from the telegrapher, Harper might say, "It's Manhattan's ball, first and ten from
their own twenty. Single wing to the right. The snap is to Galway,
who starts around right end, cuts off tackle to the twenty-five-yard
line, finally he's brought down on a fine tackle by Smith. The ball
is spotted on the twenty-eight-yard line, a gain of eight on the play.
Second and two now . . ." and so forth. All this, of course, was
accompanied by crowd noise supplied by a sound-effects man. If
you had a good imagination, which Harper did, and if you had
plenty of guts, which he also did, you could get a pretty entertaining
ball game out of it, particularly if you had the score right, which
Harper usually did. I learned a lot from being a part of those
broadcasts, as well as from the live ones from Ebbets Field. As our
1935 football broadcasts came to a close, I figured I would be
through for a while unless I got a call to take a staff announcer job.
We were coming up to the end of the year, and I was content with
my work at WHOM.

About a week before New Year's Day, I got a call from Burt

Squire, manager of WINS. He wanted to have a talk with me. He said WINS had a chance to do the famous East–West Game by ticker wire on New Year's Day. He thought it would be great for the station. Unfortunately, he added, Harper had gone on vacation, and no one knew where he was. Since WINS was a Hearst station, he had contacted Dave Walsh, ace sports columnist of the International News Service, which was owned by Hearst. I wondered why Squire had asked me over, and he explained that, first, they wanted me to be the color commentator, and second, they weren't sure how Walsh would handle a game on a ticker broadcast and wanted me to go to his office and explain the mechanics of it to him. Their reasoning was typical of the wrong-headed thinking that went on at a lot of radio stations in those days. They were taking a man who undoubtedly had little radio experience and giving him a most difficult assignment. All I could think of was that Harper must have made it all sound so easy that they thought anyone could do it. Certainly, I said, I would be happy to be the color commentator on the show. I would be glad to go to the *Daily Mirror* building where Walsh was, and explain how the broadcast worked. I had misgivings about the show, but what the heck, it wasn't my idea.

Walsh and I set up an appointment. He was a nice gentleman whose writing I had always enjoyed. He was one of the best in the business. But writing a sports column and doing a radio broadcast of a football game are two different things, and doing a radio broadcast of a football game, relying on a Western Union wire, is something else entirely. I found Dave Walsh very friendly and eager to have me explain things to him. Painstakingly, I went over again and again how a play would evolve. "East's ball, first and ten from the twenty-yard-line . . . single wing right . . . Smith on the wing, Jones calling signals, Wiley the fullback and Armstrong the tailback. Armstrong has the ball, starts around right end, gets back to the line of scrimmage, and is brought down by Harley." I went through possible plays again and again and had Walsh ask me questions if he wasn't sure of anything. I had him go through the plays, and after a while he seemed to get the hang of it. We shook hands and said we'd meet at the studio on New Year's Day. I was skeptical, but I could only do my best and hope that Walsh would come through.

The game got under way with me doing the opening color and lineups and then introducing Dave Walsh as the play-by-play announcer. It didn't work out. Walsh, through no fault of his own, just didn't have the experience or the imagination to do it. During the first few minutes of the first quarter, one of the WINS announcers was brought in to ad-lib, faking a time-out, and I was called to the phone. Squire, the station manager, said Walsh couldn't do the job. Did I think I could? I said yes, and was rushed back into the studio. When Walsh was told I was taking over, he heaved a sigh of relief, shook my hand, thanked me for what I had done, wished everybody a happy New Year, and left. I carried on the play-by-play, and did most of the color commentating too. I'd had enough experience working with Harper to know how to do it, and it was really a breeze. The officials at WINS were extremely grateful.

What I did that New Year's Day with the East–West Game had a lot to do with my ultimately being hired as a staff announcer and assistant to Harper in sports. It was an exciting and important day for me, but, come to think of it, I can't recall who won the game.

WINS

In January of 1936 there was an opening on the WINS announcing staff, and Earl Harper persuaded the station to give the job to me. It was a step upward in that I was moving from a foreign-language station to an all-English station which also had a big emphasis on sports events. I did leave WHOM with a certain nostalgia because the people there were easy to get along with, and I had many good friends. At WINS, the pay of twenty-five dollars a week was kind of standard for announcers on non-network stations and the job offered many opportunities for advancement. As a staff announcer I had a regular daily schedule of introducing programs every fifteen minutes or half hour. I was also Harper's assistant, which meant that whenever he did a sports event or special event, I was relieved of my staff duties to work with him.

Harper, a young man from the South, had made quite an impact on the running of WINS. I never really found out how he did it, but he sure was a big wheel, and I was glad to tag along. First of all, Earl was the sports director, and when he wanted to do a particular sports event, the station put it on. In baseball, he broadcast the Newark Bears baseball games. Since the Yankees, Giants, and Dodgers had agreed to a pact prohibiting the broadcasting of their games, this meant that WINS had the only regular broadcasting of baseball in 1936. The Bears were the New York Yankees' number-one farm club, and Earl thought, with good reason, that if the Yankees won the pennant (which they did for the next four years), they would put in a good word for him with the powers that were, and he would be one of the announcers on the World Series. But I'll come back to that later. Besides baseball, Earl had what was called "The Inquiring Microphone," a show done from the lobby of the Strand Theater on Broadway in New York, where people of all sorts were interviewed and expressed themselves on topics of the day. Naturally I went along with him every day and helped him with the organization and format of the show. Since I didn't have to be back at the station right away, we saw all the new films that came to the Strand. I don't think I missed an Edward G. Robinson picture of that era. Earl also had a daily sports talk at 6:00 P.M. that I helped him prepare, and I assisted on his broadcast of the St. Patrick's Day Parade and the Army Day Parade. Now this was radio, not TV, so naturally it couldn't compare with the great efforts of my friend Jack McCarthy on WPIX. And besides, Earl wasn't Irish.

I enjoyed the excitement of all the special events, and the regular staff announcing gave me invaluable experience that helped me later on. It also helped develop my poise and aided me in enlarging my vocabulary. It was an experience that I wouldn't have traded for anything. And I was traveling with the star of the station, a man who in 1936 was making four or five hundred a week while everyone else at the station, with a few exceptions, was making fifty or less.

The work was pretty difficult. Sometimes, whenever I felt down about it, I thought of the year and a half when I didn't have a job, and that changed my thinking immediately. The trip from the station to Newark for the minor-league baseball broadcasts got to be boring, and believe me, day-by-day baseball announcing sometimes became pretty monotonous, particularly on days when there were only a few hundred fans in the stands. But Harper was a good play-by-play man, maybe the best around at that time. In fact, he was the only one working locally, since Red Barber was still in Cincinnati and Mel Allen hadn't yet made an appearance in New York. My job was to open and close the show, and carry the broadcasts between innings. I liked this part of my job because at that time baseball was the sport I liked best and knew best, and the Bears, a top contender in the International League, were an interesting team. George Weiss, working his way up the New York Yankee ladder, was the general manager of the club. Later on he ran the Yankees in their big championship years, and then the New York Mets, from their founding until they became contenders in the National League. He was eventually selected for the Baseball Hall of Fame for meritorious service to the sport. When we were broadcasting the Bears games, Mr. Weiss would drop by every day, and that was a signal for either Harper or me to plug a coming Bears game. The Bears had several players who did well later in the big leagues: Spurgeon "Spud" Chandler, Marius Russo, Kemp Wicker, and Atley Donald all pitched for the Yankees in the World Series. Other past or future big leaguers were Merril May, Nolen Richardson, Bill Baker, Willard Herschberger, Dick Porter, Bob Seeds, and Ernie Koy.

Besides broadcasting the Bears home games, we did the away games in the studio by Western Union ticker. I'll bet you thought Ronald Reagan with the Cubs games and Red Barber with the Brooklyn Dodgers games invented that. Well, Earl Harper was first, and he did it in 1935.

As I look back on those days, I'm reminded of the telegrapher—we'll call him Joe—who got rich on his days off by listening carefully to Red Barber's ticker broadcasts of the Dodger games. Red's te-

legrapher was in the studio with him, and the sounds of the dots
and dashes would go out over the airwaves. "Get-rich-quick Joe"
would saunter into a bar while the game was in progress, order a
beer, and indulge in amiable conversation with the bar patrons.
While talking, he would mentally note the dots and dashes being
sent from the ballpark. Red, of course, was lagging behind the action
as he dramatized the game. Suddenly Joe would say to someone,
"Give me two to one and I'll bet Herman gets a hit," or "Ten to
five says he'll strike out." Joe was careful to be wrong now and
then, so nobody would be suspicious, but he always ended the day
with a nice profit. Also, he wouldn't patronize the same bar two
days in a row. He did all right in that season of 1939, but his bonanza
ended when Red and his assistant, Al Helfer—better known as
Brother Al—started to travel with the team and broadcast the away
games back to New York live.

Earl Harper was so pro-Yankees that when he reported the scores
of the big-league games during our Newark broadcasts, he overdid
it. He was bucking for the World Series announcing spot that he
thought the Yankees could get him, but he forgot that the New
York Giants were in action, too, and that they were contenders for
the National League flag. Actually, he did more than forget them,
he ran them down. If the Yankees won, Earl would chortle and
whoop. If the Giants won, he'd grudgingly allow something like,
"Those lucky Giants, they won another." Earl seemed to have forgotten that the Giants were in the National League race and that
they had feelings.

One day late in the season, I had a day off and the Giants were
playing the St. Louis Cardinals—the great Gas House Gang—at
the Polo Grounds. I thought I'd like to see the game, and called
the Giants office. The fabled Eddie Brannick, the Giants' secretary,
came to the phone and I identified myself as Earl Harper's assistant
on the Newark games. Brannick snarled.

"So you work with Earl Harper. So Earl Harper thinks the Giants
are lucky. Well, you tell Harper that we hear his cracks about the
Giants and we don't like them."

I protested that I had nothing to do with it, that I only worked there.

"I know you don't say things like that," said Brannick. "But you tell Harper what I said. There'll be two tickets in your name at the press gate. Good luck to you."

I knew then that if the Giants won the pennant, Harper's chances of doing the World Series were zilch. The Giants and the Yankees both won their pennants in 1936, but Harper had talked himself out of the Series announcing job.

In the fall of 1936, college football in the East was sponsored for the first time. The Atlantic Refining Company, in a massive move, signed up many local stations to broadcast the games of the East's best teams. On the schedule, as I remember it, were Dartmouth, Cornell, Holy Cross, Syracuse, Fordham, and several others. Les Quailey, an agency man, very capable in the field of sports, was one of the guiding lights in the new venture.

Today, sponsorship of college sports on radio or television is taken for granted, and no one pays any attention to it. But in 1936 it was brand-new. It had never been done before. The great institutions of learning looked with a jaundiced eye on anything that might besmirch their reputations in the slightest. It was not easy to get them to change their ways, but ultimately the collegiate opposition to sponsorship was worn down. I'm sure the contracts with the colleges contained, along with the usual *wherefore*s and *whereas*es, many restrictions on the broadcasters.

Today the tail is wagging the dog. The colleges are after the money, and TV decides everything—it has even changed bowl game schedules. In 1936 the colleges maintained a veto power. For that reason, the Atlantic Refining Company held a three-day seminar in Philadelphia for all the announcers and directors who would be involved in the airing of the games.

WINS had been assigned the broadcasts of the Cornell games at Ithaca in upstate New York; Earl Harper was to do the play-by-play while I did the color and commercials. I was thrilled at this opportunity and so was Earl. We were part of that Philadelphia gathering, and I remember seeing many of the top echelon of sports announcers there. It was there that I first met Ted Husing and his assistant, Jimmy Dolan, Bill Stern and Stan Lomax. Husing had always been an idol of mine. And one day, during a lull in the proceedings, I saw him standing alone in the room. I went over to him and said, "Mr. Husing, my name is Dunphy." Husing surprised me. "*Don* Dunphy?" he asked. I was almost speechless that the great Husing would know my first name. He said he had heard me often and liked my work. He was a very friendly and considerate man.

Stan Lomax was the number-one sports announcer for WOR in New York at that time and had a fabulous audience for his daily sports talk at 6:45 each evening. Harper and I were chatting with Lomax at the meetings, and he asked what games we were doing. When he heard that we were doing the Cornell games, he laughed. Lomax was an alumnus of Cornell. "Let me give you a tip," Stan said. "It's cold, real cold up there in the fall. When that wind blows from Lake Cayuga, you'll wish you were somewhere else."

I could see Earl Harper stiffen and maybe even shiver a little. He was from the deep South, and apparently had never been farther north than New York City. Harper, who could get things done at WINS, lost no time in responding to this warning. When he got back to the station after the Philadelphia meetings were over, he immediately met with the brass. Since we were to have a crew of six working the Cornell games, the station immediately bought six storm coats, six blankets, a giant thermos bottle, and a footlocker to put all of them in. Every Friday night during the season we would get a late train from Grand Central Station to Ithaca, and each Friday evening the footlocker and its cold-weather contents would be loaded on the train, taken off at Ithaca, and brought to Schoelkopf Field. Would you believe it?—the fall of 1936 turned out to be the mildest autumn in years, and during the entire season we never opened the locker once.

The football season was a good one, and Cornell, one of the powers of Eastern college football, won most of its games. But the game that stands out particularly in my mind is one that they lost. They were playing Syracuse, and a star halfback on that team was young Marty Glickman from Brooklyn, who had been a sprinter that year on the United States Olympic team. We had the pleasure of broadcasting a Glickman touchdown that helped beat Cornell. Marty went on to become one of our best sports announcers.

I never did get the real story, but somehow, late in 1936, friction developed between Earl Harper and Burt Squire, the manager of WINS. The situation snowballed, got worse and worse, and in December of that year Harper resigned and went over to WNEW. Not only that, but he took the Newark Bears baseball games with him. Almost immediately, I was appointed sports director of WINS and took over the evening sportscast. This was a great break for me, and sent me on the way up the ladder. But I don't know if it was so good for Harper. It was a shame that whatever was wrong between him and the station couldn't have been straightened out. Harper and WINS were ideal for each other, and until 1936 they meshed together beautifully. WINS was a small station in those days, a part of Hearst Radio, and Harper fitted in perfectly. He was a fine baseball announcer, reasonably good at football, and nothing fazed him. He came up with many great ideas, such as "The Inquiring Microphone." Once a week or so he put on a program for the veterans of World War I. (Of course, we didn't call it World War I. We didn't know at that time that there would be another.) This program put a lot of people in his corner. We broadcast the Army Day Parade and the St. Patrick's Day Parade. If you think doing a parade on radio is easy, try it sometime. In 1936 I helped with the parade broadcasts, which almost led to my leaving WINS rather than Harper's doing so.

At that time the New York State Radio Network was formed to link stations around the state—Rochester, Albany, Syracuse, and several other cities. WINS was the New York City outlet. In early March, WSYR in Syracuse needed a sports announcer. They had heard about me and asked WINS if a trade could be worked out in which I would go to Syracuse and Bill Harding would come to

New York. A Colonel Wilder was running things at WSYR, and he came to New York to listen to me on the air. If he liked my work, he would talk to me about going to Syracuse. On March 17, while Earl and I were in the middle of broadcasting the St. Patrick's Day Parade, a message came to our director: "Put Dunphy on the air alone with the parade for the next ten minutes." I got the message and did the parade by myself for a while. Another message came from the station: "Have Dunphy come back to the station immediately to talk with Colonel Wilder." Since our broadcast point was at Fifth Avenue and 63rd Street and WINS was located at 58th and Park Avenue, I didn't have to go far. I started toward the station, not sure whether I was glad or sorry. Colonel Wilder was indeed an interesting person and most persuasive. He pointed out the advantages of being in Syracuse, a reasonably large city, where I wouldn't have the competition I had in New York. And, of course, he stressed that at WSYR I would be number one in sports, not an assistant as I was at WINS. The starting salary up there would be more than I was now making at WINS. It sounded very alluring to an ambitious young fellow like myself, but something whispered in my ear that I should make haste slowly and not rush into anything. I told the colonel that I appreciated his interest in me and that I liked what he said about WSYR, but I needed time to weigh the situation. He asked me not to take too long because he wanted to fill the spot as soon as possible. I gave the matter considerable thought and discussed it with my mother and several friends. All of them thought it would be nice if I were the number-one sports announcer at a station, and I thought so too, but one big thing kept coming into my thoughts. Over and over I kept thinking that most people in radio were trying to get to New York. I was already there. I was born there. It had always been my home. Why go somewhere else? As far as being number one at a station was concerned, I felt I would eventually be that in New York. And I knew that I was liked and respected at WINS, even though they were willing to trade me to Syracuse. So I went to see our manager, Burt Squire, and told him I had decided to decline the offer. He didn't seem alarmed, but thanked me and said he would explain everything to

Colonel Wilder. As it happened, Bill Harding, who was supposed to come to New York in exchange for me, showed up at WINS the next day. Apparently no one had told him the deal was off. WINS put him on the announcing staff anyway, and in subsequent years we worked together on many sports events. When I look back, I often think about the fact that had I gone to Syracuse, I might have met Jane Hurley, but would never have met Muriel Keating.

So when Earl Harper left WINS it was a great break for me, but I couldn't help feeling bad about it. He had done a lot for me since that day in 1934 when I called him and offered to help him with the Manhattan College games. He had gotten WINS to hire me as a staff announcer, and we had done scores of events together. We got along reasonably well—not perfectly, because I too had a mind of my own—and I feel that I helped him a lot, and the station apparently thought so too.

I don't think his deal with WNEW worked out too well; after a year or so, he was out of the New York scene. Some years later, on New Year's Day, 1944, we unexpectedly worked together again for just one day. I broadcast the Cotton Bowl game for Gillette and Mutual, and Earl—ironically enough—was hired to assist me as the color commentator. After that, unfortunately, I lost track of him.

When Earl Harper left WINS and I was appointed sports director, I inherited the 6:45-to-7:00 P.M. sports talk. I thought this was a break for me, but it wasn't all that good. It brought me positive notices in the Hearst papers, but practically nothing in the others. In addition to WINS, the Hearst organization owned three newspapers in New York City: the *New York American* and the *Daily Mirror*, which were morning papers, and the *Evening Journal*. Dinty Doyle, who had come from San Francisco, was the radio editor of the *American*. He was a real sports fan and did a lot for me by mentioning me frequently in his column. Nick Kenny, who had a daily column in the *Mirror* with his brother Charley, was also very helpful. The well-known Dan Parker was the sports editor and columnist of the *Mirror*.

WINS was a part-time station, with only 1,000 watts of power.

It was competing locally with powerful network stations like WOR of Mutual Broadcasting, WJZ and WEAF of the National Broadcasting Company, and WCBS of Columbia Broadcasting. They were the network stations. Strong independents were WMCA and WNEW. Besides facing powerful competition, WINS was hampered by the fact that it was on the air part-time. We shared time on our wavelength with a station in Albuquerque and had to be off the air at sundown, New Mexico time. In the summer, we could run until 10:00 P.M., but in the winter we might be off the air as early as five.

Realizing the problem I had in facing other, better-known sports announcers on better-known and more powerful stations, I decided to do something drastic. At that time, radio sports talk programs rarely featured guests. I changed that and had a guest every night. This hardly seems radical now, but it was then, and in a week or so I was called to the manager's office. Besides Mr. Squire and his secretary, there were three gentlemen there who were introduced as Harry Lewis, the president of Seidenberg Cigars, and his two sons. Seidenberg was going to be the sponsor of my evening sports talk, and its officers wanted to meet me. Having a sponsor on WINS in those days was really something. I was walking on air and trying to conceal my excitement. The Lewises were exceptionally nice, friendly people, and they let me know that the content of the program was my responsibility. They would not interfere in any way. Mr. Lewis assured me Seidenberg's interest would be in the cigar commercials only. Bill Harding, a fine announcer, would do them. I was very happy indeed, but then the roof fell in, or almost. As the meeting was breaking up with everyone in a good mood, Harry Lewis turned and handed me one of his cheroots. "Here, Don, have a cigar." Without thinking, I said, "No, thanks, I don't smoke." As long as I live, I'll never forget the look of incredulity on Mr. Lewis's face. "How the hell can you sell cigars if you don't smoke?" he blurted out. I thought the deal was dead, but Burt Squire, the station manager, was a consummate diplomat. He assured the Lewises that I was not doing the commercials, that I would not let the audience know I didn't smoke, and that it would not affect the program in the least. Somewhat mollified, but still shaking his head, Harry Lewis broke into a smile. We all shook hands and the meeting broke up. Seidenberg Cigars was my sponsor for a long time.

Soon after I got Seidenberg as a sponsor of my show from 6:45 to seven each evening, the station sold a half-hour show to follow mine. It was a re-creation of the Yankee baseball game of that day and was to be done by a sports announcer from New England, Jack Ingersoll—a real nice guy who became a good friend of mine. I was excited and felt that WINS was now going somewhere.

But some weird things happened in radio in those days, and one of the weirdest was the restriction that WINS let this show put on me. Because the re-creation of the Yankee game followed me, I would not be allowed to give the day's Yankee score on my sports talk. I could give the Giants score, the Dodgers score, the Red Sox score, the Cubs score, any old score I wanted to give, but not the Yankee score. The reasoning, if you could call it that, was that if the audience heard the Yankee score on my show, they wouldn't stay tuned in to Ingersoll's re-creation of the Yankee game. I blew my top at this and was furious when I confronted the manager and the salesman. I pointed out that this would be unlikely to help the re-creation at all, but would certainly kill my show. I said there were four or five other sports talks on the air at that time, and anyone wanting the Yankee game score would get it somewhere else. I pointed out that they were making their own man, their sports announcer, me, look like an idiot. But they were adamant. I was not allowed to give the Yankee score—period. It was implied that if I wanted to quit, I should. I thought, "These guys are idiots. How can they expect a sports talk in New York City not to give the score of the world champions?" But I calmed down. I decided that this zany arrangement wasn't going to last long, and it didn't. For a day or two the listeners apparently assumed I'd given the score and they'd missed it, or thought maybe I'd forgotten to give it. But after a couple of days the phone calls started, and some bordered on the violent. Then the mail came, and that was even more vituperative. Then Seidenberg threatened to cancel. The station backed down, and I was allowed to give the Yankee score. If you find this story hard to believe, I don't blame you, because I could hardly believe it at the time. But it really did happen.

I worked as sports director of WINS from 1937 to 1947, and hosted an evening sports program Mondays through Saturdays. Every so often I would come up with a promotional idea to hype the program. It usually was in the form of a contest in which I gave away valuable tickets to sports events as the prizes. In the spring of 1941, I ran a contest that could have turned into the biggest crisis of my broadcasting career. It could have caused me to leave town and the business permanently. Joe Louis, then the great heavyweight champion, was matched for the title with the hulking Abe Simon in Detroit on March 21. The bout was scheduled for twenty rounds, and as far as I can recall, it was the last bout that was scheduled for that many rounds, or at least the last heavyweight title bout that was. Two weeks after this fight, on April 4, former champion Max Baer was scheduled to fight Lou Nova at Madison Square Garden.

My idea was to run a contest on the outcome of the Louis–Simon bout, and to give pairs of ringside seats to the Baer–Nova fight as prizes. Since those ducats were going for sixteen dollars each, pretty serious dough in 1941, they were good prizes indeed. Through my friend Irwin Rosee, radio publicity director for promoter Mike Jacobs, I made arrangements to give away three sets of ringside seats to the Baer–Nova fight on a contest predicting the winner and the time of the knockout in the Louis–Simon fight. In early 1941, the great Brown Bomber was in the midst of his famous "Bum of the Month" campaign. In December of 1940 he knocked out Al McCoy in six rounds. In January it was Red Burman in Five. In February it was Gus Dorazio in two. Simon was scheduled for March, Tony Musto for April, and Buddy Baer, Max's brother, for May. In other words, Simon was destined to be a "Bum of the Month," or so it seemed.

I thought I had a pretty good contest going when I asked my WINS listeners to write in predicting the winner and the time of the knockout. The prizes would go to the first three who were closest to the actual result. It was an exciting and attractive contest, and the postcards poured in. I was happy about the response, and so was the station manager. Most of the listeners predicted an early knockout by the champion. The answers ran something like this: Louis in 2:02 of the first, Louis in 1:28 of the second, Louis in the third at 1:15, and so forth. Naturally, if a couple of contestants came up with the same time and it proved correct, they would get similar prizes. The great majority picked Louis in the first five rounds. Some picked him in the middle rounds between the eighth and fifteenth. Some picked him in the nineteenth. And then were was the joker in the deck: about eighty picked Louis by a decision at the end of twenty rounds. There was not one response picking Simon—which was reasonable because he wasn't given a ghost of a chance by anybody. The people who picked Louis by decision at the end of twenty interested me and caused me a little concern. By the rules of the contest, if Louis won by a decision, there would be eighty ties for first, and I would have to give away eighty pairs of ringside seats worth approximately $2,560.00. Since the Garden would only go for six seats, and the station wouldn't go for any, it would be up to me to come up with the rest, or leave town. Since I was making only a hundred bucks a week and didn't have any money saved, the chances are I would have left town and you wouldn't be reading this.

But after briefly imagining that dire possibility, I dismissed it from my mind. The thought of Simon going more than a few rounds with Louis was laughable; the thought of his going the limit was ridiculous. I wasted no more time on the subject. I settled down in New York to listen to Sam Taub's radio broadcast from Detroit. Sam's description was vivid as always: "Louis jabs Simon, jabs him again, nails him with a left combination, measures Simon with a straight right." Simon was doing nothing but catching.

That's the way it was in the first round. It was the same in the second and in the third, with variations. Louis was all over big Abe, hitting him almost at will. The pattern changed a little in the fourth and fifth. Simon was starting to hold on. He was holding more often in the sixth, seventh, and eighth. But he was still in there, and he wasn't going down. Louis tore into Simon in the ninth and hit him with everything in the book. But when the bell sounded the end of the round, Simon was still on his feet and making his own way to his corner.

Between the ninth and tenth rounds I started to get a sinking sensation in the pit of my stomach. It suddenly occurred to me for the first time that this bout could conceivably go the limit. If it did, I would be responsible for eighty pairs of Baer–Nova ringside seats at thirty-two dollars a pair. They came out for the tenth, and once again it was Louis tearing into Simon. But from Sam's description I began to gather that the Brown Bomber was starting to get arm-weary. Also I remembered that I had seen fighters on occasion take so much punishment that after a while they were oblivious of it. Nothing changed the pattern in the tenth. Louis battered Simon, and Simon took it. The bell rang and they went back to their corners. Same thing in the eleventh. By now I was convinced that the bout would go the limit. Nothing new in the twelfth. At the end of that round I was figuring how I would get out of town and where I would go. What would I do? Certain now that the bout would go the full distance of twenty rounds, I was barely listening in the thirteenth when suddenly I heard Taub shout, "It's over. The referee is stopping the bout to save Simon from further punishment."

I thought, "He could have done it a lot sooner and saved us both a lot of punishment." I never ran another contest on a prizefight. In March of 1942, Louis fought Simon again, with the champ's purse donated to the Army Relief Fund. Louis kayoed Simon in six. I had run the contest on the wrong fight!

I sometimes think my broadcasting career really began that day years ago when Carl Calman, manager of WINS radio station, called me into his office and introduced me to Ernie Braca and Solly King. These gentlemen, it turned out, were about to publish a horse-racing sheet in opposition to the *National Racing Program*, then the reigning king of the tip sheets. The new venture would be called the *Daily Payoff*, and Ernie and Solly would buy time on WINS to air the results of the day's races at every track in this country and Cuba. Bill Harding and I would be the announcers and the *Daily Payoff* would have carte blanche as far as WINS programming was concerned. In other words, whenever Bill or I had a flash result or a mutuel payoff or a jockey change or whatever, we were to call for a microphone and put it on the air immediately.

This started a new life for me. Although I had been a sports announcer for a couple of years, I had never been to a racetrack in my life, and I was completely ignorant of the finer points of the Sport of Kings (or is it the King of Sports?). I had to learn a new glossary of terms that had hitherto been completely foreign to me, such things as "late scratches," "added starters," "no boy," "mutuel payoffs" (to be known as "muts"), and so forth.

We got the program on the air all right, and then the fun began. Bill and I threw ourselves wholeheartedly into the deal, and the campaign began to make the *Daily Payoff* a household—or rather a newsstand—word. Spot racing news had never been put on the air before, and Bill and I outdid ourselves. We interrupted anything and everything. We even went on the air when it wasn't necessary. The rest of the WINS program schedule was massacred as we broke in time and again with "They're off at Belmont," "Here are the prices for the fourth at Havana," "There's a late scratch at Hawthorne," "The horses are on the track for the first at Santa Anita," and so forth, from early morning until late at night.

I can still see the artists who appeared on WINS in those days, chagrined and embarrassed as their talents were cut to ribbons by the relentless charge of the *Daily Payoff*. Wonderful singers such as future opera star Dorothy Kirsten and the soon-to-be-popular Frankie Laine would stand at the mike, mouths wide open, as we nudged them aside to put a *Daily Payoff* special on the air. They were upset, but the racing fans loved it. Dorothy Kirsten never held it against me. We became good friends, and later she sang at my wedding. And when I met Frankie Laine at the Joe Louis Dinner in Las Vegas a couple of years ago, we had a great laugh over it.

The bookies never had it so good. The *Daily Payoff* made it easier for the bettor and made a bonanza for the bookies. Prior to the

Payoff going on the air, if a bettor wanted to know the result of a race, he had to call a telephone number found in a racing sheet and use a code word to get what he wanted. But this was laborious, expensive, and time-consuming. It was irksome to the itchy player, since most of the time the line was busy. The *Payoff* changed all that. Now if a bettor wanted to play the double, or make a parlay or a round-robin, he'd soon know if his horse came in and he could go on to bigger and better things. It was great for the betting public, and the sheet's circulation soared. But the owners of the *Payoff* weren't satisfied with success. They wanted more and more. So Bill and I started announcing winners by saying, "The winner of the sixth at Belmont is *Daily Payoff* number seven," instead of giving the name of the horse. This was apparently too much—the audience screamed, so we started giving the name of the horse too.

It was a popular program—maybe too popular. It was hard work also. And after a while it got both boring and consuming. I'd find it impossible to get numbers and horses' names out of my mind. And I couldn't help feeling sorry for the singers who were having their careers jeopardized. Kirsten and Laine survived and made it big, but what of some of the others who had talent but might have gotten so discouraged that they quit it all?

In those days there were such things in racing as added starters. In other words, a horse might not be listed in the overnight entries, but for a special fee an owner could get him entered in a race almost up to post time. So added starters and late scratches became important terms in our racetrack terminology. One day I got fed up with the whole thing, and instead of reporting a late scratch, I went on the air and reported, "In the fourth at Jamaica, there's a tardy deletion." This ad lib caused more panic than the market crash of '29. Pandemonium reigned. The WINS switchboard was jammed with calls from irate listeners who couldn't find "tardy deletion" in their *Daily Payoffs* or anywhere. Was he an added starter, a late scratch, or what? It took two hours to straighten out the mess, and I was almost fired.

About that time, I won the audition to become the announcer for the Madison Square Garden fights. The sponsor was the Gillette

Safety Razor Company, located in Boston. I had heard much about Bostonians' staid ways, and I wasn't sure what their reaction would be if they learned that I was announcing something so earthy as spot racing news, so I didn't tell them and I hoped they wouldn't find out. Since WINS didn't reach Boston, I felt fairly secure about it. Our first fight was the Joe Louis–Billy Conn heavyweight championship bout at the Polo Grounds on June 18, 1941. Bill Corum, the famous sports columnist of the *Journal-American*, was to work with me on the broadcasts, and since we were a new broadcasting team, it was decided to do a dry run simulating the broadcast as it would actually occur. The practice session took place at the regular fights at Fort Hamilton in Brooklyn. The advertising manager of Gillette, Craig Smith, and two executives of the Maxon Advertising Agency joined Bill and me at ringside. Johnny Addie, later the fine Madison Square Garden ring announcer, was doing the chores at Fort Hamilton. Prior to the main event, he decided to give Bill and me a nice sendoff by introducing us to the crowd. For Bill there was a round of polite applause. But when I was introduced, some leather-lunged wag in the back shouted, "Hey, Don, who won the eighth at Belmont?" It broke up the house and my secret was out.

The *Daily Payoff* didn't make it, proving to be another ninety-day wonder. I don't know what happened to Solly King, but Ernie Braca and I met many times on the boxing beat since he managed contenders Tommy Bell and Tony Anthony and finally the great Ray Robinson.

It's fun thinking of those days, but when I do, I also think of the sign over a restaurant adjacent to a racetrack—"Eat your betting money, but never bet your eating money."

In January 1941, I didn't realize what a fateful year it would turn out to be, for the country and for me. I was doing all right at WINS, but just all right. I was making $100 a week, which wasn't bad for a small station. Through my evening sports talks and my broadcasts of college football and the track meets at the Garden, I was becoming better known. But while I was doing a lot on the air, I didn't feel I was making much progress. The more I did, the more annoyed

I became because I couldn't seem to crack the networks. But then I got a break, maybe the biggest break anyone in broadcasting ever got. Remember those ads: "I got my job through *The New York Times*"? Well, I got my big job through a music war, and I can't sing a note.

ASCAP, the American Society of Composers, Authors and Publishers, was founded by the great composer Victor Herbert and his friend Gene Buck. They were having dinner at the Plaza in New York, when the orchestra leader, seeing Herbert, decided to play one of his compositions. Listening to it, Herbert said, "They're playing what I wrote and I'm not getting anything for it. It isn't right." Buck agreed with him and they set about founding ASCAP, of which Buck was president for many years. From then on, whenever music was played, a royalty was paid to ASCAP, which passed on a fee to the publisher, composer, and/or author. ASCAP became bigger and stronger. Radio was a bonanza for it and for the authors, composers, and publishers. In January 1941, the four radio networks (Mutual, Columbia, and the two NBC networks, Red and Blue) decided the ASCAP fees were prohibitive and left, forming their own music outfit, which they called Broadcast Music, Incorporated or BMI. I didn't realize at the time how much this would affect me! The music world and the sports world seemed miles apart.

In January 1941 I was in my sixth year as sports director at WINS, and felt I was stuck. The important broadcasts seemed to bounce around in a circle: Ted Husing, Bill Stern, Bill Slater, Clem McCarthy, and Sam Taub; for baseball, Red Barber had a lock on it. I wondered if I would ever get the chance I thought I deserved.

In those days, strangely enough, my best relationship was with boxing. Irwin Rosee was doing radio publicity for Madison Square Garden. He and I were good friends, and he came up with an idea. Why not a boxing program on WINS every Saturday afternoon to comment on the previous night's fight at the Garden, and to discuss everything else in boxing as well? It was a good idea, and the station put it on. I was the host of the show and the mainstays were Harry Markson, publicist for Garden boxing, and Barney Nagler, who wrote for the *Bronx Home News*. We called the program "Between

Rounds," and it was a fine show; Saturday afternoons on WINS became a kind of open house as far as boxing was concerned. We interviewed boxers, managers, publicity men for New York fight clubs, and sportswriters. One of those who was on many times was Ben Feingold, whom we believed was a sportswriter. It turned out later he was a mailman. He was very knowledgeable about boxing and took part in the various discussions. One Saturday after the show, Irwin asked me when I had invited Feingold on the program. I said, "I didn't invite him at all. I thought you had invited him." We both laughed, and let him continue on as an occasional guest.

A regular on the program, a man who added a lot, was Meyer Ackerman, who did publicity for a couple of fight clubs, including the Queensboro Arena. One Saturday in March, Ackerman mentioned some exciting news to me. There was going to be a change in the boxing broadcasting setup at Madison Square Garden. WOR-Mutual was taking over the fights from the Blue Network of NBC, and the Gillette Safety Razor Company would be the sponsor, not Adam Hats. This was a bombshell. The Garden fights had been aired by Bill Stern and Sam Taub for a long time. "That's great," I said to Meyer. "Now maybe I'll get a chance to do the fights." Ackerman shook his head. "I'm sorry, Don," he said. "They want Ted Husing as the announcer."

Now I shook my head. It was the same old roundelay all over again. Husing, Stern, McCarthy, Slater. Around and around. How does another announcer get a chance? How do they know I can't do it better? What about some struggling sports announcer in Topeka or Peoria? How do they know he can't do it? They don't. It made me mad.

Of course, I could understand why Gillette wanted Husing for the fight broadcasts. He was the number-one sports announcer of the day, and had a good relationship with them. His biggest job for Gillette was the broadcast of the Kentucky Derby, and he had done football for them. Husing was sports director for CBS, and in order for Gillette to use him on Mutual, CBS had to agree, which they did. My getting to the top seemed more remote than ever. The following Monday, I checked the story Ackerman had told me. I

found that the Gillette account was handled by the Maxon Agency.
Bill Von Zahle was the WINS salesman who handled Maxon. He
verified what I had heard. Mutual Broadcasting had scored a coup
and taken the Garden fights away from NBC's Blue Network. "I
go for a man who wears an Adam Hat," would be replaced by
"How're ya fixed for blades?" The first fight in the new setup would
be the Joe Louis–Billy Conn fight for the Brown Bomber's heavyweight championship. A real blockbuster. The most important fight
in years. Since there wasn't anything I could do about it, I tried to
put it out of my mind and concentrated on my work. March drifted
into April, and April into May.

May 21 was a day I'll never forget. I had the day off because my
sports talk on WINS was preempted. My phone was out of order,
which had a bearing on subsequent events.

Having nothing better to do, I stopped by the offices of the
Twentieth Century Sporting Club in the Brill Building on Broadway. It was the organization under which Mike Jacobs promoted
fights at the Garden. The place was jumping with excitement. Irwin
Rosee grabbed me. "Where have you been?" he asked almost hys-
terically. "I've been trying to get you all day."

Rosee explained the reason for the excitement at Mike Jacobs's
office, which was all caused by a "music war." Mutual had suddenly
pulled out of Broadcast Music, Incorporated, and gone back to
ASCAP. This left the other three networks, CBS, and NBC's Blue
and Red, holding the bag. They were furious—especially CBS.
"Okay," CBS told Mutual, "now you can't have Ted Husing to do
your fights." What about Gillette? Suddenly they were within weeks
of the biggest fight since Louis–Schmeling and they had no announcer. Sam Taub was around, but naturally they didn't want
him because of his close identification with Adam Hats. Now Gillette
did what I thought they should have done in the first place. They
started looking for new talent.

The next night, May 22, a big fight was scheduled at the Garden.
Anton Christoforidis was defending his NBA light heavyweight title
against Gus Lesnevich. Gillette invited many announcers to par-
ticipate in one large live audition. Irwin put in my name with Craig

Smith, the advertising manager of Gillette, but he, a Bostonian, was skeptical about someone he had never heard of. Irwin assured Smith that I was a good boxing announcer—besides, they had an open spot in the audition. Rosee had gotten my name in the audition, but now he couldn't find me, and my phone was broken. It was indeed fortunate that I dropped into his office that day.

As I listened to him explain all this, I got the feeling the job was mine and that the audition was a mere formality. Not so! When I entered the Garden the following night and got to ringside, it dawned on me that this was no walkover. Mel Allen was there. He was a top announcer, and I hadn't expected him to take the audition; he had been scheduled to be Husing's color commentator before the upheaval. His presence worried me. Then there was Bob Elson, who had done the World Series for Gillette, and Bert Lee, Jr., who had done hockey for Gillette. But most important of all of them was Paul Douglas, later a great movie star, but then a top sports announcer. No, this would be no breeze. I'd have to work for it.

The mechanics of the audition were that each announcer would do two early rounds and two late rounds, working two at a time, sitting at opposite sides of the ring. Bob Elson was the color commentator for everyone. Our voices were recorded on the big discs that were used in those days, then sent to Craig Smith. My concentration was great. I put everything out of my mind but this big effort. I thought I did well. After my first two rounds, I remember hearing Bob Elson remark to someone what a fine job I had done. I told Bill Harding, my co-worker at WINS, "I did my best. I have no apologies. If someone did better, he deserves the job." Incidentally, Lesnevich won the fight, and the WBA light heavyweight crown.

Now the waiting and suspense began. About fifteen announcers had taken the live audition, and another twenty had sent recordings of their work to the Gillette Company in Boston. It would take time for Craig Smith and his assistants to wade through the pile and come up with a selection. I waited a week. Then I called Rosee to find out what was happening. His reply was discouraging. "Don," he said, "I'd say the odds are about five to one against you. They think you did the best job, but they don't know you, and they don't think you have the experience necessary for this job."

"But, Irwin," I protested, "you know I have the experience. I've been doing fights for a couple of years."

"I know you have. Convincing Gillette that you should be their choice is the problem," he said.

Frustrated, I asked him what I should do. He suggested I call Tom Slater, who, as sports director for Mutual, was directly involved in the discussions. Tom, whom I had never met, but knew by reputation, was the brother of Bill Slater, the sports announcer. He was very sympathetic when I called, and suggested I write a letter to Craig Smith at the Gillette headquarters in Boston. I thanked him and said I would.

By this time I was seething, knowing I had done the best job on the audition but wasn't being picked. After I finished my evening sports talk, I planned what I should do. I would write that letter to Smith, but first I would have a drink. So I went to a neighborhood bar and had a Manhattan. I had two more. Then I went back to WINS and wrote to Smith. I was cool and determined. I started letter after letter, but invariably tore the paper out of the machine before it was half finished. Finally, after the floor was littered, I got the one I wanted. "You're in Boston, and I'm in New York," I wrote, "so I'm not surprised you haven't heard of me." Then I described my experience, and the fights I had done locally. Not about to let everything hang on the recent audition, I said I was doing a fight from the Queensboro Arena the following week, and I hoped he would have someone listen to it. I mentioned this because I wanted him to know the confidence I had in my ability and also to show that the Lesnevich–Christoforidis fight was no fluke. Then I thanked him for his attention.

The letter stirred up something. Two days later I got a call from Ed Wilhelm of the Maxon Agency, which represented Gillette. He asked about the Queensboro fight, the station and the time. Now I knew there was interest.

After that fight there was another week of waiting and hoping. I kept in touch with Rosee, but apparently he wasn't hearing any

more than I was. We were into June now, and the fight was scheduled for June 18. Something would have to happen soon. It did.
One day I was on my way to the studio when I met Bill Stynes,
who worked at WINS. He told me that Ed Wilhelm had called and
wanted me to call him. Now I felt that the matter was at least
resolved.

Ed was most pleasant and congratulated me. The Gillette people
had picked me to be the blow-by-blow announcer on the heavyweight championship fight. It was the beginning of a twenty-five-
year relationship with the company. At last I had made the big
time.

Joe Louis–Billy Conn

POLO GROUNDS, JUNE 18, 1941

On the day of the fight, I left Jackson Heights early to go to the weigh-in at the State Office Building. The weigh-in was very crowded. I should have been excited, but I remember I was very calm. The weights announced were Louis at 199½, Conn at 174. Later I heard from other sources, including Billy himself, that he only weighed 169¾, and that Louis was above 200, but the authorities were afraid to announce such a big discrepancy in the weights, so Louis was dropped below 200 and Conn raised to 174.

After the weigh-in, Mike Jacobs brought Bill Corum and me to an office to meet with the three boxing commissioners, General John

Phelan, who was the chairman, Bill Brown, and Walker Wear. The gist of the meeting was that they didn't want any favoritism in the broadcast. They wanted it to be fair to both fighters. Bill and I assured them that we would not have it any other way. We had no questions. We knew the rules, which were a lot simpler than they are now: scoring by rounds; a referee and two judges voting; no mandatory eight-count; no three-knockdown rule. A man could be saved by the bell.

I didn't get to see Conn after the weigh-in, but I went up to Louis to wish him luck. As always, Joe was thoughtful. He realized that this was my big night. So he said, "I want to wish you luck, too, Don." That made me feel good.

After the weigh-in, I had lunch and then dropped into WINS. Cec Hackett, the manager of the station, was going to the fight, and he invited me to have dinner with him and his wife. Afterward they would drive me to the fight. I thought it was a great idea. However, I didn't realize what a trial it would turn out to be.

The Hacketts, whose apartment was on Fifth Avenue and 70th Street, served a nice dinner, but I must say that with the Louis–Conn fight on my mind, I didn't have a great appetite. The fight was scheduled for 10:00 P.M., and I planned to be at the Polo Grounds at nine. It wasn't a long drive from the Hacketts' to the Polo Grounds at 155th Street and Eighth Avenue, and even with the expected fight traffic, we figured to make it in less than forty-five minutes. We started for the fight at about eight o'clock. Then the fun began, although at the time it was more like tragedy than comedy. We got to 125th Street, just a mile and a half from the ball park, in short order, and then ground to a halt. There was construction on Eighth Avenue for the next half-mile, something we hadn't known about, and all traffic was rerouted. We crept along at the proverbial snail's pace. At 8:45, the first feeling of alarm struck me. At nine o'clock I really got worried. I began to think of Craig Smith, Ed Wilhelm, Searle Hendee, and Fred Weber—executives of Gillette and Mutual—at ringside at the Polo Grounds wondering what had happened to me. Would they think I had met

with an accident, or—worse, maybe—would they think I had chick-
ened out on the broadcast? My mind was in a turmoil. At 9:15 we
got to 145th Street. I thanked the Hacketts, bolted from the car,
and raced down the subway stairs. A train came almost immediately. It was jammed with the fight crowd, but I was able to squeeze
in. The next stop was the Polo Grounds, and we got there in minutes.
My ticket called for entrance through the press gate, which was
jammed, but I got in. I should have entered the field by an entrance
near the bull pen, which was in deep right field (the ring was set
up over the pitcher's mound), but I thought I could make better
time by taking the route under the stands and coming out to the
field through the box seats. It worked until I got to the little gate
to the field. There I was stopped by a cop who wanted to see my
ticket. I showed it to him. "This ticket," he said, "calls for entrance
through the bull pen. You can't get out this way." I was only about
seventy feet away from my seat at ringside, and I could see Smith,
Wilhelm, and the others looking all over for me. I confidently told
the officer who I was and that I was there to broadcast the fight.
He had never heard of me (I guess he never played the horses). I
pleaded with him, but he was adamant. It was now nine-thirty. I
had to go all the way back under the stands to the bull pen, only
this time I was going against the crowd. It was a struggle, pushing
against the eager, milling bodies, but I got there and ran out on
the field. The fresh smell of the Polo Grounds turf was a tonic to
me, and I raced to ringside. It was almost 9:40. You can't imagine
the looks of relief on the faces of Smith and company. I wish I could
have seen the look on my own face.

This is the actual wording of the radio description of the first Louis–
Conn fight, taken from the recording of the fight. The first words
are from Bill Corum, one of America's great sports columnists, who
was the color commentator on the fight. I did the blow-by-blow.

CORUM: . . . and Billy is wearing those purple trunks and here
comes the champion. Here comes old Joe. Julian Black precedes
him into the ring. Listen to that cheering. Joe's got on his famous

blue-and-red bathrobe with "Joe Louis" on the back, and he's got another dressing gown and robe underneath that, a white one. I guess he thought it was going to be cold here this evening but it isn't. He's holding a towel around his head. Now a midget has jumped in to shake hands with him, the same little fellow that's always crawling into the ring to get chased out, and he's always rushing in to shake hands with the challenger. Conn is putting on the gloves first, and Billy looks in great shape, doesn't look as big as Louis, naturally, a 174-pound man couldn't. Twenty-five pounds have got to show.

[The bell rings to get attention for Harry Balogh, the famous ring announcer.]

BALOGH: Attention, please. Thank you. Thank you. . . . Ladies and gentlemen, please. Thank you very much. May I have your attention for a moment, folks. Another contest will follow. The officials as the judges: Marty Monroe, Bill Healey, the timekeeper is George Bannon. Counting for the knockdowns at the bell, Jed Gahan. The referee is Eddie Joseph. Again, ladies and gentlemen, with your kind permission, please. Here is one of the foremost of the heavyweight challengers for heavyweight championship honors, Lou Nova.

CORUM: Nova looks mighty good too, and there's a fellow that really believes, just as Conn does, that he can beat Louis. You know, Lou thinks he's got a cosmic punch.

BALOGH: Now the feature attraction on this evening's program. Fifteen rounds for the heavyweight championship of the world. Presenting the present world's heavyweight king from Detroit, Michigan, weighing 199½, he's wearing black trunks, Joe Louis. [Long ovation.] From Pittsburgh, Pennsylvania, weighing 174, wearing purple trunks . . . [Balogh is interrupted by an ovation for Conn] . . . the very capable challenger, Billy Conn. May the better man emerge victorious!

CORUM: All right, they're coming up to meet Joseph. As I say, I'm sure you got the weights, 199½ for Louis, 174 for Conn. That makes it twenty-five and a half difference. Now listen to the referee.

JOSEPH: Watch your low punches and backhands. They cost you

a round. And if a man is knocked down, go to the farthest neutral corner and resume fighting when I tell you. Shake hands and go to work.

CORUM: They're going back to their corners. Johnny Ray rubbing Conn, patting him on the back. Jack Blackburn with his hand over Louis's shoulder. Hasn't pulled the robe off yet. Now he has. Taking off the white towel. Joe just lifting up his hands. Got his back turned. Standing just putting in the mouthpiece. Kind of shoves Blackburn out of the ring himself. There's the bell, Don Dunphy.

DUNPHY: Thank you, Bill Corum. They advance very slowly to the center of the ring. Conn, as expected, is dancing around. Louis is trying to crowd him into a corner. Conn almost slips, moving around very fast. Jabs with his left. It's blocked. Conn jabs with his own left. It's short of the mark. Louis is trying to get Conn into that corner and both of the boys, as Bill told you before, are wearing purple trunks. They wouldn't give in one to the other. [This is at variance with Balogh's introduction, which said Louis was wearing black trunks. In those days before TV, fighters wore clashing colors; the champion normally wore purple. But Conn claimed he was also a champion.] Louis is short with another left jab. Not a blow landed so far. Another left by Louis is short of the mark. The wraithlike Conn keeps moving around the ring. Louis trying to get him into a corner. Still trying to crowd him in and get that crushing blow in if he can. Conn feints with a right and the referee is telling the boys to get in there and give a little action. No blows struck yet. Conn jabs with a left. It's short. Louis just waiting for Conn to lead to him so he can counter with that right. Another left by Billy Conn is short of the mark. Neither of the boys have landed a blow yet. There's Louis still stalking Conn. Conn moving around very fast. From right to left. Now he's going all the way around to the left. Louis is short with a left lead. Conn didn't even have to block that one. He wasn't there when it came. Conn short with another left jab and Louis trying to get him into that corner. Conn is down, but it's not from a punch. He jabbed at Louis and slipped. And Louis didn't even hit him on the way down. It's not going to be a knockdown. At least not in my book. There's Louis trying to get Conn into that corner once again. . . . Not a blow landed yet. A left jab by Conn finds the mark. The first blow of the fight. Another blow by Conn finds the mark and Louis crowds Conn, who goes into a clinch. In close, Louis rips two right hands to the body. There seems to be something the matter with Conn's shoes. He's slipping around the ring. Conn jabs a left which grazes Louis's chin. Conn beats him to the punch with a left hook to the body. In close, Louis brings up a right hand to the jaw. He's got Conn on the ropes. He rips a hard right to the midsection and a left hook to the jaw. Now Conn is back swinging with a left hook to the jaw and Louis rips a hard right to the body. Louis is short with a left hook as Conn goes out of range. Conn shoots a left and it's short as Louis blocks the punch. Louis crosses his right and Conn is not there, going back from the blow. Conn rips a left to Louis's head and goes into close quarters. They tie each other up. Louis gets a left and a right free and pounds Conn twice and Conn seems to be hurt. But he's out bouncing around in the center of the ring. A left hook by Conn finds the mark. In close, Louis brings up his own left hook to the jaw and they tie each other up. Conn pecks away with a left hand that finds Louis's nose. Louis very calm—so is Conn, apparently. Conn jabs a left and then goes into a clinch, finally scoring a point. They wrestle each other around in the center of the ring. And the referee, Eddie Joseph, tells the boys to separate, which they do. Conn jabs a left. Louis misses a right cross. That was a haymaker . . . had Conn been there. Louis had Conn in the ropes but Billy kept moving away and got out of range. Louis jabs a left which gets in there. Conn, continually on the move, shoots a left which Louis blocks. Less than a minute to go in round one. Not very much damage done so far. Louis is still trying to get Conn into the corner. Referee Eddie Joseph is moving around. A very fast fight with little blows landed. Louis is short with his left jab. He's still trying to get Conn in there and Conn won't accommodate him. And there's the bell for round one.

CORUM: That was a good round, but a feeler-out round.

Louis built up an early lead, but Conn whittled away at it, and the fight was pretty, even into the tenth. That round I described thus: "A right cross to the jaw thrown by Louis catches Conn as he comes off the ropes. Louis hooking a left to Conn's jaw, Conn slips to the canvas and a very gentlemanly Louis doesn't even try to land a blow. Very nice, Joe, and the crowd appreciates it."

Later in the round: "Louis gets his hands free with a left and a right to the head, another left and a right to the head by Louis." But Conn battled back. "A left hook to the jaw by Conn. A left hook to the body and a right uppercut scored by Billy Conn." But it had been a good round for the champion.

In the eleventh, Louis started the round on the attack, but then the blow-by-blow ran like this: "There's Billy fighting back with a right to the body, crossing a right to the jaw. Another right to the body by Billy Conn and now the tables are turned as he ties up Joe Louis and has his own right hand free." Then, near the end of the round:

DUNPHY: Conn comes back with a right to the body, another right to the body, and a left hook to the body by Billy Conn. A right to the body, a left hook to the jaw, another right, and Conn is still swinging. And Louis hasn't landed a blow in this flurry. A left hook to the body, a right cross to the jaw, and Louis is worried. A left hook, another left hook by Billy Conn and they lock arms in the center of the ring. And now it's Joe Louis who's a bit tired. Now the tide of battle has turned again as Conn beats Louis to the punch. And the fight gets more dramatic every minute. Louis seems to be tired. The tide of battle has turned again. Louis hooks a left to Conn's head at the bell.

CORUM: Oh boy, there's excitement for you, Don. Listen to that crowd. Louis was definitely hurt in that round, is very tired, goes back to his corner completely dispirited. Conn dances back to his corner, waving to the crowd, still looking like a million dollars, and he really hurt Louis. There's no question about it. He hurt him, and he had him hanging on, and he also had him very tired. It wasn't one punch. They just locked heads in the middle of the ring and Conn simply outfought him with sheer Irish fight. Grinned and punched, and punched and punched, hooked and slammed and banged Joe around and when Joe did hit he didn't seem to have a thing on his blows. He seemed to be befuddled by Conn. He couldn't tie him up. He couldn't get away from him. He couldn't punch at long range. He just got well pasted around in that round and that's all you can say and he looks a very dispirited champion as he puts his mouthpiece in and leans back to talk to Blackburn. He looks much more tired than Conn. [Bell rings.] But here's Don.

DUNPHY: Round twelve, four to go. . . . The boys are out in the center of the ring. Heavyweight championship of the world at stake. Conn and Louis—no blows landed in round twelve so far. Louis jabs away with a left to Conn's chin . . . Conn dances around . . . Louis is after him. He's a very serious young man now, the champion is, as he crosses a right to Conn's jaw. Conn doesn't seem to mind that blow at all and goes into a clinch. . . . There's Louis with a stinging left hook to the jaw . . . a jab and Conn takes a right cross to the jaw. . . . Conn rips a left hand to the body, and as Louis rips a left and a right to the head, Conn covers up and partially blocks the blows. Louis pushes Conn away from him. In close, Conn takes a right cross to the jaw thrown by Joe Louis and hooks his own left to the champion's chin. . . . Less than a minute to go in round twelve. . . . In close, they batter the body with lefts and rights and honors are about even. . . . Conn hooks a left to Joe's head which goes around him. Hooks another left to Joe's jaw. Louis, in close, digs a left to the body and Conn comes back with a left and right to the body of the champion. Now Louis has Conn on the ropes, crossing a right to the jaw and hooking a left to the body. Another left to the body is blocked by the challenger. . . . Louis is staggered by a left hook. Conn staggers Louis. . . . Louis is reeling around and holding on. A left hook to the jaw followed by a right cross, and the champion is hurt. Louis is trying to hold on. Conn hooks two lefts to the jaw. . . . Another left hook to the jaw by Conn. . . . Louis is hurt, make no mistake about that. . . . Conn hooks his left to the jaw and Louis paws with his left hand. . . . A left hook to the jaw scored by Billy Conn at the bell.

CORUM: And there was drama for you, if you ever saw it in any ring. What a fight this is turning out to be. Conn hooked Louis with a left, almost upset him, and Joe did just miss going down, but don't think that because Conn has been drawing the cheers and forcing the fighting that he's doing all of it. Louis hurt him two or three times in that round and cut him a little about the mouth and about the eyes, and when the round was over Billy tried to go to Louis's corner. But the big punch was that left hook that Conn landed, which definitely all but shook the champion right off his throne at least momentarily, and it tottered under him and Louis was completely dazed. He's so tired in his corner, more tired than Conn, although as I say he's still doing some of the fighting and after that punch even, he hurt Conn with a left hook of his own. A terrific round, a terrific fight. The warning bell has sounded. Joseph goes over and says something to Conn. But there's the bell and Don. . . .

Here is the way the officials scored the bout through the first twelve rounds (the bout was scored on a rounds basis):

	Conn	Louis	Even
Judge Bill Healey	6	6	0
Judge Marty Monroe	7	4	1
Referee Eddie Joseph	7	5	0

The scoring after twelve rounds of this championship bout refutes the long-accepted theory that had the fight gone the fifteen-round limit, Conn would have won and would have been the heavyweight champion of the world. Not necessarily. The bout, as I mentioned, was scored on a rounds basis with a majority vote of the three scoring officials, Judges Healey and Monroe and Referee Joseph. There were three rounds left, and if Conn had taken just one of them, he would have been the winner with eight rounds on the cards of Monroe and Joseph. However, Louis could have defended his title successfully if *he* had taken the thirteenth, fourteenth, and fifteenth rounds. On that assumption, the final scoring would have been as follows:

	Conn	Louis	Even
Judge Bill Healey	6	9	0
Judge Marty Monroe	7	7	1
Referee Eddie Joseph	7	8	0

DUNPHY: And here's round thirteen, and I wonder if it will be unlucky for either of these two great fighters. . . . They go to close quarters. Conn, after hooking a left to the body, brings up a left to the jaw. Louis staggers with a right uppercut and Conn wisely holds on. Louis hurts Conn again with a right and a left to the body. Another right and left to the body. A left hook to the jaw by Conn, a right to the jaw, two more rights as he outswings the champion. Conn jabs a left and is staggered by a right cross thrown by Joe Louis. Conn is hurt. Louis comes back with a right and left to the body and Conn hooks a left to the jaw. Conn every so often is staggered but he comes fighting back . . . he's got remarkable recuperative powers. . . . A right cross to the jaw by Louis. Louis takes Conn's head back with a right uppercut, and Conn goes to close quarters. . . . A left jab to the jaw and a right cross scored by Joe Louis and Conn is hurt as Louis rips a right to the jaw. . . . Conn is staggering but he won't go down. . . . Here's Louis jabbing a left and uppercutting his right to Conn's head. Conn blocks a left hook. He's reeling around the ring. . . . Louis hooks a left and a right to the jaw and Conn is down from a right cross to the jaw. . . . He's taking the count . . . four . . . five . . . six . . . seven . . . he's on his back . . . eight . . . nine. He's getting up at the count . . . no . . . the referee says it's all over. . . . The bout is stopped . . . The bout is stopped. The winner and still champion, Joe Louis. But what a fight Billy Conn gave. How about it, Bill?

CORUM: Ah, Don, there'll never be another one like that. No better and no greater fight did anyone ever see, and Louis came right back from the brink of defeat after Conn had made as great a fight as you could possibly imagine. Listen.

BALOGH: At two minutes, fifty-eight seconds of the thirteenth round, the winner by a knockout and still the world's heavyweight champion, Joe Louis.

I agreed with Bill. In my estimation, there hasn't been a finish like it since, and I think there never will be again in an important bout. It was as dramatic a fight as I have seen. Conn came so close to winning the title. Looking back, it occurs to me that what looked like a great punch by Conn may possibly have led to his undoing. It was the left hook to the jaw that Conn scored near the end of the twelfth round. It staggered the champion and caused him to reel around and then hold on. Up to that time, Conn seemed content to just win the fight as he was definitely doing through twelve rounds. But when he staggered Louis, it may have given him the idea to win by a knockout. That's the way he fought in the thirteenth. He tore into Louis, missed a left hook, and was staggered himself. At this point Conn could have backpedaled until the cobwebs cleared. The tired Louis may have had trouble catching up with him. But as I described the action, "Conn every so often is staggered but comes fighting back." That was it. Louis knocked him out, and the count reached ten at 2:58 of the round. Billy must have wondered what would have happened if the knockdown had occurred three or four seconds later. He would have been saved by the bell! What would have happened had there been a fourteenth and possibly a fifteenth round?

To no one's surprise, the bout proved once again what I have always thought, that Louis was the greatest of heavyweight champions. Great fighter that he was, he was great because he could come from behind when he had to.

How was it that Conn, a light heavyweight, came so close to beating the man many consider the greatest of all time? And come close he did. Could the champion have been tired from his "Bum of the Month" campaign? Could he have been overconfident against a light heavy who until then had shown no devastating punch? Or could he have been used to fighting big, lumbering men, some of whom were mentally licked before the bell for round one?

I don't know, of course, but I can surmise. He had never fought anyone as fast as Conn or, with the exception of Tony Galento, as fearless. And Conn's speed was not in his feet alone. His hands were like lightning, and once the Pittsburgh Irishman got past the early rounds' tension, he fought as though he, not Louis, were the champion. You've heard about "the old one-two" in boxing, I'm sure. It's usually a left jab followed by a straight right or a right cross. Well, Conn came up with something I'd never seen before, and possibly Louis hadn't either, for he couldn't seem to cope with it. It was a one-two-three—a left hook to the body, a left hook to the jaw, and a winging right to the head. And then repeat the maneuver. Louis's efforts to block it were not successful. Conn's speed could have won the bout for the challenger. But it didn't. As announcer, Harry Balogh had intoned "May the better contestant emerge victorious." Louis did.

Two more asides on the fight. Conn, of course, was a Pittsburgh favorite. The night of the fight, the Pirates were playing a ball game at Forbes Field in Pittsburgh. When the Louis—Conn fight got under way at about 10:30 P.M., it was piped into the public address system at the baseball game. At first the fans objected and booed the interjection of the blow-by-blow description of a prizefight into a baseball game. But after a while, when they heard how well their boy, Conn, was doing, the fans wouldn't let it be turned off. They stayed to listen even when the game was over.

The other thing I'd like to mention is that the broadcast was a tribute to the genius of Gillette's advertising director, Craig Smith. He gambled that a broadcast of a prizefight would sell razor blades, which then were five cents each. How right he was. The fight got a radio rating (there was no TV then) of 56.4, the highest of any program on a single network up to that time. It was a whopper. Gillette, Craig Smith, and yours truly were on our way!

Joe Louis–Buddy Baer

One of my most interesting post-
fight interviews followed the Joe Louis–Buddy Baer fight for the
heavyweight championship at the Garden in January of 1942. It
was a return of a bout the previous year in which Baer, by knocking
Louis out of the ring, came close to winning the big bauble. In the
interim, Louis had defended successfully against Billy Conn and
Lou Nova, winning both bouts by knockouts. Then, on December
7, we had been blasted by the Japs at Pearl Harbor and we were
at war.

For the Baer bout, Louis, who was entering the service, gave his
entire purse to the Navy Relief Fund. I'll always remember the story
they tell about Jack Blackburn, Louis's aging trainer. Just before
the fight got under way, Blackburn said to Louis, "Don't let it go

too far. My legs can't take too much of that going up and down those ring steps." Louis smiled and said, "Chappie, don't you worry. You only gonna climb them once."

And that's the way it was. The champion tore into the challenger and blasted him out in one round. In short order it was over, but my fun was just beginning. I climbed into the ring and grabbed Louis for the post-fight statement. As usual, Joe was very gracious. He said something nice about Buddy Baer and then uttered the famous words that went down in history. Referring to the war, Joe said, "We'll win 'cause we're on God's side." No one could have said it better.

Then I brought Baer to the microphone.

"What happened, Buddy?" I asked.

Buddy caught me completely off guard. "Don," he answered, "I'll explain it all on the Fred Allen program next Wednesday."

Not knowing what he was talking about and figuring that perhaps Louis had hit him harder than I thought, I thanked him and let it go at that.

But it turned out that Buddy indeed was to be a guest on "The Fred Allen Show," and although I didn't know it at the time, so was I.

It seems that Irving Mansfield, subsequently a top radio and TV producer, and the husband of writer Jacqueline Susann, was then the publicity director for the Fred Allen show, sponsored by Texaco. Irving cooked up a wonderful idea. He thought it would be great if I went on the Fred Allen show along with Buddy Baer, and I did.

When Allen introduced Baer to the audience, Buddy walked out on the stage and I walked with him. "Buddy," asked Fred, "who's that with you?"

"Oh," said Buddy, "this is Don Dunphy, the announcer. Joe Louis knocked me out so fast the other night that Don didn't have time to read the Gillette commercial on the air, so I brought him along to do it here."

So while Fred Allen feigned wringing his hands and tearing his hair, I read a thirty-second Gillette commercial on "The Fred Allen Show," sponsored by Texaco.

The Drake Relays

In 1942, Mutual Broadcasting assigned me to broadcast the Drake Relays at Drake University in Des Moines, Iowa. This was a different chore from broadcasting the indoor meets at Madison Square Garden, which I had done many times. The Garden track was 160 yards around, with eleven laps to the mile. Events like the Drake Relays and its counterpart, the Penn Relays, in which I had run, are competed over 440 yards on quarter-mile tracks, as they usually are called, with four laps to the mile. As a rule, only a few field events are held indoors: the high jump, the pole vault, the long jump (it was called the broad jump then), and possibly the shot put. Outdoors, there are all of these plus the discus throw, the javelin, and maybe the steeplechase. If you are qualified, indoor meets are comparatively easy to do;

outdoor meets are very difficult because of the size of the field and the number of events.

At the Drake Relays, I was invited to speak at the radio class at the university. After my initial remarks, I told the class that in airing the relays the next day I faced a most difficult assignment. I said that I needed volunteers to act as couriers and bring me results of various field events that were occurring at the same time as the running events that I was broadcasting. Quite a few offered their assistance, and we worked out a plan that had everything covered. The broadcast seemed to go well the next day, and everyone seemed happy.

Years later I was invited to appear on a telethon, Crusade for Europe, I believe it was, with Steve Allen as the host. Before the program I was introduced to Steve, who was very congenial. He surprised me by saying, "You don't remember me, do you?"

I replied that I didn't remember ever having met him, but I congratulated him on the great strides he had made in broadcasting. "But you don't remember meeting me," he continued. "Don't you remember you broadcast the Drake Relays years ago? And at the Drake radio class you asked for volunteers to help you. Well, I volunteered and was assigned the shot put. And during the afternoon I kept running up to you, handing you sheets of paper with the results on them. And every time I handed you a slip of paper, you'd look at it quickly, crinkle it up, and throw it away." Much embarrassed at hearing of this ancient gaffe, I could only laugh and apologize.

Imagine that, I had Steve Allen working for me. For free.

Muriel

In the summer of 1941, boxing promoter Mike Jacobs threw a big outdoor barbecue at his estate in Rumson, New Jersey. Almost everyone from the New York sports world was there. During the afternoon I was introduced to a very pretty young lady, Pearl Watts Amato, who was Bill Stern's assistant at NBC. This chance meeting was to have a remarkable effect on my future life. Among the tidbits of conversation I remembered was that she could get tickets to the great radio shows of the day.

New York, particularly Radio City, was the center of broadcasting in the United States at the time. All the big shows emanated from there—"The Fred Allen Show," "The Eddie Cantor Show," Kate Smith, Fred Waring, and Jack Benny, to name but a few. These were performed before studio audiences, and tickets to them were extremely hard to get. Since I often had guests from out of town, I thought it would be great if I could get them tickets to some of those shows. I told Pearl that I would take her up on her gracious offer.

At that time, as sports director of WINS, I did a weekly sports interview program from the Hotel Abbey in New York every Friday from 12:30 to 1:00 P.M. It was a good show. Besides me, the panelists included Jack Lavelle of Notre Dame fame, Tom Paprocki, sports cartoonist of the Associated Press, and Andy Burke and Frank Small, sports publicists. It was a most interesting program featuring important people from the world of sports. The broadcast was always followed by a sumptuous buffet lunch with an open bar. Word got around town, not so much about the show itself but about the lunch and the drinks that followed it. Soon the program was performed before an overflow crowd.

On Thursday, January 29, 1942 (the date is clear in my mind), I found that I needed tickets to one of the big radio shows. I had called Pearl on a few occasions, and she had been most obliging in getting them for me. So I called her again. She cheerfully said she would get me the tickets. I thanked her and concluded by saying, as I always did, "Pearl, I've got to take you to lunch sometime." She startled me by saying, "You always say that, but you never do."

Now I got a sudden thought. I told her about the sports program and lunch at the Abbey the next day, and invited her to join us. "And why don't you bring a friend?" I added. She did. The next day Pearl showed up at the program with a beautiful young lady, Muriel Keating, who was the secretary to John McNeil, manager of the Blue Network of NBC. I was so taken by the new entry that I could hardly do the program that day.

After lunch I walked the girls back to NBC. Later I called Miss Keating and asked her to dinner the following week. She accepted. In three weeks we were engaged, and on June 20 we were married. We have two sons, Don junior, born June 5, 1943, and Bob, born April 25, 1946. As were their father and mother, both are in broadcasting. Don is a vice-president at ABC News, and Bob is a director of sports. Muriel is as beautiful as ever, and I always feel grateful to Mike Jacobs for throwing that party at Rumson, New Jersey.

PART TWO

Great Fights

In a career that has spanned some forty-five years at ringside microphones, I've broadcast more than two thousand fights, about two hundred of which were title bouts, fifty in the heavyweight division alone. Picking the greatest fight of them all is no easy task, but I'll try, on the assumption that boxing aficionados would be curious about my opinion.

After considerable soul-searching and memory-prodding I've reduced the field to the ten that in my mind were the most outstanding. I know I risk raising hackles. Boxing experts and boxing fans will, naturally, have their own opinions. I've limited my choices to the period during which I was doing fights on a regular basis, which of course eliminates great bouts such as Dempsey–Firpo, Dempsey–Tunney, and Louis–Schmeling, which were fought before 1941.

I also expect that some will be upset because I haven't chosen Pep–Saddler, Griffith–Benvenuti, Patterson–Johansson, Gavilan–Graham, or many more that could also be considered great. But the fact is I could have written an entire book of great fights. So I apologize to the principals in other sensational scraps and to you fight fans who would choose differently. But, to paraphrase a famous personality, "I had to do it my way."

Herewith, my list of the ten greatest fights (not necessarily in order of importance):

Louis–Conn (first fight)
Marciano–Walcott (first fight)
Ali–Spinks (first fight)
Graziano–Arnold
Leonard–Hearns
Basilio–Robinson (first fight)
Zale–Graziano (first and second fights)
Ali–Frazier (first and third fights)

(The Louis–Conn bout was covered in an earlier chapter, and the Ali–Frazier set-tos will be covered in a later one.)

The Rock from Brockton: The Rocky Marciano– Jersey Joe Walcott Fight

MUNICIPAL STADIUM, PHILADELPHIA
SEPTEMBER 23, 1952

"Walcott hooks a left to the head. *Marciano is down!*"

I looked at Rocky as he scrambled to get up. He looked surprised, but I wasn't. Anyone would have gone down under the fierce attack that Jersey Joe unleashed in round one. The surprise wasn't that Rocky was down. The surprise was that he was getting up.

Looking at Rocky on the canvas, blinking the haze out of his eyes while Philadelphia's Municipal Stadium shook with the roar of forty thousand fans, my mind wandered back to the first time I met him. It was at the annual Buffalo Athletic Club Dinner the previous year. On the dais, I was seated between Rocky and the New York State Boxing chairman, Eddie Eagan. The three of us had plenty of time to talk.

I had seen Rocky in a couple of bouts in the Garden. He had won them—in fact, he was undefeated after thirty-seven bouts—but I must confess that he hadn't impressed me. I didn't have the feeling that this robust son of a Brockton, Massachusetts, cobbler could go on to win the heavyweight title. He could punch, it was obvious. Thirty-two of his fights had ended in KOs. But it worried me that he could be hit, too, and the basic objective in the fight game is to avoid that. Rocky was also very clumsy; it sometimes seemed as if he were wearing two left shoes. And when he missed a swing, it usually missed by daylight, leaving him wide open for a counterpunch.

Rocky, I thought, was a good journeyman heavyweight—he would win a lot of fights. But could all the polish and training in the world get him ready for the likes of champion Jersey Joe Walcott or the still-dangerous ex-champ, Ezzard Charles? And coming up shortly for Rocky was a bout with former champion Joe Louis, who was continuing his ill-advised comeback. Louis, faded though he was, still had that head-jarring left jab. It was hard to see how he could miss Rocky with it, hard to fathom how he could miss cutting Rocky to ribbons.

But as I chatted with Rocky during dinner, my feelings toward him began to change. He was very intense and deeply sincere in his belief in his ability. Fights and championships, of course, are won in the ring, but somehow Rocky Marciano convinced me over a steak.

"Don," he said, "I'm gonna win that title." It was as simple as that. There was no doubting that he meant it. Listening, I began to believe.

·   ·   ·

I watched Marciano carefully as he prepared for the Louis fight, which I was to broadcast. I think I watched him more closely than any fighter I'd seen since Joe Louis. In training, Rocky was a recluse, a hermit. He took himself to the mountains and shut out everything but getting ready for Louis. I've never seen a more determined, dedicated fighter. Out on the road before daylight, he ran and ran and ran. It looked as if he were getting ready for the Boston Marathon.

In the gym, whether hitting the light bag or the heavy bag or sparring, he worked harder than anyone I've ever seen. He was clumsy; he was awkward. But he was something else. On October 26, 1951, in Madison Square Garden, when the bell rang, Rocky was ready.

Predictably, Louis jabbed him. Again and again. Once, twice, sometimes as many as five punches in a row. But Rocky shook them off and came on relentlessly. Louis won the early rounds, but surely he wasn't the Brown Bomber of old. He was tiring, and it soon became a question of time. He couldn't keep Rocky off. After the fifth round, Louis was on his way. Marciano knocked him through the ropes and out in the eighth round; it was the last round Joe Louis ever fought.

After Louis, Marciano disposed of Lee Savold, Gino Buonvino, Bernie Reynolds, and Harry Matthews, all by knockouts—a grand total of thirteen rounds of boxing. Under the patient, careful training of little Charlie Goldman, the Rock improved visibly. His punching was sharper. He developed a deceptive bob-and-weave that left him less vulnerable to the jab. Day by day he got better. Then he was matched for the title with Jersey Joe Walcott.

Jersey Joe, who had been christened Arnold Cream, had a checkered career in the ring. He'd win a few, lose a few, and some years he hardly fought at all. In 1939, 1940, and 1941, for example, Walcott fought a total of five fights, but he won them all. In 1944 he recorded two bouts. Starting with 1945, he began to meet and beat better fighters. Still, to me, he hardly looked like championship material.

About this time, Joe Louis temporarily ran out of opponents and fought a series of fourteen straight exhibitions in 1947. He and the fans were chafing for some action, and Louis decided to come back to the Garden. Walcott was his selection as another exhibition opponent. But New York's commissioner, Eddie Eagan, said no to the exhibition idea. If the heavyweight champion fought at all, the crown would have to be on the line. Louis didn't mind.

Louis hardly took Jersey Joe seriously, and was an overwhelming favorite, but in a startling and memorable encounter, Walcott almost won. I remember his flashing right-hand counterpunches, which floored a bewildered Louis twice. Dancing in and out, shifting and shuffling to the right, then the left, hooking and crossing with that right, he made Joe look bad.

Most fans in the Garden felt they were about to witness the greatest upset of all time. And at ringside, looking up at the plodding Louis and the dancing Walcott, I sensed it too. Walcott thought he was winning by a mile. In the last two rounds he elected to stay away from Joe, certain he was comfortably ahead on the New York rounds-scoring basis. In those critical final rounds, Walcott threw very few punches.

Referee Ruby Goldstein voted for Walcott but the two judges voted for Louis, and Madison Square Garden echoed with boos. I don't believe that even Louis thought he won that one. Funny, though, it made me recall the criticism Billy Conn had received for mixing it up with Louis in the last couple of rounds. He'd lost. Walcott was criticized for *not* mixing it up and he lost, too.

Louis and Walcott were rematched on June 25, 1948, and Louis, in better shape and not overconfident, knocked Jersey Joe out in the eleventh, although Walcott again had him down with that sensational sneak right hand. It should have been the end for Walcott, who was now thirty-four, but it wasn't. He was still to achieve his measure of heavyweight glory.

Louis, apparently feeling that he had run out of worthy opponents, retired on March 1, 1949. In June of that year, Walcott and Ezzard Charles were matched for the vacant NBA title, and Charles won a fifteen-round decision. Jersey Joe had been denied a third time.

When Charles and Walcott were matched for the title in Chicago, Jim Norris, who was running Madison Square Garden, decided to hype the gate by installing ex-champ Louis as the nominal promoter of the bout. Louis did most of his hyping on the golf course. One day after a round on the links he showed up at fight headquarters and was surrounded by reporters who wanted to know how the ticket sales were going. Ever honest and frank, Louis startled the group by replying, "I don't know, we ain't sold none yet."

Walcott, though he lost to Charles, had made it close enough to justify a return bout in Detroit on March 7, 1951. Again it was close, and again Charles took the decision. The ever-persistent Jersey Joe got yet another shot at the crown on July 18, 1951. This time at the age of thirty-seven, Walcott startled the boxing world by kayoing Charles in the seventh round. It was his fifth heavyweight championship bout. After defeating Charles again the following year by a decision, Walcott was matched with Marciano.

Could Rocky beat the seasoned Walcott, the superior counter-puncher with deceptive footwork? Could he beat the man who had put Louis down three times with the sneak right, the man who had flattened Charles with one deadly left hook?

The title match took place in Philadelphia Municipal Stadium on September 23, 1952, before more than forty thousand wild fans. The crowd seemed about equally divided in its sentiments. Some were rooting for the wise old veteran from Camden, New Jersey, the father of six children, who had quit the ring several times in disillusionment, whose first professional fight was officially recorded in 1930. And some were rooting for the twenty-nine-year-old Marciano, born Rocco Marchegiano in Brockton, Massachusetts, the undefeated, courageous heavyweight who, through great determination, had fought mostly bigger and much heavier opponents and had knocked out thirty-seven of forty-two foes.

Walcott had a decided edge in experience, having fought the likes of Louis, Ezzard Charles, Harold Johnson, and Joey Maxim. He knew all the moves and used them. The feeling among the media people at ringside was that Walcott would be too clever for Rocky, although Marciano was a slight betting favorite at bell time.

"The main attraction, fifteen rounds, for the heavyweight championship of the world . . .

"From Brockton, Massachusetts, wearing black trunks with a white stripe, weighing 184 pounds, the challenger . . . *Rocky Marciano!*

"From Camden, New Jersey, wearing white trunks with a black stripe, weighing 196 pounds, the heavyweight champion, *Jersey Joe Walcott!*"

I could feel the electricity in the air as I waited for referee Charley Daggert to send them on their way. I felt it would be a great fight. I wasn't disappointed.

This was my blow-by-blow description:

"There's the bell for round one.

"Marciano is wide with a left hand.

"Marciano tries a left to the body. It's short.

"Referee Charley Daggert gets them out of a clinch.

"Walcott scores with a right to the chin.

"Walcott chops a right to the head . . . brings it to the body.

"At long range, Walcott scores with a jab, puts a right to the face, crosses a right, bangs both hands to the body, and Walcott is scoring heavily here in round one.

"Marciano rips a long right, hard to the body, crosses a right to the jaw.

"Marciano is hurt with a left and right to the head by Walcott, as they clinch in Marciano's corner.

"Walcott hooks a left to the head. Marciano is *down!*"

Rocky scrambled to his feet. The count had reached two. Rocky had to be in great shape, and he was. The long hours of roadwork, the many rounds of sparring, the rope-skipping, the light bag, the heavy bag, the calisthenics, all of them paid off for Rocky in round one.

"Walcott is on top of him with another left hook, rips a right to the head, misses a left jab.

"Marciano goes in and holds on for a moment.

"Walcott was within a few seconds of victory.

"Marciano gets away from a right and smashes a right to the jaw and hurts Walcott. And Walcott may have let him get away. . . ."

I didn't realize at the moment how prophetic that remark was. Marciano survived Walcott's lethal attack and battled the champion on fairly even terms from then on. And, make no mistake about it, Walcott fought his greatest fight that September night in Philadelphia. He had to. Marciano kept coming, kept boring in, kept the pressure on, never took a backward step. But Walcott's great experience helped him pile up points, and it was close.

The pace was so fast I hoped my voice would hold out. Midway through the bout, Al Weill, Marciano's manager, complained that some ointment had gotten in Rocky's eyes. The challenger was blinking and rubbing them, but it didn't seem to affect anything.

They went at it round after round, the crowd cheering every punch. Walcott picking his spots, potshotting the challenger; Marciano giving him no rest, boring in, oblivious of punishment, hoping the older man's legs would cave in. What a fight! Then Walcott started to inch away on points. He was definitely in charge of the fight.

Walcott won the eleventh round handily, and in the twelfth, he gave the younger man such a pounding that I began to wonder if Rocky would last. Rocky was all heart, but he looked all in, too. As the bell sounded for round thirteen, Rocky looked distressed. Here's how I described that dramatic round on radio:

"Marciano has been in trouble—in trouble the last couple of rounds, but he gets out there quickly and moves in on Walcott, who paws out with a left hand to the body. It's short. Marciano is short with a left jab aimed at the head. Marciano digs a left hand to the pit of the stomach of Walcott. Walcott backing away now. . . .

"Here's Marciano moving in on him again. Walcott feinting a left hand, going into a shuffle, Marciano bulling his way in close. Walcott's ageless legs keep taking him back out of trouble whenever he gets into it. Walcott is back to the ropes. *Takes a right to the jaw!*

Walcott is down on his stomach and they're counting over him! It may be a knockout. I don't think Walcott can get up! It's going to be a knockout for Marciano! A straight right-hand punch to the jaw, and Walcott rolls over. He is still out cold. It's a knockout and we have a new heavyweight champion of the world! It is Rocky Marciano, still undefeated, from Brockton, Massachusetts!"

It was just a year since Rocky had said to me, "Don, I'm gonna win that title."

Muhammad Ali–Leon Spinks (First Fight)
LAS VEGAS, FEBRUARY 15, 1978

Muhammad Ali defended his heavyweight title against Leon Spinks in Las Vegas, at the Hilton Hotel. On paper there didn't seem to be much reason for the fight except that Ali was the great champion, the great charismatic personality, and the people wanted to see him. And like Joe Louis, of an earlier boxing era, the people wanted to see him fight, no matter who the opponent was.

The statistics were heavily weighted in favor of the champion. He had won fifty-five of his fifty-seven bouts, losing two close decisions; one to Joe Frazier in a title bout and one to Ken Norton, for the NABF title. He had met the best and had scored thirty-seven knockouts.

Leon's credentials were unimpressive. He had won the Olympic light heavyweight title at Montreal in 1976, but as a pro he had had only seven fights, of which he won five by kayos and one by decision. The only well-known heavy he had met was Scott LeDoux, and that had ended in a ten-round draw. The one thing going for Spinks was age. He was twenty-four to Ali's thirty-six. I guess another thing going for Spinks was that he didn't seem to have any imagination. He wasn't the least bit awed that he was meeting one of the great heavyweights of all time. He apparently had confidence in his own ability, and if Ali was great, well, Leon came from

Missouri, and Ali would have to show him. Or maybe he thought that he would show Ali.

In any event, as the fight got under way, it was obvious from Spinks's attitude that in his mind Ali was just another fighter. It was also obvious to all of us at ringside that Spinks was no pushover. He got off quick, as they say, and won the first three rounds on all three judges' cards, using the ten-point must system—ten points to the winner of a round, and nine or less to the loser, with an even round scored ten each. But Ali's greater experience came into play, and he scored big from the eighth round through the twelfth. At that point it was anybody's fight. The heavyweight championship, the most important single crown in sports, was up for grabs. At the end of the twelfth round the scoring read like this: judge Harold Buck had it even at 114 each; judge Lou Tabat had the challenger ahead 115–113; but judge Art Lurie had Ali leading 116–112. There were three rounds and a lot of scoring points left.

Now Spinks, the challenger, put on a surge. Carrying the fight to the champion, he won the thirteenth and fourteenth rounds, which were scored for him 10–9 on all three judges' cards. As I broadcast the scrap, Mike Marley, a Las Vegas sportswriter who has since moved to New York, was getting me the official scoring by the judges. The scoring was not announced to the crowd at the Hilton Pavilion, but thanks to Mike, who knew his way around Las Vegas sports events, I was able to put it on the air.

It was obvious to me that going into the fifteenth and final round, Muhammad Ali needed a knockout to win the fight and keep his crown. At this important point in the fight, Buck had the challenger ahead 134–132, Tabat had him ahead 135–131, but Lurie still had Ali leading 134–132. I knew we were coming to an exciting moment. Were we about to see the greatest upset in heavyweight championship history? The greatest upset so far and by far was when James J. Braddock, a rank underdog, who had retired from the ring in discouragement, made a comeback, fought his way into a title bout with champion Max Baer, and won the crown by a decision. Certainly, if Spinks won this fight, it would compete with that memorable contest for honors as the biggest upset of all time.

Spinks seemed reasonably calm in his corner as he waited for the bell for the important fifteenth round. I don't know what Ali's feelings were, or how his corner men felt about his prospects at that moment, but Ali came out going for a knockout. He had looked tired in the fourteenth round, and I remarked on the broadcast over CBS Radio that Ali was making most of the clinches, a sure sign of weariness. It had been a tough and grueling fourteen rounds for both fighters, but at twenty-four, Spinks was twelve years younger and had not gone through the wear and tear of fifty-seven fights, many of them against top-notchers the likes of Joe Frazier, Ken Norton, Earnie Shavers, and Sonny Liston. I remarked, as the round began, that we had here the upset of the ages. Win Elliot, the color commentator on the show, agreed with me.

Ali may have realized that he needed a knockout to win, but Spinks wasn't exactly putting his chin out as a target. They slugged at the start of the round, but Spinks kept on top of Ali, and with about two minutes to go in the round, he was holding the champion against the ropes. Davey Pearl, the referee, who had done a good job all the way in this important fight, got them apart. Ali then hooked a left to the jaw and followed with a right that hurt Spinks. Ali took command with a left and a right to the jaw that aroused his partisans in the arena. But Spinks was not to be denied. Although seemingly very tired, the challenger took the play away from the champion, and Ali was driven across the ring. Still trying for a kayo, Ali drove a right to the jaw and scored with a right to the body. But Spinks fought back hard, and Ali was hurt after a right to the jaw. Ali was giving everything, but Spinks wouldn't back away. Now Spinks scored his best punch of the night, a right to the jaw. Both men were very tired at this point, with about thirty seconds left to go in the fight. Ali opened up with everything in his arsenal, desperately trying for a knockout. There had been no knockdowns in the fight, nor would there be. Once more, Ali brought the crowd up when he scored with a hard right to the head, making Spinks hold on. But Spinks had enough left. I remarked that this was the best round of the fight, and as I did, Spinks hurt Ali with a right to the jaw, then again with a right uppercut to the chin. Spinks scored with a right to the head at the bell.

Tension settled over the crowd as we waited for Chuck Hull to announce the fateful decision. I found out later that all three judges had given the last round to Spinks, and that sealed the verdict. It was a split decision, with Harold Buck and Lou Tabat voting for Spinks 144–141 and 145–140 respectively, and Art Lurie voting for Ali 143–142. Leon Spinks in his eighth professional fight was the winner and new champion.

But his stewardship was of short duration. In a return bout at New Orleans on September 15 of that year, Ali easily won back the title on a fifteen-round decision. It was a different Ali from the February fight, and a different Leon Spinks, too.

Rocky Graziano–Billy Arnold
MADISON SQUARE GARDEN, MARCH 9, 1945

This fight was memorable because it marked the end of one bright career and the beginning of another. Graziano at this time was a welterweight. Arnold was one of the hottest prospects to come along in years and had run up a great winning streak.

Matched with the wily and clever Fritzie Zivic, he had lost an eight-round decision, but that didn't seem to diminish interest in him too much. He was still considered one of the brightest stars on the boxing horizon. It was assumed by many that Zivic's experience and cunning had been too much for the youngster. In a similar situation years later, Floyd Patterson lost a close one to Joe Maxim before going on to win the heavyweight crown. On paper, the bout with Graziano seemed a safe one for Arnold. Graziano was a wild swinger with a good punch when it landed, but some felt that the experience gained in the Zivic bout would help Arnold immeasurably.

And Graziano's recent record had not been good. Just before the Arnold match, he had fought draws with Frankie Terry and Danny Kapilow, kayoed Bernie Miller in two bouts, and lost twice in a row to Harold Red Green in ten-round bouts. Hardly imposing.

Arnold, a terrific hitter, tore into Graziano in the first round and battered him from pillar to post. The wild Rocky fought back gamely, but hardly landed on the surging Arnold. Rocky took more punishment in that one round than he had in all his previous forty-six bouts. It was amazing that he didn't go down. Arnold pounded him around the ring. It was unbelievable.

Apparently Arnold didn't believe it, either. The bell saved Rocky, and I can remember it as though it were happening right now. At the end of the round, Arnold went back to his corner, but before he sat down he stood there for a long moment, looking over at Graziano. He seemed to be wondering what was keeping Rocky on his feet.

The second round was not quite as violent but it was all Arnold. Rocky still took a battering. But he didn't go down.

The third round began much the same way, with Arnold on the attack. All of a sudden, as if from nowhere, Rocky fired a right to the jaw. It caught Arnold flush. He staggered. The crowd came to its feet roaring. Rocky tore into Arnold. And now the wild Rocky who hadn't landed a good punch in the previous two rounds, became Rocky the sharpshooter. He measured Arnold again and again and pounded him with both hands. Arnold went down and was counted out—clear out into obscurity. Rocky went on to the middleweight championship and fame and fortune. It was the end of one career and the beginning of another.

Sugar Ray Leonard–Thomas Hearns
LAS VEGAS, SEPTEMBER 16, 1981

The Sugar Ray Leonard–Thomas Hearns fight for the undisputed world welterweight championship was the greatest and most im-

portant fight of its era. It was a unification bout for the crown, since
Leonard was the World Boxing Council title holder and Hearns
held the World Boxing Association title. Sugar Ray won recognition
as world welterweight title holder by knocking out champion Wilfred
Benitez in the fifteenth round at Las Vegas on November 30, 1979.
I did the radio broadcast of the scrap. He lost it to Roberto Duran
at Montreal on June 20, 1980, and regained it by stopping Duran
in eight rounds at New Orleans on November 25, 1980. On June
25, 1981, Leonard kayoed Ayub Kalule to win the world junior
middleweight title.

Hearns won the WBA welter crown by kayoing Pipino Cuevas
on August 2, 1980, in two rounds at Detroit. I did the closed-circuit
telecast of the bout, and it was the first time I saw the new boxing
sensation. His string of knockouts earned him the appellation "Hit
Man."

Leonard and Hearns were two great fighters as they faced each
other on September 16, 1981.

In thirty-one fights, Leonard had scored twenty-two knockouts,
won nine decisions, and lost a close bout to Duran, whom he later
knocked out.

Hearns had won all thirty-two of his fights, racking up thirty
knockouts and winning two decisions.

The scoring of the fight was done by three judges, Chuck Minker,
Duane Ford, and Lou Tabat. The referee, Davey Pearl, did not
score the bout.

Hearns, boxing beautifully, built up an early lead. I gave him
the first five rounds.

Leonard came to life in the sixth and rocked Hearns with a big
left hook. It certainly was a two-point round for Leonard. I gave
him the seventh round and called the eighth even.

Hearns regained his composure and won the next four rounds on
my card, the eleventh by a big margin.

At the start of the thirteenth, I remarked that Hearns was on his
way to victory (I had it nine Hearns, two Leonard, and one even).
I mentioned that Hearns was in great shape, if he didn't get careless

as he had in the sixth round. Sure enough, with the bout slipping away from him, Leonard nailed Hearns with a Sunday punch in the thirteenth, staggered him, then battered him around the ring. Hearns got through the round, but he was not in good shape.

Leonard tore into him in the fourteenth and floored him. Referee Pearl stopped the fight at 1:45 of the round, and Leonard was the undisputed welterweight champion.

The press was divided over who was ahead after twelve rounds. Some gave Leonard a lot more rounds than I did. And certainly there were some rounds, especially the sixth and the thirteenth, in which Leonard deserved a two-point margin. But boxing bouts have always been hard to score.

The sheet I used for the Leonard–Hearns fight is reproduced on page 94. Regardless of the official scoring system for a fight, I always used the rounds basis for the very good reason that if I wanted to take a quick look to see the trend of a fight, I didn't have to stop and add up the points. On the Hearns–Leonard fight the scoring was ten points to the winner of a round, nine or less to the loser, and an even round on an official's card was scored ten each. Invariably a round won by a fighter was scored 10–9. On a rare occasion where there might be one or more knockdowns it would be scored 10–8. I recall only two occasions in championship bouts where there was scoring of 10–7. They were the Jimmy Carter–Tommy Collins lightweight championship fight in Boston and the Sugar Ray Robinson–Jake LaMotta middleweight brawl in Chicago. I've never heard of a 10–6 or anything lower. Which makes me wonder about the ten-point must. For instance, why not just a five-point must? or even a three-point must? It would serve the same purpose.

On my sheet you will notice that I have assigned numbers to the winners of rounds. Leonard is on top of the sheet, so he would be number one. Hearns is below him, so he is number two. The eighth round scored even, so that is marked with a zero. The reason I use numbers is to confuse anyone walking behind me at ringside, looking at my score sheet, and yelling out, "Hey, Dunphy gave the first round to Hearns."

UNDISPUTED
Welterweight Championship — CAESAR'S PALACE   Sept. 16, 1981
— LAS VEGAS, NEVADA —

(1) SUGAR RAY LEONARD — PALMER PARK, MARYLAND   146
    WBC CHAMP
    multi colored white red strips

(2) THOMAS HEARNS — DETROIT, MICH.   145
    WBA CHAMP
    WHITE TRUNKS

                    15 ROUNDS

            REFEREE — DAVEY PEARL

Round	Score	Notes
1	2	Hearns after bell SCORING — 10 POINT MUST
2	2	by 3 JUDGES - REF DOES NOT
3	2	SCORE.
4	2	
5	2	MANDATORY 8 COUNT
6	1	Hearns rocked Beg LH v rounds NO 3 KNOCKDOWN RULE —
7	1	IT HAS BEEN WAIVED
8	0	
9	2	MAN CAN'T be SAVED by
10	2	BELL except IN LAST ROUND
11	2 Big	20 SECONDS TO get BACK
12	2	IN RING - No help by Handlers
13	1 Big 4 POINTS	
14	Ref stopped 1:45 stop RING 20 FT SQUARE
15		Need Mouthpiece to START

RING ANNOUNCER — CHUCK HULL   ROUND
TIME KEEPER — Charley Roth
KNOCKDOWN TIMER — Jim Broadfoot   JUDGE Chuck Minker
DOCTOR — Donald Romeo   JUDGE Duane Ford
DOCTOR — Ed Homanski   JUDGE LOU Tabbat
        Daniel Zimmer
            COMMISSIONER — SAM MACIAS
            CHIEF INSPECTOR — HAROLD BUCK

Carmen Basilio–Sugar Ray Robinson
(First Fight)
YANKEE STADIUM, SEPTEMBER 23, 1957
(Second Fight)
CHICAGO STADIUM, MARCH 25, 1958

We have four fights left on our list of great fights, and all of them were for the middleweight title: Tony Zale and Rocky Graziano in 1946 at the Yankee Stadium and their return bout at the Chicago Stadium in 1947, and Sugar Ray Robinson and Carmen Basilio, also at the Yankee Stadium in 1957, and their return bout at Chicago Stadium a year later.

Robinson was probably at his peak as a middleweight when he defended against Basilio the first time in New York. And Basilio, who, like Robinson, had also been the welterweight champion, seemed to be at his fighting best. It was an exciting battle from start to finish, with the action fast and furious, and it was hard for me to keep up with the punches in announcing the action. But I did. There were no knockdowns, and it was difficult to pick the winner of some of the rounds. Basilio, who had the heart of a lion, was completely oblivious of Sugar Ray's great reputation and gave as much as he took, and maybe a little more. At the end of fifteen I heard Johnny Addie announce that it was a split decision and that Basilio, the former onion farmer from Cannestota, New York, was the new middleweight champion.

In the return bout in Chicago in 1958, Basilio was the defender and Robinson the challenger. Again it was close. This time Basilio suffered a cut eye early in the bout, and gradually it got worse until it closed completely. But Carmen was all heart, and despite the injured eye he still carried the fight to Sugar Ray. It was another split verdict, but it reversed the New York decision and Robinson was champion again.

Tony Zale–Rocky Graziano
(First Fight)
YANKEE STADIUM, SEPTEMBER 27, 1946
(Second Fight)
CHICAGO STADIUM, JULY 16, 1947

The first two Zale–Graziano fights were blockbusters. Graziano was an exciting kid from the streets of New York who had worked his way into contendership by virtue of a terrific right-hand punch and a fighting spirit. Zale was the man of steel from Gary, Indiana, who had won the vacant world middleweight title by outpointing Georgie Abrams in 1941, but he never really had a chance to defend it. Early in 1942 he proved his mettle when he fought Billy Conn but lost a twelve-round decision. To give Zale his due, you have to recognize that Conn had come close to taking the *heavyweight* crown from Joe Louis the previous June. Zale, a middleweight, was able to stand up to him, although he lost. In 1943, 1944, and 1945, Zale was in the service and out of ring action. For that matter, Rocky, nine years Zale's junior and sporting a string of knockouts, was made the favorite in the fight.

I eagerly awaited the start of this bout and my broadcasting of it. From the opening bell it was fast, as Rocky tried to overpower the veteran champion with a first-round onslaught. But Zale, biding his time, waited for the overeager youngster to leave him an opening. Rocky obliged. Zale took advantage, and down went Rocky in round one. But he was in great shape. He bounced up full of fight and carried the fight back to the champion. It was give and take, with no quarter asked and none given. They battered each other with the greatest display of fistic fireworks I have ever seen. Through rounds three, four, and five, Rocky took over. He was hurting Zale and hurting him badly. Tony was scoring heavily too, but Rocky was wearing him down. I had the feeling that the sixth round would be the last. It was, but not the way I expected. Graziano was pounding Zale, and it seemed that Tony would soon be knocked out. And then it happened. Eager to end it with a series of head shots, Rocky left his midsection unprotected. Zale saw the opening and fired a solar plexus punch that not only floored Rocky but paralyzed him momentarily. Rocky was on the canvas, gasping for breath. He wasn't out and he knew what was going on, but he couldn't move. He was counted out and Tony Zale was still the middleweight champion. Once on his feet, Rocky recovered quickly and was all right. Not so Tony. He had taken a terrible beating and he showed it. He had won, but you wouldn't know it from looking at him. As I interviewed him for the radio audience, Tony was steadied by his managers, Art Winch and Sam Pian, and his trainer, Ray Arcel.

The return bout in Chicago the following year was almost a replica of their first fight. It was another bruiser, fought in the July heat of Chicago Stadium. This time Zale was winning the fight when Rocky and the heat felled him in the sixth round. Graziano was now the middleweight champion.

They fought a third time at Ruppert Stadium in Newark, New Jersey. This time it was no contest. An aroused Zale took back the title with a three-round knockout. He held it for about a year, till he was knocked out by Marcel Cerdan.

So many great fights. So many great fighters. Louis–Conn, Marciano–Walcott, Basilio–Robinson, Leonard–Hearns, Ali–Leon Spinks, Ali–Frazier, Graziano–Arnold, Zale–Graziano. Which one do I think was the greatest? It's not an easy pick, but if forced to choose, I'd have to select the first Tony Zale–Rocky Graziano middleweight championship fight as the greatest. It had everything that a fight should have, with an added fillip: a surprise ending.

TV and Radio

I have been asked many times the difference between doing a blow-by-blow description of a prize-fight on radio and on TV, and which I preferred.

In 1939, 1940, and early 1941 I did a few radio bouts. In June of 1941, I became the Gillette and Madison Square Garden boxing announcer and continued in that capacity until 1960. All this was on radio, of course. In the fall of 1960 I did my first TV bout, and on December 11, 1981, I did my last when Muhammad Ali lost the final fight of his career, on Paradise Island in the Bahamas. As for the first question, the difference between radio and TV is that radio is more difficult physically but easier mentally. TV is just the reverse; easier physically but harder mentally.

This deserves explanation. Doing a bout of ten or fifteen rounds on radio, using the rapid-fire staccato style that I did, is a real physical effort and can be very tiring. Just as the fighters and the referee have to be in shape to go the distance, so does the radio announcer. I was always very careful on the day of the fight. I found through experience that the worst thing I could do was to eat a big meal before a broadcast. If I did, I found myself gasping for breath after a few rounds. I took care of my voice, and especially my throat. I tried not to use them too much the day of the fight, especially as the witching hour of 10:00 P.M. approached. I always carried my kickapoo juice with me. Kickapoo juice? I'll explain it later. The main thing about the radio broadcast is being able to do it—having the voice and the ability to keep up with the action—and staying calm. The announcer should have excitement in his voice, but he should contain the excitement there, and stay calm inwardly. Why is radio easier mentally? Because if you can do the job and if you have confidence in yourself, the rest is actually easy. The announcer doesn't have to think, he just has to describe. This may seem silly, but not having to think is important. If you stop and think what you're going to say, you're in trouble.

In TV, you have to think. It's easier physically—the viewer can see the action so you don't have to describe it constantly—but it's harder mentally because you have to think about what you do say. You shouldn't talk too much, but saying less makes what you do say more important. A good TV boxing announcer will ask himself as the round proceeds, "Am I talking too much?" "Am I telling the audience what they already see?" The TV announcer should avoid doing a radio description on a TV show. Too many announcers do that. "That's a right. That's a left hook. That's a left and a right to the body." That style is superfluous and annoying to the viewer, who can see all the action for himself. Rather than "radio-ize" a TV fight, I would try to call attention to the effect of the blows, which the viewer looking at his set might not notice. I might point out that "Leonard's jab, which was short of the mark in the early rounds, is now finding its mark." A TV announcer has to have "at mouth," if I may coin a phrase, a lot of salient information about records of the fighters and so forth. The radio announcer doesn't have time to do this during the fight; he will probably do it in the pre-fight broadcast.

There is an interesting difference between announcing a fight for regular TV and for one being shown on theater or closed-circuit TV. The announcer has to be aware of the fact that when the crowd is cheering loudly in the boxing arena, they will also be cheering loudly in the theaters. If he talks at that moment, he is going to be drowned out in the theaters. The audience won't know what he said.

Do I prefer radio or TV announcing? When I was younger, I preferred radio; when I got older, I preferred TV.

With TV, it took me a long time to get used to another announcer speaking during a round that I was describing. There had been two of us working when we were doing radio fights, but each had a different job. Mine was to do the blow-by-blow description; the other announcer would handle the color and commercials. But while there was action in the ring, I was the only one talking. When I did TV fights in the sixties, I was the only one on the show. I covered the round of action, and when the round was over, the studio did the commercials. If there were no commercials, I would cover for the minute between rounds. But then the old guard changed. New producers and directors with their own ideas came in, and the way of doing a fight on TV changed. Now there were two men talking during the round, one the blow-by-blow announcer, the other the analyst. For a long time I was uncomfortable with someone else talking. Usually the so-called analyst was a champion or a celebrity who was put on the show to get publicity. He might have gotten publicity, but sometimes he got in the way. Very often, both of us would start talking at the same time, and everything became muddled. The famous boxers naturally thought they knew more about the fights than I did, but expressing themselves clearly was something else. As for the celebrities, I usually spent a lot of time asking them to be brief in their comments. I didn't want someone to get knocked out while they were in the middle of a sentence. Sometimes they would get carried away listening to themselves and they'd forget I was even there. It was tough getting back on when they had lapsed into a radio-style, blow-by-blow description of a TV fight.

The first time I ever worked on TV with someone else was on a telecast of the Floyd Patterson–George Chuvalo fight at Madison Square Garden in 1965. Lester Malitz, the father of Mike Malitz, who is now with Top Rank, was the producer of the fight for closed-circuit and theater TV. Top Rank was a boxing promotion outfit headed by Bob Arum. Mike came up with the great idea of having the champion, Muhammad Ali, be my analyst on the fight. It got us great publicity and I must say it worked very well. I spent quite a bit of time with the champ before the fight, and he listened carefully to my suggestions. He didn't overdo the talking. Neither did Joe Frazier, with whom I worked on the Ali–Joe Bugner championship bout in Kuala Lumpur, Malaysia, in 1975. Joe gave a good analysis, and his remarks were brief and to the point.

It didn't always work out that well. When Joe Frazier defended the heavyweight title against big George Foreman in Kingston, Jamaica, in 1973, Don King was the promoter of the bout for theater and closed-circuit TV. I was the ringside announcer, and Don assigned Pearl Bailey to be my color commentator. Now, I have great admiration for Pearl Bailey, one of the all-time great performers. But a fight announcer? Please! Everything went well on the telecast until the fight started. Then Pearl, who was seated in the first row ringside with me, stood up and started cheering for Foreman. By rooting for one of the fighters in the bout, she broke a long-time rule of sports announcing, which demands an impartial attitude on the part of the announcer. But when she stood up at ringside, she made matters worse. First, she wasn't paying any attention to what she should have been doing, and that was commenting on the fight, when necessary. Pearl is lovely but she is not tiny, and when she stood up in the first row, she blocked the view of sportswriters who were covering the fracas. Cries of "Sit down, Pearl!" and "Hey, Pearl, we can't see!" went unheeded as she cheered on her favorite. Finally came the coup de *swat*. As Foreman floored Frazier, Pearl screamed with joy and whacked me on the back with what she must have thought was a playful slap. I was knocked forward, and my

ringside papers went flying. I still wince when I think of that jolt.
I wondered who was defending the title, Frazier or I. Fortunately,
Pearl calmed down for the second and last round and I, if not Joe,
was able to go the distance. I didn't blame Pearl. She's an exuberant
and enthusiastic person, and we remained good friends.

I did the Larry Holmes–Mike Weaver heavyweight championship bout at Madison Square Garden in 1979. Again, Don King
was the promoter, and Home Box Office produced the theater TV
effort. Len Berman was my co-announcer, and there was an added
starter, Ryan O'Neal. Ryan O'Neal? He was a real fight fan, and
at that time was appearing in a boxing picture. But did that qualify
him to be an analyst on a heavyweight championship bout? Don't
ask me, I'm new around here.

For the "Thrilla in Manila" between Muhammad Ali and Joe
Frazier, Don King again was the promoter, and I was the announcer
on the theater TV show. Ken Norton, a fine heavyweight contender,
who also expresses himself very well, was the analyst.

I expected a good color commentator, which Ken was. Through
the years he worked many fights and handled his part of a broadcast
very well. What I didn't expect were two additional announcers,
Flip Wilson and Hugh O'Brian. Don King, the impresario, had
outdone himself. Obviously he believed that in numbers there is
strength. Like Pearl Bailey, Flip Wilson was a performer *par excel-
lence*. But was he a fight analyst? Hugh O'Brian had been successful
in the movies, and his TV series about Wyatt Earp had gone over
big. But what qualified him to be at ringside, talking about one of
the greatest fights of all time? I couldn't help thinking that while
Don King was a fine promoter, he also had a lot of friends and he
sure took care of them. I suddenly found myself in charge of a game
of musical chairs.

On any championship fight, there is always a great demand for
seats at ringside in the press section. This time the broadcast came
up one short: there were four announcers but only three seats, and
I was supposed to rotate Ken, Flip, and Hugh after each round.
This, with my own work, kept me from paying too much attention
to what they were saying. Alternating announcers never did help

the continuity of a show. I'm always annoyed by confusion at ring-side. I think it's unnecessary if things are laid out properly in advance. At times I have become upset and said to myself, "What the heck am I doing here?" or "I don't need this." But soon I'd calm down and think about how fortunate I'd been to be part of such wonderful events. Being a perfectionist and taking my broadcasting super-seriously are probably why I did so well and lasted so long. In any case, coming back to Ken, Flip, Hugh, and the missing seat at ringside in Manila, we got through all right, and the replay showed that I did very well. It was a great fight, culminating in Ali winning after the fourteenth because Frazier was having trouble seeing after sustaining a badly cut left eye.

I've done fights on radio and I've done fights on TV, and there was even one fight where I did both. You may think that it was a simulcast, but it wasn't. A simulcast is a broadcast that goes out simultaneously over both radio and TV, using the same announcers. On October 21, 1965, Dick Tiger of Nigeria challenged Joey Giardello of Philadelphia for the middleweight championship. The fight, at Madison Square Garden, was a rematch of a bout two years earlier in which Giardello had won the crown from Tiger. It was a good scrap, with Tiger emerging as the title holder again by virtue of a unanimous decision. The telecast was of the closed-circuit variety, with New York and its environs blacked out the night of the fight. Guy LeBow was the TV announcer. However, the radio description of the bout, which I did, was not blacked out, and New Yorkers could hear it over the Mutual Broadcasting System.

The fight was so interesting that Channel 9 in New York decided to play it on TV the next night. So I went to their studio in the Empire State Building and called the fight over a TV monitor as though it were being done live. It was a fascinating way to work, but I must say I missed the crowd noise and the ringside atmosphere.

It was the first of many bouts I would do for Channel 9 and Madison Square Garden Productions. In 1970, Jimmy Ellis and Joe Frazier met for the vacant heavyweight championship. The title was vacant because Muhammad Ali was still inactive owing to his differences with the draft board. Ellis had won an elimination tournament for the World Boxing Association heavyweight title. To get to the championship he had beaten some pretty good fighters, including Oscar Bonavena, Jerry Quarry, and former champion Floyd Patterson. Ellis was recognized as the title holder in most states but not all. New York went its own way and decided that the winner of a bout between Joe Frazier and Buster Mathes would be the New York champion. Frazier won convincingly and was recognized as champion not only in New York but in several other states that had working agreements with New York. So now we had two champions. It was decided that Ellis and Frazier should fight a unification bout for the title on February 16, 1970, at Madison Square Garden. Frazier won easily by a knockout in the fifth round.

I mention this bout because I did the radio broadcast of the fight for Mutual Broadcasting. When the bout was over, I decided I wouldn't do any more fights on radio. I had been doing bouts on radio for more than thirty years, and I was finding it increasingly tiring. So I decided to confine my ringside efforts to TV and bid radio fight announcing a fond farewell—or so I thought.

In 1977, Ali, who had regained the title, was matched to defend against the knockout artist Earnie Shavers at Madison Square Garden on September 29. About three weeks before the fight I received a phone call from Len Bramson of Canadian Radio, asking if I would do the radio of the bout for them. I thanked him for calling me, but told him I was retired from giving radio descriptions of prize fights. He was very disappointed and tried hard to get me to change my mind. But I remained firm.

In a day or two I began to think it over. "Look," I said to myself, "this bout can't last long. Either Ali will knock out Shavers or Shavers will kayo Ali and become the new champ. And it won't last more than a couple of rounds." According to their ring records, this seemed a reasonable assumption. And there was another factor. I had innumerable tapes of great fights I had done on radio, and at that time I was trying to make them into an album. It would be good to add an Ali–Shavers tape to the collection.

So I called Bramson back and told him that if the offer was still there I would take it. He was happy and told me that I would be working with George Chuvalo, the Canadian champ. Now I had another thought. Was I in shape to do a fast bout on radio? After all, I hadn't done a radio bout in more than seven years. Would the voice hold up?

I decided to go into training to get myself in shape, just like the fighters. I still had two weeks to get ready, and ready I must be, on the off-chance that the Ali–Shavers fight did go a lot of rounds or even, perish the thought, that it might go the distance of fifteen rounds.

So I devised a training routine. First I got out my stopwatch, which hadn't been used in a long time. Then I sat down and simulated the broadcast of a round, describing punches as I thought they would be thrown, movements of the fighters, clinches, the referee, etc., using, of course, the names of Muhammad Ali and Earnie Shavers. I did this in a moderate, conversational style for three minutes, then took the conventional one-minute rest. I repeated this maneuver twice more. Then I did three one-minute rounds at about three-quarters of the pace I would use during a real round. I repeated the operation the next day.

Feeling I was getting my voice and throat back, I speeded up the action. At the end of a three-round session I did what, in track, we used to call wind sprints. For fifteen seconds I spoke as fast as I could, rested ten seconds, and did five more sprints. Each day I would add a round to the regimen until finally I felt I was ready. It's a good thing I was. Despite the knockout power of both Ali and Shavers, the bout went its full fifteen rounds.

In February of 1978, Ali was booked to defend the crown against Leon Spinks at the Hilton Hotel in Las Vegas. Bob Arum was the promoter and CBS had the TV rights. Frank Miller, head of CBS Radio sports, called me and asked if I would do the fight for them. I thought quickly. Spinks's record as a pro showed only seven bouts, one of which was a draw. Ali would dispatch him in short order. Besides, I would have another championship tape for my album. I told Frank I would be happy to do the bout, and he said, "Great, your old mike pal Win Elliot will do the color and commercials."

So I went back in training again. You know what happened. The bout went fifteen rounds.

Ali and Spinks were rematched for New Orleans in September. This time John Chanin of ABC Radio called me and I didn't argue the point. I felt I was back in shape to do radio now, Lou Boda worked with me, and of course the bout went fifteen rounds.

I wasn't done with radio yet. On November 30, 1979, Wilfred Benitez defended the world welterweight title against Sugar Ray Leonard at Caesar's Palace in Las Vegas and—you guessed it— there I was at the radio mike, with Bob Buck helping me on NBC. Leonard won the fight and the crown on a TKO at 2:54 of the fifteenth round. In a bit more than two years I had been on a Canadian network, CBS, ABC, and NBC, doing almost sixty rounds of radio. The voice held up for this mini-comeback, and I added four championship fights to the collection I was planning for an album.

In September of 1985, co-promoters Don King and Butch Lewis matched heavyweight king Larry Holmes to defend his crown against light heavyweight champ Michael Spinks at the Riviera Hotel in Las Vegas. My friend John Chanin was now a radio producer for Don King, and sure enough, I got a call from him to do the radio broadcast of the fight for Don King Productions. Once again it had been six years since I had done a radio bout. Friendship or no friendship, I was firm with John. There was no way I was again going to do a radio broadcast of a fight.

John wouldn't accept my refusal, and called a couple of times more. My answer was still the same: no blow-by-blow description. Finally, John came up with what I thought was a fair compromise. Would I just do the first round and let Sam Nova do all the rest while I joined Lou Boda and Art Rust, Jr., as analysts for the fight? I agreed to this, and the show came out well. I wish I could say the same about the fight album. That still hasn't come out at all.

Sports Announcers

$\mathbf{B}$efore TV, the sports announcer was the bridge between the sports event and the folks gathered around their radios at home. When I was announcing, I always considered myself to be the eyes of the audience, and I am sure that Ted Husing, Bill Stern, Sam Taub, and the other premier sports voices of that era felt the same way.

There were many superb sports announcers in the thirties and forties. Besides the three I just mentioned, there were Graham McNamee, Mel Allen, Red Barber, Connie Desmond, Bert Lee, Jr., Bob Elson, Ford Bond, Clem McCarthy, Paul Douglas, and Marty Glickman, to name just a few. They were standouts in the field.

In the ensuing pages, I'm just going to concentrate on those announcers who did boxing, for that is what this book is mainly about. I just thought you might like to know something about the great sports voices of years ago as I knew them.

Larry MacPhail

There was practically no major-league baseball on the air in the New York area until 1939. Sure, the World Series was broadcast, and Earl Harper did daily broadcasts of the Newark Bears of the International League. But there was no daily broadcasting of the New York Yankees, the New York Giants, or the Brooklyn Dodgers.

The three New York clubs had been sold the idea that radio broadcasting of their games would hurt the live gate and they'd lose money. So they had a pact that there would be no daily airing of the games. Now we see the clubs making millions from radio and television, and realize how stupid they were. Larry MacPhail was important in helping them wise up.

MacPhail always had an eye for the spectacular, and he was one of the sport's all-time spectacular personalities. As a colonel in Europe at the end of World War I, he'd had a big idea. Kaiser Wilhelm had fled to the safety of Holland, a neutral country. Many felt that the Kaiser should be brought to trial for war crimes. MacPhail was one. With a couple of fellow officers he decided to go to Holland, kidnap the Kaiser, and bring him to justice. As the story goes, MacPhail and his friends got as far as the castle where the Kaiser was holed up. Then, unfortunately, the whole thing fell apart. The guards couldn't be convinced to let them in to see the Kaiser, and their efforts came to naught. But it was a heck of an idea.

That's the kind of guy Larry MacPhail was: always thinking in a positive way. When he got into baseball and became head of the Cincinnati Reds, radio was just emerging from its infancy. MacPhail was one of the people who saw the vast potential it had for major-league baseball.

He put the Reds games on the air and hired a young announcer named Walter Lanier Barber, better known as Red. This was a great break in several ways. It helped the Reds at the gate by publicizing their games and getting more fans interested in the game. It was a break for Red Barber. And it was a break for a multitude of baseball announcers who followed, for Red developed the style and the basic lexicon of baseball play-by-play.

In the New York area, the Brooklyn Dodgers were running far behind the Yankees and the Giants in popularity and gate receipts. It was 1938, and the Dodgers had not won a pennant since 1920. The Giants had won four straight from 1921 to 1924, again in 1933, and in 1936 and 1937. And they had won the World Series three times. The Yankees had won the pennant in 1921, 1922, and 1923, in 1926, 1927, and 1928, and in 1932, 1936, and 1937. They had captured the World Series six times. Truly, the Dodgers had fallen way behind, and the cry "Wait till next year" was beginning to wear thin.

Noting the spectacular efforts by Larry MacPhail with the Reds, the Brooklyn brass made him an offer and brought him east as general manager to get the Dodgers out of the doldrums. He did. When MacPhail got to Brooklyn, he found out about this silly agreement that the three New York clubs had against broadcasting baseball on a regular basis. He scrapped it immediately and brought Red Barber from Cincinnati to Brooklyn, and the New York area was introduced to real baseball announcing.

Ted Husing

Ted Husing was a giant among radio sports announcers in the late 1920s. Before him, there were Graham McNamee and J. Andrew White. I don't recall any others, though I'm sure there were some. But Husing was the one who made sports announcing a fine art form. He really used to do his homework. I heard Ted many times in the late twenties and early thirties, and there was never a time when he didn't know his subject thoroughly.

Football was his favorite, and he particularly enjoyed doing the

Army–Notre Dame game, which was second in importance only to the Army–Navy game in those days. I still recall the day in 1929 when I stood outside a radio store on Broadway in the freezing cold, hearing Ted call Jack Elder's famous interception of a Chris Cagle pass, and his eighty-yard dash for the touchdown that gave the Fighting Irish a 7–0 win over the Cadets at Yankee Stadium.

On Mondays in the fall when I was walking down the street, people thought I was talking to myself. I wasn't. I was imitating Husing in his broadcast of the previous Saturday's game. He had a mellifluous voice, perfect diction, and a masterful command of the language. He was a high school graduate (High School of Commerce) in New York City, and I never heard that he went to college. He didn't have to; he was self-educated and self-assured.

His descriptive powers were beyond compare. Words flowed easily from his lips. The listener knew what was happening and where at every moment. If the plays were exciting, Ted didn't have to shout to convey it; he just raised his voice a notch and spoke a bit faster. His speech was never garbled.

I never broadcast tennis, but I think it would be most difficult to do on radio. I listened to Ted do a famous match between Helen Wills and Helen Jacobs. It was amazing. From Ted's description, I knew where that ball was on every bounce.

I recall a spring day when I was running for Manhattan College in the Penn Relays. There was Ted in the infield like a Martian, with a big transmitter that looked like a stovepipe on his back. He was walking around, doing one event after another all by himself. My race being over, I was fascinated and followed him around, listening. It was then that I probably got the idea of becoming a sports announcer myself.

Late in the twenties, William Paley formed the Columbia Broadcasting System, and Ted Husing was its biggest star. Not only had he now been accepted as the number-one sports announcer (I almost wrote "sportscaster," but Ted abhorred the word) in the country, but he was great in many other facets of broadcasting. For instance, CBS used him as its anchorman at the Democratic and Republican

conventions of 1932, and also as its anchorman the night Franklin
D. Roosevelt was elected to the first of his four terms.

Speaking of 1932, it was that year when Max Schmeling defended
his heavyweight championship against Jack Sharkey. Gene Tunney
had relinquished the title in 1928, and Schmeling and Jack Sharkey
had fought for the vacant crown in 1930. In a wild finish, Schmeling
was awarded the title on a foul when he went down from a blow to
the midsection in the fourth round. After much indecision on the
part of the referee, Jimmy Crowley, the German was declared the
winner while still down. It wouldn't happen today, because now
you can't win on a foul.

Schmeling and Sharkey met for a rematch in the Madison Square
Garden Bowl on June 21, 1932, and Ted Husing was at the microphone. With him to do the color was a writer named Socker Coe.
It was a very close fight, and I remember one other thing about
that evening. I don't know when it started, before or during the
fight, but Husing and Coe spent the evening contradicting each
other. This was unheard of among sports commentators. Mildly
disagree, maybe, but contradict, never. Husing and Coe were strong-
minded personalities, and neither would give an inch. It was back
and forth, blow for blow, all night. Sharkey won a controversial
decision over Schmeling, but Husing and Coe ended their bout in
a draw. As far as I know, they never worked together again.

Husing was also an expert race caller, and the Gillette Company
used him to broadcast the Triple Crown races, the Kentucky Derby,
the Preakness, and the Belmont Stakes.

In the late 1940s, Husing also became a disc jockey for New
York's WHN. Oddly enough, although Ted had been the bright
star of the sports announcing firmament, he is supposed to have
made a lot more money playing records than he did describing
athletes. In the late forties he started doing TV broadcasts of fights.
As a matter of fact, the last thing I can remember this great announcer doing was the classic Jake LaMotta–Sugar Ray Robinson
fight for the middleweight championship at Chicago on February
14, 1951. Robinson, at the start of his career as a welterweight, had

won his first forty fights, including a ten-round decision over the Bronx Bull, before LaMotta handed him his first defeat on February 5, 1943.

In all, they had met five times before the title bout, with the Sugar Man taking four decisions. But all the bouts had been close. In the meantime, Robinson had won the welterweight crown and LaMotta had won the middleweight title from Marcel Cerdan. It had been almost six years since their last ring meeting.

This February 14 fight in Chicago became known as the Second Valentine's Day Massacre, Ted Husing's vivid description of the bout caught my attention as I watched it on TV. The bout had been close in the early rounds, but Robinson began pulling away. After the eleventh round it was no contest as Sugar Ray battered the game and courageous LaMotta.

LaMotta was proud of the fact that, although he had lost some fights, including four to Sugar Ray, he had never been floored in a bout. Nor was he in this one.

I recall Ted's description of the last round: "Round number thirteen. The hard-luck number. Robinson is hurting LaMotta now. LaMotta is on queer street, holding on. This is some of the most damaging evidence of punching I have seen. How he can survive, no one knows. No man can take this pummeling. The fight is stopped in the thirteenth round, the hard-luck round. Jake wouldn't want to quit. There you see a champion gone down to defeat."

Robinson had won the title to become a dual champion, but LaMotta had remained on his feet in an unexampled exhibit of bravery.

Bill Corum

I first met Bill Corum in 1937 at the press headquarters of the World Series between the New York teams, the Yankees and the Giants. At that time I was just making some strides in the business as sports director of WINS.

Bill was a nationally renowned sports columnist of the Hearst papers. The flagship newspaper in New York was the *Journal-American,* where his daily column appeared. I had always admired Corum's writing, not only because the columns were well written but also because of his eminent fairness. He was a decent person who had a consideration for the feelings of others.

He rarely ripped a sports figure in his column, but if he did you could be sure the subject deserved it. In this way he differed from acerbic columnists of the time such as Dan Parker of the *Daily Mirror* and Joe Williams of the *World-Telegram* who had the ax out constantly. Years later, when we were working together, Bill would say to me almost plaintively that he couldn't understand why Williams and Parker were constantly on the backs of sports figures.

"They're hurting sports," he would say, adding, "They're writing themselves out of jobs." The papers they wrote for ultimately folded, but I wouldn't blame it on them.

The night I first met him, Corum was standing at the bar of the Waldorf. I introduced myself and found him a very friendly person. Little did I know then that our careers would be so enmeshed four years later and that we would work together on sports broadcasts for so many years.

A graduate of the University of Missouri, Bill entered the service in World War I and left it as the youngest major in the U.S. Army. He was gassed in that conflict, and it took a severe toll on his lungs in the long run. An addicted smoker, he died of lung cancer in 1958 at the age of sixty-five.

In his early career, Bill had studied journalism at the University of Missouri, which Mary Margaret McBride attended at the same time. He was interested in sportswriting and took a journalism course at Columbia University in New York. Then he got a job with the sports department of *The New York Times*. His coverage of sports was so impressive that Arthur Brisbane, who ran things for Hearst and initiated a policy of always looking for and hiring the best, grabbed him for the *Journal* when the top sports columnist's job became open.

Bill was popular and widely read from the beginning. It's interesting to note his continued interest in Columbia University and also his friendship with Lou Little, its fabled football coach. In 1933,

Columbia had a good but not great football team, and Corum came up with an idea that seemed zany at the time. How about Columbia for the Rose Bowl? It almost seemed laughable. Columbia was a great institution of learning, but its team in the Rose Bowl? Despite cries of derision from coast to coast, Corum doggedly mounted a campaign for the Lions.

Soon other great writers around the country began to see merit in the idea. Do you know what happened? The Selection Committee for the Rose Bowl picked Columbia to play the great Stanford University team on New Year's Day 1934. Do you know what else happened? Columbia startled one and all by beating Stanford's Indians 7–0, using the immortal KF79 play engineered by quarterback Cliff Montgomery, who sent Al Barabas around the end for the only touchdown, scored in a morass of mud. Corum's dreaming really paid off.

In 1941, when I was selected by the Gillette Company to be their blow-by-blow announcer on fights, much to my surprise but also to my pleasure, Bill Corum was selected as the between-rounds and color commentator. Our first show was the heavyweight championship battle between champion Joe Louis and Billy Conn. In an earlier chapter I described that fight and the vital part Bill Corum had in its production.

Bill and I had never worked together on a show. As a matter of fact, there was skepticism in some quarters about our doing that most important fight, particularly since this was a great venture— a gamble, if you will—on the part of the sponsor. There was doubt about Bill because his appearances on radio had been as a guest and some felt that he was therefore not qualified to be the color man on a championship fight.

There was also doubt about me. Certainly I had the experience, but the shows I had done were of small stature. Might I not cave in at the thought of a show of this magnitude, of being on a network for the first time, describing a fight to millions? And, of course, Corum and I were a new team and would be working together for the first time. I could understand the doubts.

One who also understood them was Irwin Rosee, who was doing radio publicity for promoter Mike Jacobs. Irwin came up with the smart idea of our going to different New York fight clubs on fight nights and practicing for the Louis–Conn fight. I would do the blow-by-blow, using the names Joe Louis and Billy Conn instead of those of the real contestants. Bill would then pick it up at the bell and talk as if it were Conn–Louis. We took our practice show on the road to several fight clubs that were great in their day but have been out of existence for a long, long time—the New York Coliseum at Starlight Park in the Bronx, the St. Nick's Arena, Fort Hamilton in Brooklyn, and the Queensboro Arena, where I got my start on pro bouts. It is now a parking lot at Queens Plaza, where I park my car when I drive to the city.

The practice sessions worked reasonably well, and things seemed to be going smoothly until one night at the Queensboro. That night we were joined at ringside by Craig Smith, the advertising manager of Gillette, the man who was responsible for the whole operation. Also present were Searle Hendee and Ed Wilhelm of the Maxon Advertising Agency, which represented Gillette. Irwin was there, of course, and so was Tom Slater, sports director of the Mutual Broadcasting System, which was going to air the big fight. I noticed that Bill seemed to have a bit of trouble putting it together that night. I don't know, maybe I did, too. As we were leaving the arena, Slater seemed depressed. This was a radical change because he was usually so upbeat. He called me aside. Quietly he told me to keep my cool, but there might be a change in the broadcast setup. Corum might be out.

This bothered me not only for Bill's sake but also for mine. It occurred to me that if they might change Corum, they might change me, too. After all, they hardly knew me. Besides, they were from Boston and I was from New York. As a matter of fact, they had met me only a couple of weeks before. Sure, I had won their audition on the Christoforidis–Lesnevich fight, but might that not be a one-time shot, a fluke? Might I not crack under the pressure of such a titanic broadcast? Perhaps they might go back to a big-time announcer like Bill Stern or Clem McCarthy or even Sam Taub, whom

Mike Jacobs would prefer. Naturally, these thoughts troubled me. For a while I was very uncomfortable. Then I calmed down. I began to realize that my work on the simulated fights was as good as anything I had done. And besides, they had sent out terrific amounts of publicity on the fight and it had made the papers and radio stations all over the country.

"No," I said to myself, "they can't change me." They didn't, and thank goodness they didn't change Bill, either. Tom had been unduly alarmed. Corum and I did the Louis–Conn fight on June 18. It was a great thirteen-round fight. The broadcast was a smashing success, with an all-time-high rating of 56.4. Gillette sold millions of blades. Bill worked on the fights for twelve years until he left to become head of the Kentucky Derby, and I was with Gillette for twenty-four years.

Toots Shor, the famed restaurateur, was a very close friend of Bill Corum. The innkeeper who served the great of the sports world and Hollywood had the pleasure of having the Friday-night fight crowd close his shop on many a Saturday morning. After that we might go to Bill's suite at the Park Lane Hotel for a nightcap.

Bill's favorite sports were baseball, boxing, and horse racing. He was extremely knowledgeable in all three, and Gillette, which broadcast not only boxing but also the World Series and the Triple Crown of racing, used Bill as a color commentator on all three. Bill, who was very close to Matt Wynn, the president of the Kentucky Derby from its beginning, or so it seemed, coined a phrase that seems likely to live as long as the Derby. He dubbed it "the run for the roses." When Matt Wynn passed out of the picture, Bill was named president of Churchill Downs, host to the Derby. At this time, to honor his dear friend, Toots gave one of the great sports parties of all time. Don Ameche was the toastmaster and Frank Sinatra and Ethel Merman sang for the assembly. The only other woman present was a regal woman from the South, the proudest person there, Bill's mother.

When the great sportsman died in 1958, the funeral service, at Campbell's parlor, was jammed with celebrities. Bob Considine, the noted columnist, spoke about Bill's life and career, and Red Barber gave a most touching and unforgettable eulogy.

Graham McNamee

The American Sportscasters Association annually gives the Graham McNamee Award, as well they should. This gentleman of the old carbon microphones of the 1920s was the pioneer of sports broadcasters. He was a very likable person with a great voice and an infectious laugh. Later he became even more famous as the straight man for Ed Wynn's radio show, possibly the most popular program of its era. By today's standards, McNamee would not be considered a good sports announcer, nor was he. He made mistake after mistake in the events he covered, but no one seemed to mind. He was the only show in town. How did the listeners know whether he was capable or not? They had no one with whom to compare him. In his defense, it must be said that as far as sports announcing was concerned, he had to blaze the trail and set the standard.

McNamee did many important events in his time. I recall his famous broadcast of the seventh and deciding game of the 1924 World Series, which the Washington Senators won for Walter Johnson over the New York Giants of John McGraw. Graham did football games and the Poughkeepsie Regatta, the latter from a blimp. In boxing, he did the famous Dempsey–Tunney championship bout.

McNamee, Ted Husing, Bill Stern, Red Barber, and I were the first inductees to the American Sportscasters Association Hall of Fame. The Graham McNamee Award is given to a former sports broadcaster who made good at something else. The first winner was President Ronald Reagan.

Win Elliot

When Bill Corum left the Gillette broadcasts in 1953, he was replaced by Win Elliot. This was a most fortunate move for the Gillette Company, and for Win himself. He was a very talented radio and TV personality. He had a good voice and a good mind, knew sports, and was quick to grasp the importance of a situation. We got along very well. He was the between-rounds and color commentator on the fights until they went off radio in 1960. Win did a lot of different sports capably. He was good at hockey, having played the game while at the University of Michigan, and was on the New York Rangers broadcasts for many years. He loved horse racing and worked on the Kentucky Derby radio broadcasts, and was also a TV host at the New York races. For his horse-racing endeavors, Elliot was honored with two Eclipse awards. Spencer Drayton, the head of the Thoroughbred Racing Association, asked me if I would go to Los Angeles to make the presentation to Win for the second award in 1975. I was happy to. Win was on the CBS radio broadcasts of the World Series for many years, including 1986. His weekend sports reports on CBS Radio were a feature for a long time. And he loved the fights.

I interviewed Win last year at his home in Weston, Connecticut, and our conversation brought back some nice thoughts of memorable events. I reminded him of the time we did the welterweight championship bout in Syracuse between the local favorite, Carmen Basilio, and the champion, the bolo puncher, Gerado Gonzalez, known better as Kid Gavilan. I thought Basilio had won the fight and deserved the decision. Unfortunately, the officials voted for Gavilan. The big local crowd was incensed, and we were surrounded at the cramped ringside. The crowd started to get nasty, and we had the feeling that they thought we had something to do with the decision, which, of course, we didn't. Fortunately, Norm Rothschild, the promoter, got us out safely. Basilio didn't win the title that night, but he took it from Tony DeMarco two years later in Syracuse at the Onondaga War Memorial Auditorium. It was a bruising seesaw battle with Basilio prevailing by a knockout in the twelfth round. Win had a comment on Basilio, the former onion farmer: "I've never forgotten when I asked Carmen Basilio—he was such a nice guy, you remember, and he had the scars on his hands where he'd been an onion picker and used the knife—and I said, 'Carmen, you're such a sweetheart, how come when you're in the ring you're such a terrible person? God, you're a killer.' And he said to me,

'Well, it's very easy, Win—the ring is so many feet by so many feet. There's him, there's me, and there's the referee. And that leaves no room for pity.' "

Basilio was, indeed, in his ring career, a rough and tough individual. I guess it makes a difference when you get paid for it. As a matter of fact, after retiring, Carmen was in the Athletic Department of Le Moyne College in upstate New York. There, when dressed in a blue suit and wearing eyeglasses, he looked very professorial.

In horse racing, Win recalled doing the famous match race in Chicago between Nashua and Swaps in 1955. Jack Drees did the call and Win the color. Win told me: "It was the first time I can remember that they saddled the horses on the inside, right in front of the tote board. Just the two. The Woodwards owned Nashua and Rex Ellsworth and Mish Tenney were with Swaps. Old Sunny Jim Fitzsimmons was the trainer of Nashua. He was so stooped over he couldn't see anything. All Jack Drees did was call the race. He was the star, but he was only on for a minute and a half. I carried everything else. Then the race—I was in the winner's circle on the track. Sunny Jim was there but he couldn't see the race, so I called it for him. After all, it was just two horses. It was no problem.

"The start of that race was the most sensational I ever saw. Eddie Arcaro whipped Nashua so hard that he came out of the gate with his legs up in the air and running sideways. The whole theory of a match race is 'I'll get out in front and I'll run just as fast as I have to to keep ahead.' I've never forgotten that. Nashua, of course, won handily. Sunny Jim's strategy had prevailed!

"I've often thought of walking into the old Garden on 50th Street and Eighth Avenue—through the old lobby, seeing all those familiar faces, walking down through the crowd getting to the ringside. Boy, how many fights a year would we do there?"

The fact was, we were doing fifty or so fights a year in those days, and at least thirty of those came from the Garden.

Win reminded me that on one occasion we did separate fights for Gillette on the same night. Bill Corum and I were at Yankee Stadium for the heavyweight championship between title holder Rocky Marciano and Ezzard Charles, while Win and Al Helfer were in

Washington at the Uline Arena. The promoter, a man whose restaurant we used to frequent whenever we did a fight in Washington,
was Goldie Ahearn. I remember many of those nights when Bob
Dunphy (no relation), who was the sergeant-at-arms of the Senate,
Larry Laurent, who was the radio-TV columnist of the *Washington
Post*, and Bobby Baker would join Win, Joel Nixon, and me for a
post-fight steak. Bobby Baker, a nice, brilliant young man, was a
confidant of President Lyndon Johnson and was really making political strides at that time. It was said that he was on his way to
becoming governor of South Carolina. If he got that, who knows,
he might have been President. The bottom fell out of everything,
and he disappeared from public life. Bobby was a real fight fan.

Another famous person who attended the Washington fights at
Uline and at the new Capitol Arena was Alice Roosevelt Longworth,
the daughter of President Theodore Roosevelt and the widow of
Nicholas Longworth, the Speaker of the House. I remember her
driving up to the door of the fight club, Washington's answer to the
St. Nick's in New York, all by herself in a brand-new white Cadillac
convertible. This grand lady would leave the car at the door, go in,
enjoy the fights, come out, and go home. She was really something!

The night we did the separate fights for Gillette, Win was in
Washington and had to fill the air with a fight until it was time for
the Marciano–Charles fight to take over from New York at 11:00
P.M. As Win described it, "The promoter, Goldie Ahearn, kept
circling the ring. The fighters were Holly Mims, who was very good,
and somebody else—I don't remember his name—who wasn't. Goldie would walk around and look at me and say 'Now?' I'd say, 'Not
yet.' I was supposed to tell him when to unload because you guys
were going to take the air after us. We didn't want to end too quickly.
Now, this wasn't crooked. It was just that one guy, Mims, was so
good and the other guy was so bad that the good guy could end it
anytime he wanted to. Goldie kept circling and every so often asking,
'Now?' And then we heard on the phone it was okay, New York
could take it in about five minutes. I nodded to Goldie. Goldie gave
the signal, and Mims said, 'Hey, fellow, look at this. Look at this.'
Bam. Washington yielded to New York."

Bill Stern

Bill Stern was probably the most dynamic sports announcer of his day. After a serious auto accident in 1936 that cost him a leg, he was appointed sports director of NBC, which at that time consisted of two networks, the Red and the Blue. He was equal to the task. Ted Husing had succeeded Graham McNamee as number one in the sports announcing field. Now Stern was gaining on Husing and ultimately surpassed him. Husing, of course, was the big wheel at CBS. It was a real war between the two top-notchers and it lasted several years. They had contrasting styles, which made the contest more exciting, and their networks were the giants of the business. Husing was calm and deliberate, painstakingly accurate in his descriptions. Stern had a great and exciting style. He had come to sports from show business, and, judging from his broadcasts, he believed that the show was more important than the score. On football, Husing arrived at the game thoroughly prepared. He knew the coaches and the players. He had just one man, Jimmy Dolan, helping him on his broadcasts. Stern had a retinue working with him. Husing and Dolan were so prepared for a game that they rarely made a mistake, but not Bill. Every so often on a long gainer, Stern would call the wrong man as the ball carrier. But his spotters would get his attention before the man crossed the goal line, and Bill would blithely describe a lateral pass to the real ball carrier, who would then score the touchdown. This was radio, of course, and the listeners were none the wiser. But Husing was a purist, and this bit of ledgerdemain on Bill's part annoyed him no end. Years later, as the story goes, Husing was doing a horse race at Belmont Park, and Bill came up to see him in the announcer's booth. Bill listened in fascination to Ted's description of the thoroughbreds, and when it was over he said, "Ted, that was great and it was exciting. I'd like to try horse racing." Ted replied quickly. "Don't do it, Bill, you can't lateral a horse."

Nevertheless, Stern soon surpassed Husing as the country's number-one sports announcer. Besides his broadcasts of games and other special events, Stern did a half-hour sports show on Friday nights called "The Colgate Sports Reel." It was written by some of the best writers in the field, and Bill's great voice and exciting delivery made it for years one of the most listened-to shows on radio. Rumor had it that Stern received $2,000 a week, at a time when both a subway ride and a phone call were still a nickel.

One of the features of the half hour was what came to be known as the "And that man was . . ." segment. It was a part of the show that detailed the doings of some sports hero past or present, without mentioning his or her name. It wended its way through the program with one heroic exploit after another until, just after the final example, Bill would relieve the listeners' anxiety and anticipation with "And that man was . . ." One night it was, believe it or not, Cardinal Spellman, who had played baseball for Fordham University. Another time it was former heavyweight champion Primo Carnera, who, Bill said, had strangled German sentries in the Alps during World War II. And so it went with hero after hero, week after week. It may have been theatrical, but that was what made Bill so popular. He was theatrical, he was dramatic, and he became more popular than ever. When TV surpassed radio in importance in the late fifties, Bill went to the new medium and was a success there, too, with his various shows.

Naturally, since we were both in the same business, my path crossed Bill's many times during those years. Two instances are particularly vivid. In the first, I was doing the blow-by-blow description of a championship fight, and later that evening Bill was on the air with former heavyweight contender Tony Galento. Naturally, Bill and Tony talked about the fight. Tony was very critical of my handling of the blow-by-blow and said so on Bill's program in very emphatic terms. Bill didn't criticize me, but he didn't defend me, either. This annoyed my wife, Muriel, who was listening to the program and who took to heart anything derogatory that was said about me. She immediately called Stern at the studio and got him on the phone. She made her case to an attentive Stern, who became very apologetic after listening to her superb logic. Bill told her that he was sorry about what Galento had said, and that he would like to have me as a guest on his show that following night to give my side of the story. He called me the next day and I went on his show and everything turned out fine.

The other incident concerned a football game that I was supposed to broadcast for WINS at Baker Field, the home of Columbia University's football team. CBS with Ted Husing, NBC with Stern, and WOR with Stan Lomax were also airing the game, a very important contest between Columbia and Navy. When I got to my broadcast booth about two hours before kickoff time, I found to my horror that the WINS crew was standing around looking very crestfallen and defeated. I was too, a moment later. It seemed that someone in authority at WINS had forgotten to order our lines from the telephone company, and there we were, on top of the stadium with an audience and a sponsor waiting, and no outlet. It was a disaster. Husing and Lomax were very sympathetic, but they quickly went about their own work. Not Bill Stern. He was most concerned about me. He thought about it for a moment, then said, "Don, NBC has an extra phone line here, which your engineers can hook up and patch into the WINS control room as a broadcast line. Why don't you use it?"

I did, and our broadcast was saved. I was forever grateful.

In 1984, Bill was one of the first inductees into the American Sportscasters Association Hall of Fame.

Mel Allen

I first met Mel Allen in 1937, when I was sports director at WINS in New York. The station had been signed by a sponsor to do the Fordham University football schedule, and Mel was brought in to do the play-by-play. I was signed to do between-halves commentary on the game. It was the era when the Fordham Rams had the famed "seven blocks of granite" in the line, featuring, among others, the great Vince Lombardi. It was an exciting season that climaxed in a tie game with Pittsburgh. The Rams were one of the country's

football powers, and because of that great season, their hopes were
high for a Rose Bowl invitation. As a matter of fact, their slogan
was "From Rose Hill to Rose Bowl." It wasn't to be, though. Fordham was not invited.

Allen, a young announcer at the time, did a fine job on the games,
and we got along well. We remained good friends through the years,
particularly in the Sports Broadcasters Association, where both of
us served as president at various times. Mel was one of the best of
the baseball announcers and became known as the Voice of the
New York Yankees. He had a great voice filled with vibrancy and
enthusiasm. He and the Yankees met and joined at a good time for
both. The Bronx Bombers had such great stars as Joe DiMaggio,
Phil Rizzuto, Joe Gordon, Mickey Mantle, Yogi Berra, Allie Reynolds, Whitey Ford, and a host of other greats. Allen's style fitted
the Yankees well. The team was winning pennants, and Mel was
selling a lot of tickets. In those days it was usual for a team that
won the pennant to supply its number-one announcer as the play-
by-play man on the World Series. Therefore, Allen did fifteen World
Series between 1942 and 1963. I doubt that anyone else, including
the fabled Red Barber, ever did that many. And Allen, despite a
pronounced bias, did the games well. I heard from men who worked
with him that it was not easy being in the booth with him day after
day for a 162-game schedule. But his ability must have rubbed off,
because some of his associates, especially Curt Gowdy and Russ
Hodges, went on to greatness. Gowdy left the Yankees to do the
Boston Red Sox games and then became a top-notcher on the networks, doing a variety of sports. He is now in the American Sportscasters Association Hall of Fame.

Russ Hodges also moved on to broadcast greatness after working
with Allen. He moved across town to do the Giants baseball broadcasts from the Polo Grounds. Russ became a legend in 1951 when
he was at the microphone to describe Bobby Thompson's famous
home run off Ralph Branca of the Dodgers to win the pennant. His
cry, "The Giants win the pennant!" will never be forgotten.

Mel did well on several other sports besides baseball, especially
football. He did the Rose Bowl a couple of times. He had and still

has a great voice for commercials. Even now, he does them for major-league baseball.

I mentioned that Mel and I were good friends, and we still are. But sometimes he just can't stop talking. Back in 1942, Mel and Connie Desmond were doing the Yankee games on WOR radio. Practically all the games then were in the afternoon, starting around three o'clock. WOR sold a five-minute commercial sports spot to follow the games, and hired me to do it. The catch to the deal was that if it didn't get on the air by five minutes before six on a given day, it didn't get on at all. Invariably, the games would finish somewhere between 5:30 and 5:45, which allowed enough time to get my show on before 5:55. Unfortunately for me and WOR, no matter when the game ended, Allen and Desmond would keep talking, giving scores of other games over and over again, and when they ran out of scores, they would talk anyway. Meanwhile I sweated, watching the clock edging toward 5:55. At WOR, they sweated too, especially the poor salesman who had sold the spot. The station brass met with Mel again and again. I don't know how Allen explained it, but I do know it happened once too often. The sponsor lost heart, and the show was canceled.

Like many sports announcers, Mel hankered to do fights. He was signed to do the 1948 middleweight championship bout between champion Rocky Graziano and Tony Zale. The bout was held in the Newark Bears Park. It was the third title bout in three years for these two great warriors. Zale won the first, and Graziano the second. This was the bout where the famous dwarf who used to hop into the ring at big fights jumped in and ran over to Zale to wish him well. Then he crossed over to Rocky, who, remembering Tony's punching power, tapped the little fellow on the head and said, "Geez, wish I was fightin' you tonight, 'stead of Zale." As it turned out, Zale won the fight by a third-round kayo, but Allen lost out as a fight announcer.

After a change in the Yankee front office, Mel was out for some time. But new ownership came to the Yankees and Mel was brought back to television on cable. The ability is still there, and so is the voice. Also, it's a pleasure to be at the stadium on Yankee Old-

Timers' Day, when Mel still handles the introductions in his in-
imitable style. Nobody brings on the old-timers the way Mel does.
Allen has always been Hall of Fame material, and now he's in four
of them: The National Broadcasters Hall of Fame, the Baseball Hall
of Fame, the National Sportscasters and Sportswriters Hall of Fame,
and the American Sportscasters Association Hall of Fame.

Ford Frick

Those who remember Ford Frick probably recall that he was a
sportswriter for the old *New York Journal*. He was a good writer who
concentrated on baseball, and was subsequently hired as publicity
director of the National League. He did that so well that they made
him the league president, succeeding John Heydler in 1935. In 1951,
Frick reached the ultimate as he replaced Governor A. B. "Happy"
Chandler as commissioner of baseball, a post he retained until 1965.

In 1933 the New York Giants were involved in a hot pennant
race with the St. Louis Cardinals, the Gas House Gang. Unable to
get permission to do the games live on radio, the *New York Journal*
came up with the idea of doing the games by ticker wire. That's
the way another sports announcer, Ronald Reagan, used to do the
Chicago Cubs games. The *Journal* staff hit on the idea of having
Frick do the games. He did a great job and he had a vast New York
audience as the Giants fought their way to the pennant.

I mention this because in the fall of that year the *Journal* assigned
me to cover a Manhattan College–St. Bonaventure football game
at the Manhattan Field in Riverdale, New York. I was seated in
the press row a few seats below the broadcast booth where Ford
Frick was broadcasting the game over WINS. Seeing me there, Ford
called down to me and asked if I would like to go on the air between
the halves. I was very happy to. I must have done well, because
the following week I was called down to the *Journal* office, which
had a WINS studio in the building, and was asked if I would do
the noon newscast. I said I certainly would. This was more or less

an audition because they didn't want a newscaster; they were thinking football.

The *Journal* had a contract to air the Princeton football games over WINS that year, and they weren't sure of their announcing setup. Apparently pleased with my rendition of the news, they assigned me to do a Princeton game the following Saturday.

Working with me were Benny Friedman, the immortal Hall of Famer from college and pro football, and Bob Stanton, a professional announcer who later did a lot of sports for NBC. The Princeton athletic director was Asa Bushnell. Our paths would cross many times in the years to come when he was head of the IC4A, which controlled Eastern college athletics. Friedman, Stanton, and I divided the game, which featured, as I recall, Princeton's great Gary LeVan.

The critical broadcast reports were that Friedman gave the best analysis, Stanton had the best voice, and I gave the best description. It turned out later that the report, as far as I was concerned, was neither good nor bad. It was just innocuous, which to me was much worse. I never heard from the *Journal* people again, and Friedman and Stanton did the rest of the schedule. And I didn't do another play-by-play on football for a couple of years.

But I thank Ford Frick for putting me on the air at that Manhattan game, for it whetted my appetite for sports announcing. It was the final convincer as far as I was concerned.

Clem McCarthy

Clem McCarthy was probably the most colorful racing announcer of all time. Fred Caposella and Bryan Field in New York, Jack Drees in the Midwest, and Joe Hernandez on the west coast were also among the best. Of them all, however, it was Clem who captured the imagination.

Like Ted Husing on football, Graham McNamee on baseball, and Sam Taub on boxing, Clem was a trailblazer in his descriptions of horse races. His word pictures of the Kentucky Derby and other big races were classics of their time. He had a gravelly voice, and his "R-r-r-racing fans" will never be forgotten by those fortunate enough to have heard it. I distinctly remember one of his early Kentucky Derbies. Someone must have written in and said it should be *Darby*, not *Derby*. To which Clem replied, "I don't know if it should be Derby or Darby, but mine's a bowler."

Clem McCarthy is on this list because, in addition to the races, he did many of that era's big fights, some of which featured Joe Louis. There weren't many boxing announcers in the thirties, when Clem was at his best. He worked for NBC at the time, and when a big fight came along, naturally the network wanted him to be at ringside. But they usually had to audition for a sponsor, and their idea of an audition for a fight broadcast went something like this:

The sponsors and the agency people would be seated in a client's booth to hear Clem. A script had been written according to the way they thought the fight broadcast should be done.

First there would be an introduction by a big-time staff announcer. Next a commercial. Next the color commentator, setting the scene from the script. Another commercial. Then the staff announcer would say, "Here's our veteran boxing announcer, Clem McCarthy."

Clem also had a prepared script, and he began, "Good evening, ladies and gentlemen of the radio audience. This is Clem McCarthy at ringside in Yankee Stadium. We're only moments away from the first round of the long-anticipated return bout between the challenger and former champion from Germany, Max Schmeling, and the heavyweight champion of the world, the great Detroit Brown Bomber, Joe Louis. [Crowd noise from sound-effects man.] At the weigh-in today, Louis was one-ninety-eight and three-quarters; Schmeling one-ninety-three. The referee is Arthur Donovan. We're waiting for the bell for round one. [Bell sounds.] Louis out there quickly, Schmeling backs off . . ." And so forth, all from a prepared script.

It must have worked, because Clem was picked for several big fights. The biggest of them all was the return match between Louis and Schmeling for the title in 1938. This was a real grudge match, for Schmeling had kayoed Louis in twelve rounds in 1936. In the intervening year Louis had knocked out champion Jim Braddock to take the title. Feelings were running high as Louis defended against the German. With Nazism on the march, and the clouds of war hovering over Europe, Max was looked on as a representative of Hitler. When Schmeling kayoed Louis in 1936, the Nazis had claimed it as a victory for the master race. Clem McCarthy gave a classic description of Louis's demolition of Schmeling in round one. Clem described the fight in these words:

"A left to the head, a left to the jaw, a right to the head and Donovan [Arthur Donovan, the referee] is watching carefully. Louis measures him. Right to the body, a left hook to the jaw, and Schmeling is down. The count is five, six, seven, eight—the men are in the ring. The fight is over on a technical knockout. Max Schmeling is beaten in one round." Harry Balogh (the ring announcer): "The time, two minutes, four seconds, first round. Referee stops it. The winner and still champion, Joe Louis."

Incidentally, Clem didn't mention that when Schmeling's handlers saw the fierce beating he was taking from Louis, one of them threw a towel in the ring. Referee Donovan quickly picked it up and threw it out of the ring. At one time you could stop a fight by throwing in the towel, but that led to a lot of chicanery and a rule was passed that only the referee could stop a fight. Donovan did so on his own.

Sam Taub

Sam Taub was the premier boxing announcer of his time, that time being the 1930s, when the broadcasting of sports on radio became so important in the United States. Like Ted Husing and Graham McNamee before him, Sam had to develop a technique and a vocabulary for the description of boxing. A few had tried boxing, notably McNamee and J. Andrew White, but they never really caught the feel and flavor of the ring game. A few others came and went, like the sportswriter hired to do a bout on radio at Madison Square Garden. His trouble was that he had a bet on one of the fighters—let's call him Smith. The blow-by-blow went something like this: "And there's a right, and Smith is down. Get up, you son of a bitch!" Quickly realizing his terrible gaffe, he continued, "Get away from here. Ladies and gentlemen, I'm sorry. Some spectator just yelled into the microphone." Meanwhile Smith was counted out, and so was the writer.

By today's standards, Sam Taub might not have been very literate, but he knew boxing and spoke the lingo of the game. He was able to portray capably in words the action in the ring. Sam, a little guy, had immense vitality and supreme self-confidence.

Angelo Palange was a broadcast entrepreneur in the mid-thirties. He had good connections and was a good salesman, and one of his clients was Adam Hats. He joined Sam at the ring mikes, and the two were tireless. They might do as many as six boxing or wrestling bouts a week. The "hatter" did very well. "Thank you, Sam," "Thank you, Angelo," became a famous exchange on the airwaves as Taub with his blow-by-blow and Palange with his color comments and salesmanship took the broadcasts to practically every fight club around New York, including Madison Square Garden.

Unfortunately for Palange, he had to have a short stay in the hospital. While he was incapacitated, it became "Thank you, Sam," "Thank you, Bill." Bill Stern had replaced Palange as Sam's partner, and the latter disappeared as a fight announcer. He did surface briefly in 1939 to help me with my broadcast of the Diamond Belt bouts at the Garden. Then he went into the restaurant business.

Stern, as the sports director for NBC, had the fights transferred to the Blue Network, where they got national attention. Bill Corum and I replaced Taub and Stern as the Garden boxing announcers in 1941. This hurt Sam a lot more than it did Bill, because Stern still had a lot to do at NBC. Taub initiated a very popular sports show on WHN call "The Hour of Champions." It was presented every Sunday morning, and almost everyone of prominence in the sports world was a guest on it at one time or another.

My replacing Taub as the Garden's blow-by-blow announcer must have been a terrible shock to him. But he never held it against me, nor did he hold it against Craig Smith, the advertising director of Gillette, whose decision it was. Sam and I became the best of friends, and I was delighted when he called to tell me his friends were throwing a ninetieth birthday party for him, and asked me to be the toastmaster. It was a great moment for both of us.

You often hear talk about how cold-blooded boxing promoters are. Bob Arum was the promoter of the Muhammad Ali–Leon Spinks return bout for the heavyweight title in September of 1978. Hearing of Sam's ninetieth birthday, Arum gave the announcer a wonderful birthday present. He brought Sam as his guest, all expenses paid, to the fight in New Orleans. And he hired an off-duty policeman to watch over Sam all the time he was there.

I have to add one more notable story about this great boxing figure. In Sam's early days he was a sportswriter for one of the New York papers. The sports editor was Bat Masterson, the famed marshal of Dodge City, portrayed as Marshal Dillon on TV's "Gunsmoke." Masterson came to New York, refereed a few fights, and then became a newspaperman. Coming back from an assignment one day, Sam went into Bat's office and found him dead, of natural causes, at his desk.

Steve Ellis

In 1940 I had the bug for fight announcing. In 1939 and again in 1940 I had done amateur bouts, the Diamond Belts and the Golden Gloves. People told me I did well on them, so I decided to pursue boxing. In the spring of 1940 I read that there would be professional bouts at the Queensboro Arena, an important outdoor fight club at that time in Long Island City, New York, not too far from Manhattan. Checking further, I found that the promoters at the Queensboro Arena were Marty Cohen, who is still around as a boxing official, and Bill Heydorn.

I dropped over to see them and to tell them of my plans. I wanted to broadcast their weekly bouts over WINS. The station couldn't afford to pay them rights fees at this time, but would give their bouts a lot of publicity. Naturally, if the station sold the bouts to a sponsor, they would be remunerated accordingly. They agreed with my idea. They knew, of course, that I would do the blow-by-blow descriptions, but also I told them that Bill Harding, a very capable WINS announcer, would take care of the between-rounds chores. They made a suggestion. They wanted Armand Yussem to be the between-round commentator.

Stunned, I asked, "Who?"

"Armand Yussem," they repeated.

I had never heard of Armand Yussem, and I wasn't about to put him on a fight broadcast with a name like that. But they were firm. They wanted Armand Yussem. Now we were at an impasse, and I knew that I needed the Queensboro more than the Queensboro needed me. So I made a suggestion for a compromise. We'd use Harding after one round and Yussem after the next round and so on. They agreed, and the Queensboro bouts went on the air. The biggest fight on that summer's program was an over-the-weight match between middleweight champion Ken Overlin and Harry Balsamo, who was known as "the belting brakeman." Balsamo must have had railroad ties, if you will pardon the pun. However, it was Overlin who did the belting, as he stopped Balsamo in nine.

You may be wondering what all this has to do with Steve Ellis. Well, soon after the Queensboro bouts got under way, Yussem changed his name to Steve Ellis, which seems to have been a smart move. As Steve Ellis, he did very well both as a sportscaster and as a disc jockey. He was smart enough to latch on to Art Flynn, an advertising man, who was very capable and well-known in the business. Flynn, a close friend of Horace Stoneham, owner of the New York Giants baseball team, was able to get Ellis the play-by-play job on the Giants games.

But let's get back to boxing, where he was much better, as either Yussem or Ellis. Steve had a lot of smarts, as they say in the trade, and was a clever maneuverer. Either through Flynn or by himself, he got close to the Gillette Company and they used him on the Friday-night fights if a substitute was needed either for Corum or me. From there he branched out and did the Wednesday fights on TV.

Steve did some big fights on closed-circuit or theater TV. The biggest was the heavyweight championship bout in Miami in 1964, when Cassius Clay (who became Muhammad Ali) took the heavyweight crown as Sonny Liston quit in his corner after the seventh round. Ellis also did the closed circuit of the Ali–Patterson championship in Las Vegas in 1965.

But Steve couldn't stay away from the proverbial conflict of interest. While announcing fights on TV, he was also a fight manager and one of those he managed was Chico Vejar, a fine welterweight contender of that era. When doing a Vejar fight, Ellis apparently forgot he was supposed to be impartial. The relationship reminded one of the famed Corsican brothers. If you remember the story, no matter how many miles apart they were, they were inseparable. When one was hurt, the other felt pain, too. So it was with Ellis and Vejar. One night Vejar was in a tough fight and Ellis was at the mike. The opponent hauled off and belted Chico with a solar plexus punch that was like a missile fired to the midsection. Forgetting the mike, Ellis must have felt pain, too. He yelled, "Ooh!" in a loud voice. To the announcer's embarrassment, the groan went from coast to coast.

Major J. Andrew White

I'm quite sure that not many readers, if any, have ever heard of Major J. Andrew White. But millions heard of him in the 1920s. White was a contemporary of the fabled Graham McNamee. In fact, White and McNamee were practially the only nationally known sports announcers of that decade. They competed against each other in doing the big events. McNamee was the better known, but White did his share of the big events, too. Among others, he had done the World Series. I should repeat that in the early 1920s there was, of course, no television, and radio was comparatively new. Like everyone else in the new medium, the sports announcers were plodding a pilgrim's trail into or out of the wilderness. They had to blaze a path for the future spielers.

White figures in this story because, in a rather remote way, I was connected with his broadcast of the famous Dempsey–Firpo fight for the heavyweight championship at the Polo Grounds in New York on September 14, 1923. An amazing crowd of almost 90,000 saw this classic, paying $1,250,000 at the gate. Had there been TV then as there is now, it would probably have brought another fifty million. (This was in 1923 dollars, which bought a lot more than today's dollars do, by far.) In a later chapter there's more about the Dempsey–Firpo brawl and its famous first round, which will go down in boxing history as one of the greatest, if not the greatest, important round of all time.

But back to announcer J. Andrew White. I was a kid on 103rd Street in those days, and we had one of the new crystal radios. It was a wallet-size instrument that looked like a billfold when closed, but when opened consisted of a coil of wire and a very thin piece of wire called a cat's whisker, touching a small piece of crystal. When you manipulated this little wire to touch different parts of the crystal, you got different stations, of which, I might add, there weren't many in those days. Every so often, the wire would annoyingly slip off the crystal or onto a dead spot. However, ours worked well. For amplification there was something called a Dubilier Ducon, which was a pair of earphones connected to the set and plugged into an electric light socket.

There was great interest in this fight between the great heavyweight champion who had taken the title from Jess Willard four years before, and the Giant Argentinian, the Wild Bull of the Pampas, who had knocked out this same Willard earlier in the summer of 1923 in an elimination bout to see who would fight Dempsey.

My family gathered around the little set in the living room, anxiously awaiting the broadcast by Major White. Since there was only one set of earphones, I was nominated to use them and relay what the announcer said to my mother, my uncle, my aunt, and my grandmother. I guess you might say it was the first bout I ever broadcast, even though Major White was my proxy at ringside. The bout, as I recall it and as I relayed it, began with pyrotechnics. Almost with the first punch, Dempsey was driven to his knees by the challenger. Right after that, all I remember is the announcer saying, "He's up! He's down! He's up! He's down!" This went on and on. But White didn't say who was up and who was down. Finally someone was knocked out of the ring, and while he climbed back into the ring, or was helped, as some say, White had time to collect himself and identify Dempsey as the flying body that ended up in the press section. From that point, as I recall, the announcer calmed down and I could follow his description better and relay it to my folks. The second round was easier to follow as Dempsey knocked out the game challenger. It was some fight and some broadcast. And I have happy memories of it.

Most record books show that the Jack Dempsey–George Carpentier bout for the world's heavyweight championship was the first fight ever broadcast. It was supposed to be, but it wasn't. The event was held at a place called Boyles' Thirty Acres in Jersey City on July 2, 1921. On a Saturday afternoon the bout drew a crowd of 80,183, at a time long before the George Washington Bridge or the Holland and Lincoln tunnels were built. The only way New Yorkers could get to the fight was by ferry or the Hudson Tubes under the river. If you are wondering about an outdoor bout on a Saturday afternoon—well, it was a custom in those days. Dempsey had won the title on a Saturday afternoon when he knocked out Jess Willard in Toledo. For Dempsey–Carpentier, the crowd paid a record $1,789,238, making it the first million-dollar gate.

The championship would have been the first fight ever aired, but White and his technical staff decided to check out the equipment on a preliminary bout. The result was that the contest between

Packey O'Gatty and Frankie Burns, an ordinary prelim, became immortal, being the first ever broadcast.

Jimmy Powers

Jimmy Powers was very prominent as a sports announcer in the forties and fifties. He was originally a sportswriter and worked his way up to columnist, then sports editor of the New York *Daily News.* Because of the *News*'s great circulation, he was probably the most powerful sports columnist in the New York area at that time. When the *News* made a deal with one of the independent New York stations, Powers got his foot in the door as a sports announcer and made the most of it.

For a short while, TV coverage of the fights was a problem for me. Gillette added TV coverage of the Friday-night fights to their radio coverage, for which NBC was the outlet. Gillette figured I would be more effective on radio, where I had been established for several years, and kept me there. Bob Stanton became the TV voice. In a sense, people were now getting two Garden fights for the price of one. Many listeners and viewers turned down the sound on the TV and listened to my radio broadcast while watching the picture—which was flattering to me. But naturally with TV they would see each blow struck before I could describe it. Subconsciously, I was concerned about this and found myself talking faster and faster to try to catch all the punches. This was silly. One day after a Friday fight, a fellow came up to me and said, "I watched the fight last night and listened to you on the radio. You know, you were behind the action." Annoyed, I told him, "The time to worry is when I get *ahead* of the action." That's when I realized that I had to do the fights on radio in my own style and at my own pace, which had proven successful. I decided to forget about television.

Powers's column and status were effective for him, and he made great strides. Making skillful use of his column, he became friendly with Jim Norris, who took over the Garden after the death of Mike

Jacobs. Soon, Powers was the TV voice of the fights. Gillette also dropped radio coverage of the fights, and when they resumed in the fall of 1960, on ABC-TV, I was the announcer.

Chris Schenkel

The first time I heard Chris Schenkel on the air was in the 1950s, when he did New York Giants football games on CBS. He had a likable manner and very pleasing style. He caught the eyes and ears of those in charge at ABC, and they signed him as their number-one sports announcer. He was a fine announcer, and versatile enough to cover several different sports as well as the Olympic Games. He was the announcer on many of the big fights of that era, on both home and theater TV. As will happen, though, new announcers came along and chipped away at him, though they couldn't nudge him off ABC's long-running bowling show. Chris became known as the Voice of Bowling.

The Sports Broadcasters Association

Prior to 1941, the sports broadcasters had no organization. They were a loose group that went their separate ways with no thoughts of organizing. We would meet each other at sports events or at luncheons, dinners, or other affairs to which we were invited. Meanwhile, the sportswriters had several organizations—the boxing writers, the racing writers, the hockey writers, the basketball writers, and, strongest of all, the baseball writers. In September 1941, New York City was seething with baseball excitement as the Brooklyn Dodgers—"Dem Bums," as they were named by the sports cartoonist Willard Mullin—were winging their way to their first National League pennant since 1920. Put together by Larry MacPhail and managed by the irrepressible Leo Durocher, the Dodgers that year were probably the most exciting team of all time. Brooklyn was truly a state of mind. The town erupted when the Dodgers clinched the pennant and prepared to meet the New York Yankees in the World Series. The Bronx Bombers, managed by Joe McCarthy and aided immensely by Joltin' Joe DiMaggio's fifty-six-game hitting streak, had won their flag earlier and more quietly.

What has all this to do with the sports broadcasters? Plenty. It led to our organizing. When it came time for the Series, the top sports announcers felt that they were entitled to press credentials. The baseball writers, who had control of the press credentials, felt otherwise. The most adamant of them were Charley Segar of the *Daily Mirror* and Arthur "Red" Patterson of the *Herald Tribune*. (This was ironic, for in later years Segar and Patterson would be in publicity jobs for baseball and made sure that the sports announcers got all their press releases.) Being turned down for press credentials angered the announcers, and we took our case to a higher level. I recall that we got together informally to decide what we should do. A committee was appointed, of which I was a member, and we called on MacPhail and Ed Barrow, the general manager of the Yankees, and told them our thoughts. They were very sympathetic to us but replied that at the moment their hands were tied because of the major leagues' agreement with the Baseball Writers Association. However, they were kind enough to give all of us tickets for the Series games at both parks. This mollified us a bit, but only temporarily.

After the Series was over, Ted Husing sent invitations to all the local sports announcers to meet at Toots Shor's for lunch, and there we formed the Sports Broadcasters Association. The first officers were Ted Husing (president), Paul Douglas (vice-president), Stan Lomax (vice-president), Bill Stern (vice-president), Sam Taub (secretary), and Tom Slater (treasurer).

Some of the better-known announcers in the group were Mel Allen, Red Barber, Al Helfer, Jack McCarthy (of St. Patrick's Day Parade fame—he was then a sports announcer), Bert Lee, Jr., Marty Glickman, Joe O'Brien, Clem McCarthy, and yours truly.

This SBA gathered momentum and did well for many years, with weekly meetings at wonderful eateries such as Shor's and the "21" Club. The feature of the year was the annual dinner, which was not only a sensation but always a sellout. Unfortunately, the best dinner we had was one I missed. It was held in 1957 at the Roosevelt Hotel. Mel Allen and his dear friend Len Dillon, then president of the organization, thought it would be great if we had a dinner honoring Ted Husing, who was very sick at that point. With Edward R. Murrow as the toastmaster and a dais lined with celebrities from every walk of life, it was an unforgettable affair, a great and sad tribute to the man who had done so much for the profession of sports announcing. Win Elliot and I had just done a fight in Florida and were on our way to New York for that dinner when fate intervened—a blizzard hit the Northeast. Win's plane missed New York and put down in Boston. Mine got as far as Washington. It's always been a regret of mine that I couldn't be there to honor Ted.

Time took its toll of the Sports Broadcasters Association. Of those who helped found it, some retired, some moved to other cities, and some lost interest. And Ted passed away. Sad to say, their places were not taken by the new breed of sportscasters (I'm sorry, Ted. I know you always detested that term). The result was that the Sports Broadcasters Association folded in 1958. Over the years there were several unsuccessful attempts to revive it, but the latest effort seems to be succeeding.

So far so good. Lou Schwartz, a Brooklyn native who was secretary of the Department of Public Works in New York City during the Wagner mayoralty, has been the catalyst. After leaving New York City, Lou went upstate and became president of the Finger Lakes Broadcasting Corporation. He has long been interested in sports announcers and their need to have a strong organization. In the fall of 1980 he formed the American Sportscasters Association with the help of some friends and associates. It was hard work in the beginning, but the idea caught on and the organization became strong enough to have its first annual dinner and ASA Hall of Fame inductions in 1984. The dinner was held at the Starlight Roof of the Waldorf Hotel and was a rousing success. The first inductees into the Hall of Fame were Ted Husing, Bill Stern, Graham McNamee, Red Barber, and me. In 1985, Curt Gowdy, Mel Allen, and Jack Brickhouse were inductees to the Hall, and in 1986, Lindsey Nelson was so honored. Also formed was the Sportscasters Charitable Trust to aid in the fight against drug abuse.

The Gillette TV Years, 1960–1964

The radio broadcasts I did for the Garden began with the Louis–Conn fight in June 1941 and ended June 3, 1960, in the old St. Nick arena with Emile Griffith, then in the early part of his career, taking a ten-round decision from Jorge Fernandez, whom he later fought for the welterweight title. What I remember most about that night was that it was hot, terribly hot and humid. It had been that way for days, and every window and door in the place was open in an attempt to circulate a little air inside. At about nine-thirty there was a sudden cloudburst. It didn't help. You could actually see steam drifting into the fight club as the rain pounded the overheated sidewalks outside. The fighters, Win Elliot, and I all struggled through the evening, and thus ended nineteen years of Gillette fight broadcasts on radio. The TV age had begun.

TV coverage of the fights had begun in 1944 with Bob Stanton announcing, then Steve Ellis, then Jimmy Powers, with Powers at the helm, when I took over in the fall of 1960.

As I've noted, TV and radio announcing require different styles, so it was fortunate for me that there was a lapse of almost four months between the end of radio and beginning of TV. If I had done radio one week and started TV the next, I'm sure it would have been hard. But with a long passage of time I was able to formulate my ideas and plan how I would approach TV announcing. I realized that the old blow-by-blow descriptions and constant filling the air with words would be out. There had to be a new style, and I developed one, using that interval period to attend fights at local clubs, sitting at ringside and announcing the fights to myself, imagining I was on TV. This helped me immeasurably. When I finally did TV, which was live at that time, I was mentally ready.

Starting in the fall of 1960, I announced the Garden fights for Gillette for five years. Some great fighters paraded before our cameras and spoke into our microphones, including Sugar Ray Robinson, Gene Fullmer, Carmen Basilio, Carlos Ortiz, Luis Rodriguez, and, of course, Emile Griffith. Robinson, while still good by ordinary standards, was no longer the great Sugar Ray—his brilliance was eroding. Unfortunately, like many great champions, he had overstayed his leave. He had been fighting for over twenty years, and some who couldn't have laid a glove on him in the old days were now catching up. He lost the middleweight title to Paul Pender of Boston and lost again in a return bout. He fought a draw with Gene Fullmer in Los Angeles in a bout for the NBA middleweight title, and on March 4, 1961, he lost a close fifteen-round title bout to Fullmer. Although he continued to fight until November 1965, the Fullmer fight was his last title bout. When he finally did retire, he had been fighting for twenty-five years. Ray Robinson, Joe Louis, Muhammad Ali. What a shame these great ones stayed around too long! But who knows? In similar circumstances, we might have done the same thing. When I was a kid there was a brilliant featherweight champion named Johnny Dundee. The fabulous Jimmy Walker was mayor of New York at the time—it was he who as a state senator introduced the Walker Boxing Law, which legalized boxing in New York State. So you knew he was interested in the game. Johnny Dundee stayed in the ring for twenty-two years. One day near the end of his career, Mayor Walker said to him, "Johnny, why don't you retire?"

Johnny looked the mayor in the eye and startled one and all by saying, "Why don't *you* retire?"

We had some interesting title bouts in the years 1960 through 1964. Outstanding I think was the Emile Griffith–Luis Rodriguez welterweight series. They fought four times and Emile copped the decision on three of those occasions. But, as I recall, all of the decisions were hotly contested, they were that evenly matched. Both were good boxers, hard hitters and very strong. And both had the best of trainers—Gil Clancy with Griffith and Angelo Dundee with Rodriguez. I've discussed Rodriguez with Wilbert "Skeeter" McClure, a fine middleweight from Toledo, Ohio, who'd fought Rodriguez, a welterweight, twice, dropping a ten-round decision each time. Skeeter shook his head. "That Rodriguez, he's too strong for the welterweights, and he's too fast for the middleweights." I guess you could say the same about Griffith.

Rodriguez won the welterweight title on a decision over Griffith, but Emile regained it in a return bout. They fought again for the crown, with Griffith again the winner. Even though they went at each other tooth and nail, out of the ring they were the best of friends. I interviewed Griffith after their last bout, and he was gracious enough to say, "It's too bad that Luis and I came along at the same time. He could have been a great champion."

I've always felt that you can't give too much preparation when getting ready for an important broadcast. It paid off for me in an important Griffith bout in Las Vegas in December 1962. Griffith was defending the welterweight crown against tough, hard-hitting Jorge Fernandez. Whenever I broadcast a fight out of town, I made a point of going to the weigh-in the day of the fight. That's where you find out things. The session was almost over when I asked the commissioner what would happen if a man was fouled and seemingly unable to continue. There were different rules in different states, and it was important to me to know how it might be handled if a man went down from a low blow. In New York, for instance, where they have a no-foul rule, the man would be counted out unless it was decided that the foul had been deliberate. In that case the perpetrator could be disqualified. The commission members thought about my question for a moment and then got out the Nevada rule book. It stated that if a man was fouled, he would be allowed five minutes to recover and then if he couldn't continue he would be considered knocked out.

Sure enough, that night, Fernandez, the challenger, went down from a low blow. There was instant confusion when he failed to get up immediately. Even the referee didn't seem to know how to handle the situation. Fortunately, I remembered what the rule book had said and told it to my audience. There was a lot of confusion in and around the ring. Finally, order was restored and everyone including Fernandez was told of the rule. He got up before the five minutes were up but decided that he had had enough. End of fight, end of incident.

The Griffith persona seemed to dominate the 1960–1964 period in boxing. In April 1961, he captured the welterweight crown by knocking out Benny "Kid" Paret in thirteen rounds in Miami Beach. In June he kayoed tough Gaspar Ortega in Los Angeles, and in September he lost the crown back to Paret in New York. It was a controversial decision, and I agreed with those who felt that Griffith should have been declared the winner and still champion.

Paret and Griffith were matched again for the title on March 12, 1962. It was an exciting week. On Monday I was asked to come to the ABC-TV studios. There I learned that a videotape replay had been developed and that I was invited to take part in a demonstration for a great many important ABC executives and members of the press. Jim McKay, the host of "ABC Wide World of Sports," was also there. A ring had been set up, and two boxers were there, ready to trade punches. They fought a one-round exhibition, and with the videotape cameras rolling I described the action as I would in a real fight. When the round was over, it was replayed again and again for the studio audience, and pronounced a success. The new system was ready to make its debut at the Paret-Griffith fight the following Saturday night.

It turned out to be a tragic beginning. The fight was a bruising one. The men had faced each other twice before and knew each other's styles. In the sixth round, Griffith backed Paret into the ropes of a corner and was really working him over. Paret had a habit of playing possum and letting Griffith pour punches on him. Ruby Goldstein, the referee, was about to move in to get them out to the center of the ring when suddenly Paret opened up with a blistering attack, stunned Griffith, and floored him. Griffith beat the count but was in bad shape. The bell probably saved him. Gil Clancy, Griffith's co-manager (with Howard Albert) and trainer, told me later that he thought if the round had lasted much longer Griffith might have been knocked out.

Emile was in superb condition, and the minute's rest revived him. The bout continued with blistering action into the twelfth round. In the sixth round Paret had backed into Griffith's corner on my right. Now in the twelfth, he backed into the neutral corner on my left. Again Griffith rained punches on him. For a split second I wondered if Paret might be playing possum again. I don't know what referee Goldstein's thoughts were as he bounced around the ring. Could he also have thought the champion was playing possum? He wasn't. Griffith continued to rain punches on him. Paret made no return. As Goldstein rushed in to part them, Paret sagged to the canvas. The commission doctors rushed in to try to revive him. They couldn't. A stretcher was brought in and he was taken to the hospital.

All this was now on videotape. The replays went on the air and showed the beating Paret was taking. Again and again they were repeated. I heard later that the ratings for the post-fight show were higher than for the fight itself. Apparently people were calling friends

Don Dunphy in 1941.

Bill Corum (left), famous sports columnist for the Hearst papers, with Dunphy broadcasting the first Louis–Conn heavyweight championship fight.

Top right: Round twelve of first Louis–Conn fight. The Fighting Irishman was really enjoying it, but his joy was short-lived as he was kayoed in the thirteenth.

Right: Joe Louis is acclaimed "the winner and still champion." Left to right: ring announcer Harry Balogh, Joe Louis, referee Eddie Joseph, Louis's manager Julian Black, announcer Dunphy, and Tom Slater, director of Mutual Sports.

Announcement of a new fight contract between Madison Square Garden,
Mutual Sports, and Gillette. Left to right: Don Dunphy; former heavyweight
champion Jim Braddock (with glove); Craig Smith, advertising director of
the Gillette company; and Bill Corum.

Top left: Don Dunphy interviewing Judge Landis, baseball commissioner, at
the 1943 World Series between the New York Yankees and the St. Louis
Cardinals. Thanks to British Broadcasting, soldiers in England, Africa, and
Italy could listen to Dunphy do the play-by-play announcing. Left to right,
front: Dunphy, Judge Landis, Colonel Larry MacPhail. In background: Billy
Southworth, manager of the Cardinals, and Joe McCarthy, manager of the
Yankees.

Left: In Times Square, at a 1943 parade in support of the war effort. Don
Dunphy (third from left, bareheaded), former Governor of New York and
former presidential candidate Al Smith with his famed Brown Derby, and
(second from right) New York's Mayor Fiorello La Guardia.

Don, Don junior, Muriel, and Bob in 1946.

Above right: Tony Zale knocking out Rocky Graziano to retain the middle-weight championship at Yankee Stadium in 1946. Dunphy considers it the greatest fight he ever saw.

Right: Don Dunphy interviews welterweight champion Sugar Ray Robinson at Madison Square Garden ring.

Dunphy points out how Rocky Marciano won the heavyweight championship from Jersey Joe Walcott. *United Press International*

Above left: Famous sports announcers at Gillette meeting at Wentworth by
the Sea in New Hampshire; left to right: Mel Allen, Bill Corum, Boston announcer Jim Britt, Don Dunphy, and Clem McCarthy.

Left: At a charity telethon, c. 1951; left to right: famed orchestra leader Guy
Lombardo, columnist and TV host Ed Sullivan, middleweight contender
Steve Belloise, and Don Dunphy.

When "The Fight of the Week" TV broadcast shifted to ABC in 1960, Don Dunphy was at the mike.

Above right: Dunphy is surrounded by two great champions at "Salute to Boxing Greats" night at the Downtown Athletic Club. Muhammad Ali is on the left, Joe Frazier on the right. *Bert Smith*

Right: A famous fistic photograph: the first fight ever broadcast, between Packey O'Gatty and Frankie Burns at Boyle's Thirty Acres in Jersey City in 1921. The feature was the heavyweight championship bout between Jack Dempsey and George Carpentier. Major J. Andrew White, a pioneer sports broadcaster, was the announcer.

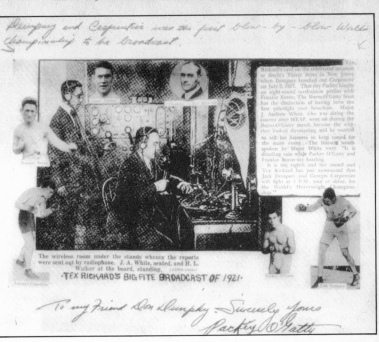

Dempsey and Carpentier was the first blow-by-blow World's Championship to be broadcast.

Tex Rickard's card on the celebrated occasion at Boyle's Three Acres in New Jersey when Dempsey knocked out Carpentier on July 2, 1921. That day Packy fought an eight-round preliminary prelim with Frankie Burns. The Burns-O'Gatty bout has the distinction of having been the first friendly ever broadcast. Major J. Andrew White, who was airing the contest over WEAF, went on during the Burns-O'Gatty match because the weather looked threatening and he wanted

to tell his listeners to keep tuned for the main event. The historic words spoken by Major White were "It is drizzling rain while Packey O'Gatty and Frankie Burns are battling.

It is the eighth and last round and Tex Rickard has just announced that Jack Dempsey and Georges Carpentier will fight at 5 P.M. rain or shine, for the World's Heavyweight Championship."

The wireless room under the stands whence the reports were sent out by radiophone. J. A. White, seated, and H. L. Walker at the board, standing.

·TEX RICKARD'S BIG FITE BROADCAST OF 1921·

To my Friend Don Dumphy Sincerely Yours
Packey O'Gatty

Don Dunphy is inducted into the American Sportscasters Association Hall of Fame at New York's Waldorf Hotel in 1984. Right to left: Don and Muriel, Don junior and Sheila, Bob and Sharon. *Matthew Mauro*

Above left: Sports announcers Don Dunphy and Bill Stern flank ring announcer Johnny Addie on the occasion of the release of an album, *The Heavyweights*, at Toots Shor's restaurant.

Left: A group of famous sports figures at an HBO broadcast at Madison Square Garden. Left to right: announcers Marty Glickman, Larry Merchant, Don Dunphy, welterweight champion Sugar Ray Leonard, and announcer Spencer Ross. In the background is Dave Meister, director of HBO sports.

THE BOSTON SUNDAY GLOBE JANUARY 4, 1920

64 TIMES 'ROUND CAPE HORN
BROOKLINE CAPTAIN'S RECORD

Capt William H. Dunphy, Who Went to Sea in 1855, Pictures the Delights of Pitcairn Island, That Lonely Pacific Isle Where Sin, Booze and Profanity Are Unknown, and Whose Greatest Longing Is for Scented Soap and Women's Clothes

By GEORGE NOBLE

Dunphy greeted by President Reagan at the White House. Famed sports announcer Vin Scully is at center.

Top left: Story in the *Boston Sunday Globe* in 1920 about Don Dunphy's grandfather's sailing adventures. Captain Dunphy is credited with rediscovering the famous Pitcairn Island of *Mutiny on the Bounty* fame.

Left: Dunphy gets a lesson from golf great Tony Lema.

Don Dunphy at ringside.

and telling them to tune in, that a guy was getting beaten to death on the TV.

Paret never regained consciousness. He died in the hospital on April 3.

Aileen Eaton was the top boxing promoter in Los Angeles for a good many years. For March 16, 1963, she booked a welterweight championship bout between title holder Emile Griffith and challenger Luis Rodriguez. Earlier that week I had been at the ten-round bout between Cassius Clay and Doug Jones at Madison Square Garden. I was a spectator at this closed-circuit affair, which Chris Schenkel was announcing. About this time, Clay caused a lot of excitement in boxing circles by predicting the round in which he would knock out his opponent. He had first done it at a bout I aired in Louisville in 1961, predicting that he would kayo tough Alex Miteff in the sixth round. I thought the former Olympic champion was going a little too far with this one, and that he'd be fortunate to beat Miteff at all, let alone predict the kayo round. But he was right, Miteff went out in the sixth and Cassius Clay went on to greater glory.

For the bout at the Garden, Clay predicted he would knock Jones out in the sixth. It was a close contest all the way, with the sixth round coming and going and Jones still on his feet. As a matter of fact, Jones was still upright at the end of the tenth and final round. Many thought he deserved the decision, but Clay was declared the winner amid a cascade of boos. I think many people who said Jones deserved the decision actually felt that Clay deserved to lose since he had failed to knock Jones out in the sixth as he predicted. I personally thought Clay had won it on a squeaker.

Griffith and Rodriguez were scheduled to fight the following Saturday in L.A. As usual, I went to the weigh-in around 10:00 A.M. It was a lovely morning, sunny and mild, but the weather turned sour. Around noon there was a sprinkle of rain. Then it rained harder. Then it poured. At about four o'clock I grabbed a cab and headed for the ballpark. On the way, I had the cabbie stop at a shoe store and I got a pair of rubbers. I figured the fight would be called off, since it was an outdoor affair, and I was surprised to learn that no decision had been made. The bout was scheduled for 7:00 P.M., California time. All day long, behind-the-scenes maneuverings had been going on between the boxing people, the Gillette people, and the network brass. At six-thirty, while the rain poured down and flashes of lightning ripped across the sky, I was told what had been going on. Mrs. Eaton, Harry Markson for Madison Square Garden, Chet Simmons of ABC, and Joel Nixon representing Gillette had been pulling strings, or should I say wires, ever since late in the morning, when it became obvious that an outdoor fight couldn't go on. Here's what they came up with. A monitor would be set up in the ring, and the Clay–Jones fight of the previous Wednesday, which had not been on live TV, would be shown on the monitor and would go out over ABC. This was a great idea, since there had been so much controversy about the decision. I would sit in the open ring and describe on the air the action of the Clay–Jones fight as I watched on the monitor. The fight would come from New York City, and the commercials would come from Chicago. They explained all this to me as another flash of lightning skittered across the California sky. Now the rain wasn't coming straight down. It was slanting into the ring. They got me a raincoat, and Angelo Dundee, Rodriguez's trainer, loaned me a rain cap.

I shook my head. It may have been an electronic marvel, but I wasn't about to sit in an open ring with a live microphone in my hand, an inviting target for the lightning. Markson got me a pair of rubber gloves. So the telecast started with me in the ring, a lonely figure except for associate producer Bill Lilling, who was giving "go" and "stop" cues. The show went on and we all got wet, except Clay and Jones. Naturally, as we signed off the rain stopped, and ten minutes later the moon was out. The next day my wife received a telegram from my son Don, who was a junior at Notre Dame. It read, "Has Dad gone nuts?"

I wouldn't want to give the impression that Emile Griffith and Luis Rodriguez were the only great fighters performing on Gillette TV during my days on the microphone. Cassius Clay appeared for us several times and, of course, won all of his bouts. Gene Fullmer, a fine middleweight title holder, was in there and so was his friend and sometime opponent, Carmen Basilio. Denny Moyer also was prominent on our fight cards, as were Harold Johnson and Willie Pastrano, light heavyweight champs. In the lighter weights we had champions Joe Brown, Carlos Ortiz, and Kenny Lane.

Boxing is a cyclical sport. Its popularity zooms, then wanes; it has its good periods and its bad ones. Sometimes it seems to be groggy and on the ropes, and you wonder if it can survive. But it always rebounds, sometimes with an incredible burst of energy. It is a basic sport and has an amazing hold on its fans. But every so often it goes into a deep slump. The years 1962 and 1963 were such a period. Although some say boxing, like the poor, will always be with us, there are those who would like to see it banned. In 1962 and 1963 they came out en masse and boxing went down for the count.

The popularity of boxing is often linked to the popularity of the heavyweight champion. Floyd Patterson was the champion from 1956 to 1962, until Sonny Liston took over. Patterson became one of the most popular of ex-champions. Whenever ex-fighters were introduced from the ring, Floyd always got the biggest ovation. He has retained that popularity to this day. He was my color commentator on many of the shows I did for HBO, and we became good friends. But he was not nearly so popular when he was actually champion. He was managed by Cus D'Amato, who overdid it in shielding him from worthy opponents. This was not Floyd's fault. He would have fought anyone. But the boxing public didn't understand this, and Patterson's approval rating dropped. Finally he fought Sonny Liston and was kayoed in one round.

If Patterson was an unpopular champion, Liston was more so. He came to the title with a fine boxing record but a terribly tarnished personal reputation. In fairness, it may not have been his fault. There were other factors. Liston was the best heavyweight around at the time, and he fought the best available opponents and beat them convincingly. But he never really caught the public's fancy, and became a prime target for those who would ban boxing.

The death in 1962 of Benny "Kid" Paret brought on an investigation of boxing and brought out more reformers. It was a tough time for the old game. In March 1963 came another boxing death. Davey Moore, the featherweight champion, died following a defense of the title against Sugar Ramos, and the attacks on the sport grew in intensity. Finally, in December 1963, the American Broadcasting Company announced that it was not renewing the fight contract. The series would be terminated in September 1964. This was a blow to me, like when the *Morning World* had folded when I was just getting started. But boxing survived and so did I. Following the cycle through, boxing later returned to the same network and became one of its most popular programs.

But the end of the Gillette fights in 1964 was, in a sense, the end of an era. For many years the slogan "Look sharp, feel sharp, be sharp," followed by "How're ya fixed for blades?" had been familiar to millions, and left an indelible mark on TV history. The sad end came in Cleveland on September 11, 1964, when Dick Tiger defeated Don Fullmer (Gene's brother) in a ten-round bout. To me, the bout, which was not a rouser, seemed secondary as I spent the evening saying goodbyes and thanking the multitude of sportswriters, radio and TV people, promoters, boxing officials, and others who had contributed to making that program so vital and important. Wistfully I thought of the first bout, Louis–Conn, and then of the last one, Tiger–Fullmer. I wondered what the future would bring. I didn't know it at the time, but it proved to be even more interesting and exciting than the preceding twenty-three years had been. Just before saying good-bye, I thanked the viewers and listeners. I told them how much I appreciated their support and their letters, even the critical ones. I thanked them again, telling them it was they who had made it all possible. I only wish Joe Humphries could have been there to sing "Auld Lang Syne."

Ring Announcers

At this point, I would like to make the distinction between a ring announcer and a ring*side* announcer. A ring announcer is the man who makes announcements in the ring. He introduces the fighters and the officials, such as referees, judges, doctors, and timekeepers, and informs the audience of other details, such as coming bouts. The ringside announcers are there to cover the fight for television or radio. Having said that, I'd like to talk about a few ring announcers who worked during my time.

Joe Humphries was the first ring announcer I remember. He preceded the ring microphone, depending, as did the orators of the day, on the force of his stentorian voice. He was a colorful figure who invariably carried a hat into the ring, using the chapeau as a prop, as George Burns does a cigar. But the advance of science and electronics did him in. He never felt comfortable with a microphone. He always felt, and probably rightly so, that the fan in the farthest reaches of the gallery or the bleachers could hear him distinctly without a mike. Besides, Humphries couldn't hold his hat, the mike, and his papers with only two hands.

As you may know, there have been four Madison Square Gardens, and Humphries was the official announcer in the first three. In the latter days of the nineteenth century and the early days of this one, boxing was ruled legal and illegal by turns in New York State, probably depending on the composition of the state legislature. It seemed that whenever it was to be banned, the Garden would put on a big "final bout," and when it was over, Humphries would lead the crowd at the finish in the singing of "Auld Lang Syne." But boxing came back to life in the third Garden, at 50th Street and Eighth Avenue, which was built especially to house boxing. And Joe Humphries was there, too.

On May 20, 1927, heavyweights Jack Sharkey and Jimmy Maloney met at Yankee Stadium. The winner would fight Jack Dempsey later that year in an elimination bout to see who would fight Gene Tunney for the heavyweight crown in the fall. Joe Humphries, the premier ring announcer of that time, officiated at the introductions. I was listening to Graham McNamee's radio broadcast of the fight. Before introducing the principals, Humphries called for silence and asked the huge crowd to please stand. As one man they stood. Everyone there sensed what Joe was going to say, for it was the night when Charles Lindbergh, all alone in the uncharted heavens, was flying over the Atlantic toward Paris. Humphries's powerful voice reached to every corner of Yankee Stadium as he said, "You all know that up there somewhere, there is a brave young man doing something that has never been done before. Let us have a moment of silent prayer for a safe accomplishment." The crowd was silent for a moment and then it broke into a thunderous roar.

The last big fight at which I remember Humphries officiating was the return bout between Barney Ross and Jimmy McLarnin at the Madison Square Garden Bowl in 1934. The Bowl was located in Long Island City, New York. Ross had taken the welterweight crown from McLarnin earlier that year. These men were master boxers and good, sharp hitters. It was a perfect match and was very close, going the fifteen-round distance. You could hear the proverbial pin drop as Humphries's voice filled the vast arena.

"The judges have disagreed, and the referee's decision makes it possible for the Fighting Irishman to regain the welterweight title."

Incidentally, in a return bout the following year, Ross took back the crown from McLarnin.

Humphries was followed by Harry Balogh, the most colorful of New York's many ring announcers. Harry could have been an actor, and he certainly did his share of emoting at center stage in the famous ring at Madison Square Garden. He improvised colorful phrases that are still talked about today. One of the most remembered of those came at the end of his introduction of the fighters. "And may the better contestant emerge triumphant."

Dan Parker was a noted sports editor and columnist of the *New York Daily Mirror*. He loved "Baloghisms" and quoted nearly every one of them. Harry, however, misread the columns, and thought the quotes were praising him. He loved to see his name in print, which occurred practically every Monday morning in the *Mirror*. As for Dan, he could hardly wait for Friday night at the Garden so he could hear Balogh's bon mots and write them up for Monday's column. This relationship lasted as long as Balogh introduced the Garden fights.

In those days of the Friday fights, sponsored by Gillette, the main event could not go on the air until 10:00 P.M. because of network schedules. Sometimes the preceding prelim would end five or ten minutes before ten, and there was not enough time to put on an extra fight, which was called an emergency bout. So that the crowd would not get restless at the sight of a ring with no fighters in it, it was up to Balogh to stall and kill time until we took to the air. This was not too easy, although as a rule Harry was equal to the occasion. Incidentally, Polyclinic Hospital was across from the Garden on 50th Street. It was the same hospital where early New York Rangers hockey players would be taken to be stitched up during games.

There was one in particular, the great Ching Johnson, who often would be taken there after the first period, and would be back on the ice fit and trim in time for the third period.

One night it was necessary for Balogh to do some stalling, and he did it as follows:

"Ladies and gentlemen, if I may have your attention please. Thank you. Thank you very much. I'd like to remind you that Polyclinic Hospital is just across the street from the Garden. And of course, when you leave here it will be a little bit late and the patients need their sleep. So please, when you leave the Garden tonight and reach the street. will you please do it quietly. Thank you very much."

That sounded so good to Harry that he repeated it the following week. The next day the Garden received a call from the hospital that went like this: "If it's all right with the Garden and Mr. Balogh, the Polyclinic doesn't need the publicity and it would appreciate it if Mr. Balogh would refrain from mentioning the hospital at the fights."

Balogh seemed to reach his apotheosis the night Joe Louis fought his first big main event. It was June 25, 1935, and the scene was Yankee Stadium, with eighty thousand expectant spectators on hand to see the young black man from Detroit take on the huge former champion, Primo Carnera. My friend Irving Rudd, who has been part of the boxing scene since 1937, when he was a young publicist for boxing at Rockland Palace, a fight club in Harlem, and who does such a great job for promoter Bob Arum's Top Rank organization, reminds me that the tenor of the times in 1935 was a lot different from what it is now. New York had not had a big mixed fight in years, if indeed it had ever had a mixed bout this big. New York was not without an occasional race riot then, and there was plenty of tension in the House that Ruth Built as the fighters waited for Harry to introduce them. No one was sure what would happen when the scrap got under way. Could a boxing bout between an Italian and a black be something to dread? There was a hush as Balogh reached for his ring microphone. The moment of truth was at hand. What would the announcer say?

"Ladies and gentlemen," he began, "before proceeding with this most important heavyweight contest, I wish to take this opportunity of calling upon you in the name of that fine and great spirit of American sportsmanship so conspicuous of you that it has made us world famous, and by that I mean that I sincerely hope and trust that the thought in your mind and the feeling in your heart shall be that regardless of race, creed, or color, may the *better* man win."

There was a stunned silence, and then the stadium rocked on its foundations as the fans cheered and whistled so loudly and so long that one wondered if the long-awaited contest between Carnera and Louis would ever come off. Irv Rudd, in an article he wrote for *Boxing News Record*, says that Harry Balogh had completely stolen the show and, what's more important, had perhaps saved the day.

Jim Braddock had taken the crown from Max Baer in a stunning upset in 1935. Meanwhile, the young Joe Louis, out of the cotton fields of Alabama by way of Detroit, was the sensation of the heavyweight division. He was beating everyone, and easily. Recognizing his great ability and potential, Mike Jacobs had taken him under his wing and was guiding him. He got him matched with ex-champion Primo Carnera, whom Baer had beaten. Before a huge crowd at Yankee Stadium, Louis annihilated Carnera, kayoing him in six rounds. The win not only meant that now Louis had to be reckoned with, but it also meant that Jacobs, with Louis under his wing, was the dominant figure in boxing.

True, Braddock was the champion, so Jacobs tried to match him with Louis for the title. He found out that Braddock was already under contract to fight ex-champ Max Schmeling for the title. Schmeling had credentials, too. Until that time he was the only man to beat Louis, having kayoed him in 1936. So Jacobs pursued the Braddock people to get him to fight Louis. They pointed out, however, that they were under contract for Schmeling. But apparently Jacobs's offer to the Braddock people was so good that they became interested in fighting Louis. Schmeling's contract was in the way, though.

So Sol Straus, Jacobs's attorney, went to work. He went over the Braddock–Schmeling contract with the proverbial fine-tooth comb and, as the story goes, he found a misplaced comma somewhere, and that apparently was grounds enough for Braddock to get out of fighting Schmeling and to take on Louis. Louis kayoed him in eight rounds in Chicago. Joe was now champion, and Jacobs was king of the heavyweights because of an eagle-eyed attorney well versed in grammar.

Johnny Addie was the next Garden ring announcer, and he was a pleasure to work with. Johnny's tenure was during a time when the announcements were coordinated with the television coverage of the fights. Timing was of the essence at this point, and Johnny had a feel for the job and made it work. During Johnny's introductions of the fights, I worked several years on radio followed by five as the TV announcer. My memory of events may be slightly shaded by the passing of time, but I don't remember one instance when Johnny didn't give one hundred percent cooperation to the electronic media. He was always genial and willing to help. What is more important he was patient, and I think that of all the attributes needed for that job, patience is the most important. You must remember that the TV and radio audiences reached a total of many millions. As I have noted, timing was important. The various networks took the air at exactly 10:00 P.M. and Johnny had to have his minor introductions out of the way before that. Then he had to remain mute until he got the go-ahead from the radio and TV producers and also from Teddy Brenner, the Garden matchmaker. Johnny had to make sure in advance that the main-event fighters were in their corners, waiting for their intros. Ditto the officials. Looking back now, it doesn't seem to have been so difficult, but maybe that was because Johnny Addie did it so smoothly.

And at the final bell it was Johnny in center ring, holding up the hand of the winner. At the end of the fights, Johnny really shone.

Tim Barry, a fine gentleman, was the trade relations director for the Gillette Company, the sponsor of the fights. Week after week it was Tim's chore, or pleasure, to entertain various clients who were important to the company. They came from all over the country. It was a big deal when the fights were over to get them together with Addie at ringside. Singly, one after another, they would be photographed with Addie holding up the hand of the guest, as he had just done with the winner of the fight. This made a big hit when the pictures were sent back home to the local papers.

One of Addie's biggest nights was when the Garden threw a huge birthday party for Jack Dempsey. Everybody was there: former heavyweight champions Gene Tunney, Jim Braddock, Floyd Patterson, and Joe Frazier, as well as Sugar Ray Robinson, Emile Griffith, and Willie Pep. The list was endless. Even George Carpentier, who had fought Dempsey in 1921, came over from France. It was some group of introductions.

The last big event at which John Addie officiated was, as I've said, the greatest sports event of all time, the first fight between Joe Frazier and Muhammad Ali, the titanic battle between two great undefeated champions. The Garden was electric that night, and so was Johnny. It was his swan song.

Two other ring announcers worked capably in the far West. They were Jimmy Lennon and Chuck Hull. Lennon, the uncle of the famed Lennon sisters, worked with us both in Los Angeles and Las Vegas, while Chuck did the big ones in glitter town.

Lennon had done a few of the Gillette fights whenever our travels took us to L.A., but it was really the movies that brought us together. Jimmy was the ring announcer in so many pictures that he seemed a part of the scenery. When I was asked to be the ringside announcer in the movie *Matilda*, I joined Jimmy in Reno, where the filming was being done. This one was a real ball. It was the story of a kangaroo named Matilda, a master boxer, who was brought to this country from Australia in quest of the heavyweight championship. Produced by Al Ruddy, it starred Elliott Gould, Robert Mitchum, Harry Guardino, and Karen Carlson. Besides the stars and Jimmy Lennon, the movie featured that catchy number, "Waltzing Matilda." The film never won an Oscar, but we had a great week doing it.

A few years later, Jimmy and I teamed up on a real blockbuster, *Raging Bull*, starring Robert De Niro and directed by Martin Scorsese. De Niro won an Oscar for his portrayal in this picture of former middleweight champion Jake LaMotta. Lennon, who always had a great ring presence, was outstanding in his introductions of such LaMotta foes as Sugar Ray Robinson, Marcel Cerdan, and Laurent Dauthille. Coley Wallace was there, too, in a cameo appearance as ex-champ Joe Louis. Wallace, a onetime heavyweight contender, had played the featured part in an earlier picture, *The Joe Louis Story*.

Making *Raging Bull* was a pleasure for me and my wife, Muriel, who was an extra in the picture. We were supposed to be in Los Angeles for two weeks, but because one of LaMotta's opponents suffered rope burns in an exciting ring tussle, the shooting schedule was thrown off and we were there for six weeks at the picture's expense. Since we did no shooting on weekends, we took those occasions to visit friends in Santa Barbara and San Diego. As Sydney Skolsky used to write many years ago, "Don't get me wrong, I love Hollywood."

Starting in 1980, Lennon did many real fights with me. Tony Trudnich, a fine promoter and a superb color commentator on boxing, put on fights at the Showboat in Las Vegas for two years, and Lennon and I worked together on them. We also did fights those years in Los Angeles, San Diego, Sacramento, San Antonio, Miami, and Detroit. In the latter city, Thomas Hearns won the WBA welterweight title by kayoing Pipino Cuevas in two rounds. I miss those fights at the Showboat. Tony and Jimmy were great guys.

And so is Chuck Hull, who has dominated the ring announcing at Las Vegas for so long. I first met Chuck when we did the welterweight championship bout between title holder Don Jordan and Benny "Kid" Paret in the Las Vegas Convention Center in May 1960. Paret took the crown that night. Hull officiated in many big championship bouts in Las Vegas promoted by the top promoters; Mel Greb in Vegas who was often part promoter with Madison Square Garden, Don King, Bob Arum, and Main Event. The last two I worked with him were the Leonard–Hearns fight in 1981 and the Holmes–Spinks title bout in 1985. This meant that Hull was part of the Spinks brothers' taking the heavyweight crown, for he also announced Leon Spinks's defeat of Muhammad Ali.

I remember Chuck officiating at many Las Vegas matches, but the fight I remember most in Las Vegas was one that didn't have him at the ring microphone. I don't know what happened, but there was an announcer on that night whom I never saw before or since. It was the fourth bout between Gene Fullmer and Sugar Ray Robinson for the middleweight title, and it came close to being a disaster for me at the TV mike. Fullmer had won the crown from Robinson in a close fifteen-rounder at the Garden in January of 1957. In a return go at Chicago in May of that year, Robinson took back the title when he kayoed Fullmer in five. In December 1960, they met at Los Angeles and fought a fifteen-round draw. Prior to this, Robinson had lost the undisputed middleweight title to Paul Pender, and Fullmer had won the vacant NBA title by stopping Carmen Basilio in fourteen rounds. I know it's complicated, but that's the way it was. Now they met for a fourth time in the Las Vegas Convention Center, with Fullmer defending. The bout went the fifteen-round distance and it was fairly close, but I thought it was Fullmer by a shade. As I said, Chuck Hull was not the ring announcer on this occasion. After the final bell I climbed into the ring to be ready to interview the winner. Two things went wrong. First, the announcer giving the results of the ten-point must system did it in a confusing way as he read off the cards of the three judges. And much, much worse, the people on our side of the ring apparently interpreted the announcer's words differently. When the decision was announced, it seemed that Robinson had won. Certainly George Gainford, Robinson's big trainer, must have thought so. I saw him pick up Sugar Ray in a victory hug. I was just about to exclaim, "Well, the great Sugar Ray has done it again! He has outpointed Gene Fullmer!" But I looked at Marv Jensen, Fullmer's manager, who was as calm as he could be, and smiling. It occurred to me that something was amiss. If Jensen had thought the nod had gone against his boy, he would have been tearing out his hair and ranting and raving. So I hesitated before saying anything. It's a good thing I did. I walked over to the announcer and asked, "Who won?" "Why, Fullmer, of course," he said. I nearly collapsed, thinking of the gaffe I had almost pulled, and went over and congratulated

Fullmer on the air. I wasn't the only one who heard it wrong. Jesse Abramson, covering the bout for the *Herald-Tribune*, flashed the paper "Robinson wins." So did Jack Cuddy for United Press. Apparently there was something wrong with the ring mike. The people at home watching TV heard the correct verdict. Wouldn't it have been something if I had told them Robinson had won!

There you have my story of the famed ring announcers from Joe Humphries to Jimmy Lennon and Chuck Hull. There were others, possibly as talented, but I didn't get to work with them as often. Offhand I can think of superb ring mike men such as Frank Freeman in Miami, Ben Bentley in Chicago, and Frank Shain and Ed Derian in Atlantic City. My apologies to any I may have overlooked.

The Making of
a Prizefight

To my way of thinking, the Muhammad Ali–Joe Frazier fight of 1971 was not only a great fight but the greatest single sporting event of all time. I knew Madison Square Garden wanted to promote the fight. I also knew that although the Garden housed this great epic, it was not the promoter. Jerry Perenchio was the promoter. In 1971, who in the East had heard of Jerry Perenchio? Harry Markson was the president of Madison Square Garden Boxing at the time, and I asked him to fill me in on the details. He did. Said Harry, "Obviously, Madison Square Garden was very eager to make that match. It was the number-one fight of our time. These were two undefeated fighters. Each had a legitimate claim to the world's heavyweight championship. It was a very dramatic kind of a fight. Our relationship with

Frazier was excellent. Our relationship with Muhammad Ali was also very good. Teddy Brenner, who was the matchmaker at the Garden at that time, and I made an appointment to see Yancey Durham, the manager of Frazier in Philadelphia."

Going down on the train, Markson and Brenner discussed what they could offer these two fighters. Markson knew the Houston Astrodome people were trying very hard to sign this fight. "We thought," said Markson, "that they would figure the Garden would offer a million dollars each." At that time, this was unheard of; no fighter had ever been offered that much. "And we expected the Astrodome would top our offer by guaranteeing a million, one hundred thousand each. We decided we would tell Yancey Durham we would offer a million, one hundred and twenty-five thousand dollars each to Frazier and Ali. Yancey met us in Philadelphia, and he had a huge limousine. He was very proud that he had a telephone in the car. They weren't too common at that time."

Markson, Brenner, and Durham went to the Joe Frazier gymnasium, and found no one there but Joe. They met in a little office and Yancey told them he had an understanding with Herbert Muhammad, who was doing the business for Muhammad Ali. Whatever Frazier might be offered, the same offer had to be made to Ali. If Herbert Muhammad received an offer from a promoter, he was to make the same explanation, that Frazier was to receive the same amount. Joe Frazier was sitting behind a desk and Durham was sitting across from him. Each had a yellow pad in front of him.

After some discussion, Markson said, "We are prepared to offer two and a half million dollars for this fight: a million and a quarter each." As Markson told me:

"Both Yancey and Frazier turned to their pads and started to write. They wrote and they wrote and they wrote. I walked around the room looking at the pictures they had on the gymnasium wall. It seemed to be taking an unconscionable amount of time for them to figure out what we had offered. Finally, Yancey got up and came over to Joe. He pulled the pad away from Joe and said, 'Joe, let me figure this out.' Now the two of them worked on the yellow pad, and I looked over their shoulders. They did not know how to write one million, two hundred and fifty thousand dollars. They wrote one, comma, two, comma, five, comma, zero, comma, and after every zero there was another comma. Years later, whenever I attended a dinner and Joe Frazier was there, he would always say to me, 'Tell them the story about the offer you made to me.' Both he and Yancey soon learned how to write one million, two hundred and fifty thousand dollars."

Durham said that the offer made by the Garden sounded very good to him, and he knew it would be good with Herbert Muhammad too. But before he could give his final okay, he had to talk to Bruce Wright, who was their lawyer. He called Wright and put Markson on with him. The lawyer said it sounded all right, but he had something important to tell Markson: "Some guy called me on the phone and begged me not to accept any offer until he came to see me. You go back to New York. If he's not here at six o'clock, you will hear from me at five after six, and you can announce the fight."

Markson and Brenner returned to New York. They went to see Alvin Cooperman, who was running the Garden operations at the time, and explained the situation. He said, "Let's wait for the call." A little after six o'clock, the phone rang. It was Wright, who said, "Harry, some guy has just shown up here, and he put a hundred thousand dollars on my desk. He said whether we make the fight or not, this belongs to the fighters, but I'm prepared to offer you two and a half million dollars guaranteed, and two and a half million dollars to Muhammad Ali."

This was double the offer the Garden had made for the fight. Wright asked Markson what he thought he should do.

Harry said, "Bruce, if you don't grab this offer, you're crazy. We cannot match it."

The reason Markson had to take that position was that the Garden had a television department. He had asked it to make a survey and give him the most optimistic estimate of how much this fight would draw on closed circuit around the country. He had the report in

front of him, and the total of two and a half million that the Garden
had offered for the fight was based on the report. Even that was
playing it pretty close.

Wright said this huge offer had come from a man named Jerry
Perenchio. None of us had heard his name before. According to
Wright, Perenchio was from California and wanted to come to New
York and talk to the Garden.

Perenchio came in the next morning, and they met in Cooperman's office. He was an actors' agent, who represented Burt Lancaster, Andy Williams, and Kirk Douglas, among others. He was
very dynamic, a man of great charm. Contrary to the suspicion that
he was a reckless person throwing money around, Perenchio gave
the impression that he was a gentleman and an excellent businessman. He explained that he had put together a syndicate and was
in a position to make this large guarantee, with only one problem.
Yancey Durham had insisted the fight must take place at Madison
Square Garden. Yancey was a real stand-up man. He felt the Garden
had been so instrumental in giving his fighter the opportunity to
become world champion that he had a moral obligation to see that
the Garden got his fight. He said it had to be. So Perenchio and
the Garden made a deal under which the Garden was to give him
the building and all its facilities in exchange for a percentage of the
gate receipts. The Garden would have one or two theaters in the
area for the closed-circuit showing, plus the Felt Forum, which, of
course, was part of the Garden complex. Perenchio got everything
else.

Perenchio returned to California to discuss the setup with Jack
Kent Cooke, owner of several sports franchises, who was willing to
put up the guarantee. Then they talked to Mr. Felt (Irving Mitchell
Felt, head of Madison Square Garden, for whom the Felt Forum
was named). Felt said the fight must be fought under the Madison
Square Garden license, which meant, according to Felt, "We are
responsible for everything, and while I know Jack Kent Cooke very
well through hockey and I know he's a very successful businessman,
as a matter of business, we would have to have this money in escrow.
That's just plain business. I think Mr. Cooke will understand this."

So, with a little protest because he thought it was a bit of reflection on his integrity, Jack Kent Cooke put up the money, and the Garden announced the fight. As Markson explained, "That's how Jack Kent Cooke got into the act. And Perenchio for this money retained for himself and his associates all the ancillary rights, all over the country. His gamble paid off very well. I would say that whoever made the estimate for him was far more efficacious than the people who made the estimate for me, because they went well beyond the guarantee."

Muhammad Ali–
Joe Frazier
(First Fight)

On December 30, 1970, I had an appointment with Alvin Cooperman of the Garden and an agency man to talk about the fight album I hoped to produce. It was important that the Garden be part of the deal because it had promoted about 90 percent of the fights that would be on the album, and I needed its permission to use excerpts of the blow-by-blow descriptions I'd done. I'd had a few meetings with Alvin about the project, and he seemed very receptive to it. Now it seemed we were close to a deal with a distributor.

My appointment was for noon at his office. At ten o'clock that morning I received a call from his secretary, saying that the meeting about the album would have to be postponed, but that I was invited to a press conference to be held at Toots Shor's restaurant at 1:00

P.M. that day. I didn't know what the conference was about, but I was glad to go. When I got to Shor's, the place was jammed. Garden officials, officials of the boxing commission, sportswriters, announcers, and cameramen from every radio and TV station in town were there. I soon found out what it was about. The Garden was announcing that it had signed Muhammad Ali and Joe Frazier to fight for the world's heavyweight championship on the night of March 8.

This announcement of the greatest fight in years was a big surprise to everyone, including me. Naturally, there had been rumors about it, but the news still landed like a bombshell.

There was a terrific air of excitement and anticipation at the luncheon, and a roar went up when Muhammad Ali strode dramatically into the room. Over the din, I thought I heard him say, "Now we'll see who the real champ is." Both men had a claim to the title. Ali had been the undisputed heavyweight champion, but when he refused to take part in the draft during the Vietnam War, many commissions, including New York's, had stripped him of his title. As a result, an elimination tournament was held, and Joe Frazier won it and the title recognition. Later the Supreme Court ruled that Ali, as a Muslim minister, in fact had the right to claim exemption from the draft as a conscientious objector on religious grounds. Ali had returned to the ring in 1970 after an absence of three years, and had knocked out Jerry Quarry and Oscar Bonavena. What made the idea of a fight between Ali and Frazier so intriguing and exciting was that it would be a battle for the championship between two undefeated fighters, neither having even a draw to mar their records. This was the first time such a face-off had occurred in heavyweight championship history. Although John L. Sullivan and James J. Corbett were both undefeated when they fought in 1892, both had draws on their records.

A few minutes after the raucous reception of Ali's appearance, Joe Frazier came out and was greeted with equal applause and excitement. He was quiet and struck me as much more serious than the irrepressible Ali. Now I saw Jerry Perenchio for the first time. He was rather tall and slight of build. Aside from the principals in this great extravaganza, Perenchio received most of the attention from the assembled guests. The clamoring mob of media people didn't seem to faze him. He was used to the limelight and took the flood of questions in stride. After being introduced by John Condon, the toastmaster, Perenchio was interrupted by Ali's jabbering, but took control of the situation nicely by turning to the Great One and saying, "For five million, Muhammad, I think I have the right to talk without interruption." Ali stopped interrupting. I guess even he was impressed by the fact that their guarantee of two and a half million each would be the largest purse ever received by prize-fighters.

By that moment all my concerns about producing a fight album had disappeared from my mind, replaced by wondering if I would be the blow-by-blow announcer for the closed-circuit TV broadcast of what unquestionably would be the single greatest sports event of all time. Every sports announcer would want the job, and that included me. Normally there wouldn't have been any doubt about my doing a Garden fight. But this wasn't a Garden promotion. A figure I had never heard of before, Jerry Perenchio, was calling the shots. I knew that Alvin Cooperman, Harry Markson, and Teddy Brenner would prefer that I be the announcer. But I didn't know how much influence they would have with Perenchio. How far would they be willing to go in pushing me with the stranger? I was in the midst of a reverie along those lines when I heard a voice call me. "Hey, Don!" it said, "Come over here for a second." It was Alvin Cooperman. "Let me introduce you to Jerry Perenchio." I knew Cooperman liked me personally and had a high regard for my ability. I knew that by this introduction he was letting Perenchio know how he felt.

Perenchio was very friendly but I couldn't tell what he was think-ing. We had a nice, polite conversation, but our true thoughts re-mained concealed. All the columnists were anxious to come up to him with questions, so I didn't overstay. I wished him luck with the promotion and excused myself.

You may wonder at this point why I had any doubts about being selected as the announcer for the Ali–Frazier fight. After all, I was recognized as the number-one boxing announcer in the country. But this was 1970, and although I did most of the fights, I wasn't at that time in any hall of fame. And I knew that not everyone listened to the fights. I figured there was a chance that Perenchio had never heard me. I also knew that every big-name sports announcer in the country would be pulling every conceivable string to try to get the job. And Perenchio was an actors' agent. Suppose out on the West Coast where he came from, there was a boxing announcer in his stable of talent—Chick Hearn, for instance. And then there was Howard Cosell. If I were a gambling man, I would have bet that he was the man to beat for the job, for though I was doing the Garden fights, Howard was doing fights for ABC, and he had done big ones. His ability or lack of it was not the only factor. He was on the scene and he had connections, and his biggest connection was Muhammad Ali. He was close to the fighter, and not without good reason. When Ali was being stripped of his title during the Vietnam War, Cosell had fought for him continually. It was my feeling that Ali would make every effort to see that he got the job. Also, Cosell had been at the mike in Ali's previous fight with Bonavena. The more I thought about it, the less sanguine I became about my chances.

After leaving Shor's, I went to see my agent, Bill Cooper, whose office was nearby. It was only a short walk, but during those few minutes I became obsessed with the idea that I had to do the fight. I've always had a lot of confidence in my ability. I knew that announcing the Ali–Frazier fight would be easy. I had done several fights in which either Ali or Frazier were principals. This one wouldn't be any different. No one was going to invent a punch that I hadn't seen. No, the fight would be easy. What would be difficult would be to convince Perenchio that I was the man for the job.

I told Cooper about the press conference, and he whistled when he heard what the fighters were getting. It was unnecessary for me to tell him how much I wanted to be at ringside for this one. He knew that. But I told him anyway. He agreed with me that Perenchio was the problem. He said he would try to find out more about him by speaking to agents on the West Coast. One thing I knew about

Bill Cooper was that he was a straight shooter who would lay things on the line and wouldn't try to build up my hopes with a lot of fancy talk. I knew that he meant what he said, and when he said this might be an uphill fight, it didn't surprise me. But I also knew that he would give it his best shot, and that was all I could ask.

The road to ringside became a little steeper the next day, when I got a phone call from my son Don junior, who at the time was assistant news director at ABC's "Eyewitness News." He wasted no time in bringing me up to date. He knew how much this fight meant to me and he was upset.

"Dad," he said, "you won't believe this. I've just come from a luncheon, and Howard Cosell was there. He came up to me when it was over and said, "I'm not going to do the Ali–Frazier fight and neither is your father. They're going to use Andy Williams, Kirk Douglas, and Burt Lancaster."

I thought of Barry Fitzgerald in *Going My Way*, when he found out that Bing Crosby was to be his assistant priest and said, "No, the Bishop wouldn't do that to me." I said to myself, "No, Perenchio wouldn't do that to boxing." Or would he? Burt Lancaster, Andy Williams, and Kirk Douglas at ringside, for a fight of this magnitude? If Cosell had said that he was going to do the fight, it wouldn't have bothered me that much. Or if he had said that Bill Mazer was the choice. Or Chris Schenkel, or Curt Gowdy. But Williams, Lancaster, and Douglas? Why not the Marx Brothers, at least they're funny. But it wasn't that farfetched. Perenchio represented Douglas, Williams, and Lancaster, and it would be understandable for him to see this great event as an irresistible opportunity to get them vast exposure.

A couple of gloomy days later, Cooper called me and said that Howard Rose, Perenchio's assistant, wanted a biography. At least, I thought, they're talking about me. Perhaps the tide would somehow yet be turned.

A few days later, Cooper, still plugging away, told me he had gotten in touch with Perenchio and set up a meeting for the following day. This was good news. Now we could lay our case before him. The meeting was to be at 5:00 P.M. at the St. Regis Hotel. When we got there we found a message that Mr. Perenchio had called and apologized for being late, and said he would be there at five-thirty. Bill and I used the half hour to talk over what we would say to the promoter and to discuss a fee, if I should get the job. Mike Malitz had paid me $2,500 for doing the Ali–Cleveland Williams fight in Houston in 1967. It was, I believe, an all-time high for a single sports event. I know that these days there are sports announcers who get more than a million dollars a year. But that's for a whole year. This was 1971 and a single event. They weren't paid anything like that then.

I had built up the importance of the Frazier fight, and I guess Bill got the idea that Perenchio was going to make a tremendous amount of money not only from the sale of tickets, but from a slew of ancillary rights as well. Maybe he got the idea that I was an equal partner in the promotion, for when he told me he was going to ask $10,000 for my fee, I almost fell off the chair right there in the St. Regis lobby.

I stammered, "Please, Bill, I haven't got the job yet. Let's not put a money block in front of my chances."

Before Bill could answer me, Perenchio arrived, greeted us well, and escorted us up to his suite. I suddenly thought better of my chances. I knew Perenchio was awfully busy and wouldn't have us over to his suite just to say hello. What was his purpose? Had he made up his mind? While he busied himself with something else, I looked around the room. Tables were stacked high with documents that were obviously contracts for the closed-circuit showing of the fight. There could have been a couple of million in those documents. As later returns on the finances of the bout would show, that was indeed a low estimate.

After a few pleasantries, we got down to cases. Surprisingly, I felt very relaxed, more relaxed than I had felt any day since the announcement of the fight. It has always been my nature, I think, to worry and be pessimistic before any business crisis, but once I'm in the middle of the struggle, my attitude seems to change. When that happens I become very calm and always feel in complete control of myself. It had been that way before my first big assignment, the

Louis–Conn fight thirty years before, and had proved true time and again.

Perenchio was very friendly and well aware of my career. He had heard me many times. As the three of us talked, the atmosphere was light, almost airy. Trying to find out just where I stood in his plans for the broadcast, I put out a leading question. "Didn't I read somewhere that Andy Williams would be one of your broadcasters?"

"Oh no," Perenchio laughed. "If Andy does anything on the show, maybe he'll sing the national anthem."

Scratch Andy Williams as a rival.

Bill led the conversation into Perenchio's interest in sports, and inquired into his sudden desire to promote this great fight. Along the way he mentioned his close friendship with Burt Lancaster. The two of them had watched the Ali–Bonavena fight together on closed-circuit television. "Would you believe this, Don?" he said. "Burt and I were turned off by Howard Cosell's description of the fight. After a few rounds we kept yelling, 'Howard, will you shut up?' By the way," he continued, "Ali has been calling me nearly every day about Cosell, and I keep telling him there's no way I'll use him."

This was cheering me up. I had considered Cosell my chief competitor and apparently overestimated the influence Ali would have.

Perenchio now turned the conversation to Burt Lancaster, talked about how long he had known the star, of how Burt had been a fine athlete and was a real fight fan. I got the distinct feeling that Lancaster would be in the broadcast setup for Ali–Frazier, regardless of who did the blow-by-blow.

Suddenly, Perenchio turned to me. "Don," he asked, "how do you visualize this telecast—if you were doing it?"

I answered without hesitation. I said I could think of Burt Lancaster opening the show as a host. He makes a fine presence. He handles himself well as a rugged yet charming actor. Naturally, I would do the blow-by-blow. I continued, "I think that someone like Ray Robinson could do the color and analyze the fight as it goes along." I had heard that he was being considered for the show. "Before and after the fight, Lancaster could be an anchorman switching to the dressing rooms with me in one and Robinson in the other." Perenchio, who had been pacing the room all this time, suddenly stopped and said, "That makes sense. I like it."

The meeting was over. We shook hands and left. My confidence had come back and Bill was smiling. He said, "The assignment is yours. It may take a while, but I'm sure I'll be called to tell me he wants you."

"I think you're right," I said, "but when you talk about a fee, please don't hit him over the head with it." Money was less important to me than the job. Of course, an agent, who works on commission, will naturally try to get as much as he can.

A few days later, Cooper called with good and bad news. "Don," he started, "I think you've got the job."

"Great!" I exclaimed.

"However, there's a catch. Perenchio thinks we're asking too much money."

I chuckled to myself at Bill's use of the plural. He was the one asking for the money. I told him to compromise as much as he could, and that's the way our phone conversation ended. We talked again several times in the ensuing week and he kept assuring me that everything would be all right—if he could just get the promoter on the phone. "I call him and leave messages," he said, "but he never returns them. I'm sure he's got so much on his mind he keeps putting off answering me. Just hang in there."

To me it was déjà vu. I knew Perenchio wanted me, but for some reason he was putting off telling me. Thirty years before, after I had won an audition for the Joe Louis–Billy Conn fight, I knew that Gillette wanted me, but they too kept me dangling. I began to feel like a participle.

I put in a call to my friend Alvin Cooperman, who assured me that the Garden was keeping in touch with Perenchio on my behalf. This was heartening.

Then Chris Dundee, the Miami promoter, brother of fight trainer and manager Angelo Dundee, called me from his home. He explained the situation. "Muhammad Ali is down here training at my gym, and Jerry Perenchio was here yesterday to watch him train. Perenchio says he likes you, but he thinks your agent is asking for too much money. I'm telling you this as a friend. Understand?''

I certainly did, and thanked him. Now I tried to get Cooper on the phone. It was Saturday, and I tried to get him all morning. There was no answer. Finally I gave up, figuring I'd just have to wait until Monday.

That evening, Muriel and I were having dinner at our son Don's house in Westbury, Long Island, when the phone rang. Don went to answer it and was back in ten seconds.

"It was Bob," he said. (Bob is my other son and a sports director at CBS.) "He said Cooper called, Dad's got the fight job, and he should call him Monday." That was Bob. Quick and to the point. Outwardly I didn't show any emotion, but I got up, grabbed the phone, called Bob back, and asked him to repeat it. It was so. The biggest single announcing job ever was mine.

I was happy. So were Muriel, Don junior, and his wife Sheila.

First thing Monday morning, I got a call from Cooper confirming what Bob had told me on Saturday. "I finally reached Perenchio in Miami on Saturday, and after considerable haggling we got together on a price. I think you'll like it. Five thousand dollars." Like it! I certainly did. I believe it was the highest amount any sports announcer had ever received for a single night's work up to that time. I thanked Cooper for his fine efforts on my behalf, and he suggested that I come into the city to meet with Ted Deglin, who was doing the publicity and promotion for the fight. Ted was no stranger to me. Years earlier he had done publicity for the Garden, and our paths had crossed many times. His congratulations to me were warm, and I looked forward to a good relationship with him, working on the fight. I gave him all the information he needed, went to the Garden to thank Alvin Cooperman, Harry Markson, and Teddy Brenner for what they had done, and then went home.

The next day it was announced that Burt Lancaster would be working with me, and shortly thereafter I learned that former light heavyweight champion Archie Moore, not Sugar Ray Robinson, would be the third man in the setup. Around February 17, Burt Lancaster arrived in town and Jerry Perenchio asked me if I would

meet the acting star in his suite at the St. Regis. Also on hand were
his longtime writer-associate Roland Kibbee and Jimmy Jacobs,
who owned the most extensive fight film collection in the world.
Jimmy is an old friend of mine.

When Lancaster opened the door to greet me, it was like walking
up and jumping into a movie screen. There he was, that full head
of hair, that strong, rugged face, an acre of teeth. Burt Lancaster
in living color. But once inside the suite, his initial charm evaporated. Although I knew Jacobs quite well, his presence wasn't enough
to still an unsettling discomfort, a feeling of alienation, as I listened
with awkward attention to Lancaster's palliatives. The rhythm between us just wasn't there. Like a boxer against a slugger, it was a
bad match.

I read somewhere that Lancaster had grown up in New York, so
I tried to open an avenue of communication that would put us on
common ground.

"I understand you're originally from Manhattan."

"Yes. I lived on East 104th Street."

"Well, that's most interesting. I was brought up on West 103rd
Street, right across the park from you. I guess you might say we
were practically next-door neighbors."

"Hm-m-m."

"I also know your brother, Dutch, slightly. I used to watch him
play sandlot baseball, and remember him as a fine football and
basketball player at New York University."

"Is that so?"

From there on, the conversation went downhill. Fortunately, Jimmy
was setting up a screen during my monologue and, thankfully, the
room was finally darkened so we could view a print of the Bonavena–
Ali fight. During the showing, Jacobs pointed out to Lancaster the
various moves of Ali and Bonavena.

"Watch the hook, Burt. See how he's throwing it. . . . Watch this,
as Bonavena backs into the ropes. . . . Notice how Ali sets him up
for his right. . . . Look at this move, Burt. . . ."

The film rolled on, with Lancaster asking a lot of questions and
Jacobs supplying the answers. When it was all over, I knew I had

seen a rerun of the Bonavena–Ali fight and I was beginning to understand something I had not been aware of until then. Jacobs was Socrates and Lancaster was Plato. In less than a month's time the pupil would be at ringside, trying to fulfill his role as a fight announcer. Well, maybe that's how Hollywood did it.

In any case, Lancaster was drumming up all kinds of publicity for The Fight. He had been booked, along with Perenchio, Frazier, Ali, Moore, Ray Robinson, Rocky Graziano, Willie Pep, Joe Louis, and other great fight figures on innumerable television and radio shows. Lancaster spoke with obvious relish and intensity about the upcoming bout on the Johnny Carson, David Frost, Dick Cavett, and Mike Douglas shows.

During this concentrated flurry of activity, my wife, Muriel, entered the scene with her own determined intensity. She had learned that I had been dropped from a David Frost taping at the last moment. I had been scheduled to appear with Perenchio and Lancaster. On the day of the taping I had dropped in at Perenchio's Chartwell Agency office, having a little time to kill before the broadcast. Ted Deglin was there and immediately registered a long frown as he delivered the news that I had been chopped from the show because they had overbooked the guests.

Ted was very apologetic. It seems that one of the show's bookers had penciled Rocky Graziano in at the last minute, and then it was decided that two guests would be sufficient. Someone apparently thought I was expendable. "I'm sorry it turned out this way," Deglin offered. "I tried to reach you at home but you had already left."

I tried to understand the reasoning. After all, not everyone is a fight fan, and although I had been at ringside for most of the major fights of the last thirty years, there just weren't many televised anymore. It had been seven years since "The Fight of the Week" had gone off the air. People forget.

My first impulse was to get angry, to blow my top. But I've always been able to cool off quickly and weigh a situation. In the first place, what good would it do? The die had been cast. It was now four-thirty in the afternoon. The taping was scheduled for seven. Things like that happen every so often. And besides, getting upset and pulling rank might cause me to say something I would regret later. My damaged pride would survive this slap in the face. After all, my main objective was to be the announcer of the greatest sporting event of all time. Forget the detours and the bumps in the road. Announce the fight!

I said something or other to Deglin to indicate that it wasn't the end of the world, and then walked over to Toots Shor's to have a drink before going home.

I phoned Muriel from Shor's. She had received Deglin's call and was absolutely furious. Before I could say a word, she sounded off. But good.

"They can't do this to you," she fumed. "After all, you're more important than anyone else."

It was catching. Now I started to do a slow burn.

I *was* important, but obviously the producers of the show didn't think so. I hung up with one hand, while the other was extracting a dime from my pants pocket so I could call Perenchio.

Luckily he was in his office. I couldn't mask the irritation in my voice as I related the circumstances to him.

"That's terrible," he said. "They can't do this to you. If you don't go on, Burt and I won't go on. Where are you, anyhow?"

"At Toots Shor's."

"Okay. Give me the number and hang around for five minutes. I'll call you back."

I walked over to the bar to order a drink. Before I had the glass in my hand to take a first sip, the phone rang. Perenchio's voice was even and commanding. "Everything's straightened out," he intoned. "They caved in. So just relax and we'll see you at the studio around six."

It was a satisfying moment. Perenchio had been sincerely concerned about the way I was handled by the Frost producers, and I guess he also realized I would be an asset to the show, which meant even more to me.

As for Muriel, I must admit she is the most tenacious member of the Dunphy household. She doesn't say very much when it involves my business affairs, but Lord help the person who knocks my broadcasting ability. When I recounted how Perenchio had stepped into the breach to make sure I got on the show, she simply said, "Well, after all . . . it was only right." That's Muriel.

Lancaster was far from through with his media commitments. He continued to make local radio sports call-in shows, all over the country, and everywhere he went there was sure to be a newspaper reporter putting Burt's comments on lined paper, helping them make their way into the sports pages the next morning. Perenchio's Hollywood buddy had totally involved himself in the pre-fight ballyhoo.

Nonetheless, I still felt dubious about Lancaster. Although he was a fine actor, he possessed no experience as a fight commentator. His crash course in boxing, even under the tutelage of film collector Jimmy Jacobs, had just produced an accumulation of data and material that filled three or four notebooks, all for the purpose of giving Lancaster a good accounting of himself on the night of March 8. If he felt this was the way to become a fight expert, it was his own affair. But my observation is that it's like someone trying to become a Shakespearean actor by hanging around Sir Laurence Olivier.

A few days before the fight, Lancaster invited me to accompany him to Philadelphia to watch Frazier train. I welcomed the idea because I felt it would give me some time to really get to know him. Our first meeting had hardly been inspiring.

He was waiting for me at the St. Regis along with Kibbee, when I entered the lobby promptly at nine in the morning.

"Hi, Don," Lancaster grinned through those marvelous teeth of his. "There's a car waiting at curbside to take us down."

We wheeled out of the hotel as quickly as I had entered, and with me in the back seat with Lancaster, and Kibbee up front with the uniformed driver, our limousine headed out of the city toward the New Jersey Turnpike and Philadelphia.

There was a light but oily rain falling as we sped past the huge Esso refinery outside Elizabeth. Now the ribbon of slick highway cut through dairy country that could have been carved into the landscapes of Indiana or Iowa. Unfortunately, the scenery occupied most of my attention, because Lancaster was engrossed in other things. As we went through the first toll booth on the turnpike, he had commented that he liked crossword puzzles, and asked me if I did too.

"Sure, I like to do them once in a while."

"That's nice."

Whereupon he folded *The New York Times* to the crossword page, took out a pencil, and began to work on the puzzle. By the time we approached Trenton he was snoring peacefully and I was staring into the gray rain that hung over the Jersey hills.

The challenge, by now, was to get to the gym as soon as possible, to say hello to old friends and feel and smell the familiar trappings of the fight game. To see Yancey Durham, Frazier's manager, to watch the champion go through his sparring session and get caught up in the moves: the rat-tat-tat of leather against the heavy bag, the skip-skip-skip of rope against ancient hardwood flooring, the sound of the bell at the start of a training round, and the timeless, rasping voice of managers, trainers, fighters, writers, and fight mob people; my milieu, my territory, my world, where I'd be able at last to hold a conversation with someone.

The gym was located close to the 30th Street railroad station. After a quick lunch, which, for the most part, was spent watching the trains go by, Lancaster, Kibbee, and I went to see Frazier's workout. He looked good, sharp, ready as one should be who is training for the most important heavyweight fight of all time. After his workout, Frazier climbed down from the ring, face glistening with sweat, and laughingly greeted Lancaster and me with a friendly poke at our midsections.

The photographers and writers quickly moved in. They wanted to get some shots of Frazier and Lancaster together. John Condon, who was in the crowd, suggested I get in the picture with them, and I happily obliged.

Now it was the writers' turn. Frazier had taken center stage. For the moment, Hollywood was relegated to second billing. That is, until one of the writers fired off a loaded question to Lancaster.

"Why isn't Howard Cosell doing the broadcast, Burt?"

"Well," he answered, doing a great imitation of himself—head cocked one way, hands moving, palms down, in another—"he's not going to do the broadcast because Jerry Perenchio and I watched him describe the Bonavena–Clay fight some time ago and he was terrible. Why, we were laughing at him and kept shouting, 'Shut up, Howard.' "

I looked for a window, a door, a crack to slide through. Nobody asked me the question, but if it had been posed, I probably would've answered, "I guess it's because we have Don Dunphy, and we feel he's the best man for the job." Or something like that. But Lancaster, with all his sophistication, managed to insult Cosell's ability and, at the same time, completely ignore my own particular gifts. The press scattered right after that remark and I took off for another part of the gym, as far away from Lancaster as I could get. What gall! Who the hell was he to criticize Howard Cosell?

Dave Anderson of *The New York Times* came over in a minute or two, his face a signpost of incredulousness.

"Say, did you hear that? I don't believe it," he murmured.

The next day Dave had a column in the *Times* dealing with Frazier, and he made a point of including Lancaster's boorish assault on Cosell. I could picture Howie reading all about it over coffee in the morning. What a snapshot!

Maybe I was oversensitive. Maybe not. But I really resented Lancaster at the time. It was a pleasure to take his rented limo back to New York without him, while he stayed in Philadelphia to appear on "The Mike Douglas Show." The folded copy of the *Times* was still in the back seat. I picked it up and finished Lancaster's puzzle about fifteen miles beyond Camden.

Despite my personal criticisms, I must acknowledge Lancaster's effectiveness in building interest in the fight. The movie star garnered millions of dollars' worth of free publicity during his countless appearances and interviews. He was indefatigable in his commit-

ment to squeeze every last ounce of value out of the event. It seemed
he was everywhere—Miami, Chicago, Boston, Atlanta, Detroit—
to plug The Fight. For that I must give him all the credit in the
world. But I can't condone his insensitivity or consider him a gracious person.

Just like that, it was Sunday, March 7, the morning of the day
before the battle for the heavyweight championship of the world. A
last production meeting was scheduled. The final scripts were to be
gone over, the bugs were to be worked out, and everyone was to
learn about his own particular broadcasting role.

The meeting took place in Lancaster's suite at the St. Regis.
Roland Kibbee, who wrote the script, was there along with Art
Fisher and Neal Marshall, the telecast producers. Also on hand,
besides me, were Archie Moore, Stan Spiro, an associate director,
Chris Wallace, a production associate, and Jim Appell, who represented Jack Kent Cooke. It seemed Cooke had a firm if distant
hand in each phase of the promotion. Between him and Perenchio,
they had gobbled up every last territory that was available for closed-
circuit television. Their one-shot franchising of locations stretched
from New York to Canada to Bangkok and the North Pole. And beyond!

Somehow, to everyone in the room, looking at Appell was like
peering into the sagacious countenance of Jack Kent Cooke. Appell
needed to do nothing else but sit there and smile.

The scripts were brought out. I'll never forget my initial reaction
when I saw the first words on the top of page one.

SHOW AND SCRIPT RUNDOWN

1. Pre-fight film "The Fighters" (VTPB)

2. BLACK :05 (VTPB)

3. Opening ANIMATED FILM (VTPB)

4. CU—Don Dunphy (VTPB)

> DON:
> (wearing headset)
> Live from Madison Square Garden, the Heavyweight Cham-
> pionship of the World—featuring the former Heavyweight
> Champion of the World, Muhammad Ali, versus the current
> Heavyweight Champion. Good evening, ladies and gentlemen,
> this is [I changed that later to "I'm"] Don Dunphy, I'll be
> calling the blow-by-blow for this championship match, an event
> of such magnitude it has been referred to around the world as
> "the *fight of the century*." Working with me to provide color
> commentary and fight analyses are Mr. Burt Lancaster and
> the former Light Heavyweight Champion of the World, Archie
> Moore. . . . And now we take you [changed to "let's go"] to
> the dressing room of Muhammad Ali.

I'd never doubted that I would do the blow-by-blow. But it had
never dawned on me that I would also open the show as the host.
How it came about, I still don't know. But I was happy.

There it was: Dunphy throws it to Lancaster in Ali's dressing
room, Dunphy throws it to Moore in Frazier's dressing room. After
some 1,500 fights, I was now throwing my usual post-fight interviews
to someone else. I was the Ed Sullivan of boxing, and inside I was
glowing.

It was at this point that I turned to Lancaster and tried to disarm
him with a slight needle.

"I'm happy one of you finally made it."

"What's that?"

"I'm thinking of something my son Don said to me two or three
weeks ago. He called from his office at ABC News to tell me Howard
Cosell came up to him at a Channel 7 luncheon and told him, 'Your
dad isn't going to do the fight, and neither am I. It's going to be
Andy Williams, Kirk Douglas, and Burt Lancaster.' "

Lancaster looked at me, then through me. For a moment I thought
he might turn into one of his favorite Indian characters, Cochise,

and go for my scalp. Then he brightened and let out a hearty laugh.

"You're happy one of *us* made it? Listen," he shot back with a mirthful jab, "I'm happy one of *you* made it!"

Suddenly, Lancaster had become quite human, and I liked him for it. From then on it was all business, and we dug deeper and deeper into the production details. Lancaster read his part with precision, inflections just right, intonation perfect. Moore also sounded okay. He was no actor, but his reading did have a quality of honesty. As for me, with all those fights behind me, the script was like an old familiar friend. I walked up to it and felt right at home.

Just before we broke from the session, which lasted until midafternoon, Marshall asked if anyone had anything else to say, any last-minute thoughts.

"Yes," I spoke up. "Just one thing. I don't care what anyone says before a round or after a round. But when the actual round is in progress, I want it understood—nobody talks except Don Dunphy."

Marshall, Fisher, Lancaster, and Moore quickly gave me their assurances I would have the mike all to myself during each round. On that note, the production meeting closed. I walked out into the Sunday afternoon with a bounce in my step and a surge of adrenaline in my system.

Monday night was coming on like a Kansas tornado.

The Ali–Frazier Fights

Ithink the first Ali–Frazier heavyweight championship fight was the greatest individual sports event of all time. Greater than the World Series, greater than the Super Bowl, greater than any sports event you can think of. It held the interest of more people in all walks of life than anything else you can imagine. Around the world, it had an audience of some 300 million. By word of mouth, radio, television, and magazines and newspapers, it dominated the news for weeks. Madison Square Garden was electric on the night of March 8, 1971, as it has never been before or since. The audience of eighteen thousand who were fortunate enough to get tickets included a veritable *Who's Who* of the entire world. Politicians, stars of the entertainment world, business tycoons, and ordinary fight fans were keyed to a high level of excitement.

It was an honor to be the TV voice that evening. I've broadcast other great fights, I've done the World Series, bowl games, track meets, and other sports, but never have I had the feeling I had that night. It was indeed a night to remember.

I guess it's paradoxical to say the first Ali–Frazier fight was great, then say it wasn't. But I think both statements are correct. It was great because of its importance, because of the participants, the stakes, the scale. But as a contest it was not the "fight of the century." Those present that night, myself included, hung on every punch. It was a good fight. But as you look back on it from a prizefight standpoint, as you review the tapes and concentrate on the punches, it was ordinary. I think both young men, realizing they were making history, were very tense. It's an open question who was more so. After a slow start, they both loosened up—Ali the master boxer, Frazier the slugger, the great left-hooker. But Ali may have cost himself a round or two. He would back into the ropes, hold Frazier with one hand, and playfully tap him on the head with the other. It may have stirred the Ali fans, but, looking over the scoreboards, I think the judges were unimpressed. Also, Ali would take a punch, turn to the audience, and grin as though it hadn't hurt him. He had to be acting. Frazier's punches always hurt.

The great drama came in the fifteenth round. There had been no knockdowns until then. Suddenly, with a whistling left hook, his best punch, Frazier dumped Ali on the canvas. When it landed, I didn't think Ali would get up, but he did. At this point Ali was hurt, and both were drained emotionally after fifteen rounds of combat. They were drained physically, too. Frazier couldn't land another punch; Ali was happy to hear the final bell. The scoring in New York at the time was on a rounds basis. Johnny Addie read the scorecards to a hushed audience. Referee Arthur Mercante gave eight rounds to Frazier, six to Ali, and one even. Judge Arthur Aidala gave nine to Frazier, six to Ali. Judge Bill Recht had it wide, eleven rounds to Frazier, four to Ali. Joe Frazier was now the undisputed champion of the world.

. . .

The second Ali–Frazier fight at the Garden in 1974 was definitely not a great fight. Neither man was the world's heavyweight champion at the time. Frazier had been knocked out by George Foreman a year earlier, and Ali was defending the NABF title, which was then a secondary bauble. Ali won a close decision in a bout that Tony Perez refereed.

The third Ali–Frazier fight was really something. The "Thrilla in Manila," as Ali called it, certainly rates with the all-time great fights. It had a slow start, but from the fifth round on, it was a battle of attrition. I don't think two men ever took so much punishment in a heavyweight championship bout. Ali had an edge after four rounds, but Frazier then dominated the fight. It was generally agreed that Joe Frazier was winning the fight after ten rounds. Ali is reported to have said he felt so bad after the tenth that he wanted to quit the fight. But naturally this great champion had too much pride for that. Both men were spent in the ensuing rounds, but Ali had a little more left. Frazier suffered a cut eye, and the bout may have turned on that. I don't know. I do know that as I called the fight I wondered what was holding them up and what was keeping them going. In the thirteenth round, Frazier was having trouble seeing, and was coming at Ali wide open. Ali was potshotting him, but his punch was now gone.

It was obvious to me in the fourteenth round that Frazier had no chance of winning the fight. I was relieved to see Eddie Futch, Frazier's handler, call a halt to the proceedings at the end of the fourteenth. It took a lot of courage on Eddie's part to stop a fight of this magnitude with but one round to go, but his main concern was the welfare of his fighter; he should be applauded for that. Ali was to be applauded, too, for outlasting Frazier and retaining the world's heavyweight title.

After the fight, a bruised and exhausted Ali said, "You've seen my last fight. Money or no money." I think he meant it, too. After the physical punishment he had endured, he wanted no more of it.

Muhammad Ali

I did Muhammad Ali's first fight on TV, which was a ten-rounder versus Alonzo Johnson in 1961 in Louisville. Then he still went by the name Cassius Clay. I did his last fight, sadly, on the tube when he lost a ten-rounder to Trevor Berbick in Nassau of the Bahamas on December 11, 1981. In between, I aired twenty-three Ali fights, saw him win and lose the heavyweight championship a couple of times, and literally followed him around the world: Toronto, London, Frankfurt, San Juan, Paradise Island in the Bahamas, Malaysia, Las Vegas, New Orleans, and the Philippines.

I didn't mind his bragging at the beginning of his career, when he was saying he was the prettiest and when he was predicting in verse the round in which he would upend his opponent. Many people disliked him for that, but I thought he was showing his genius as a promoter, building up the gates of his fights. Then he won the title.

I thought it was a shot in the arm for boxing after the sullen years of Sonny Liston. When he became a Muslim and changed his name to Muhammad Ali, I figured that was his own business. But his new name did cause problems in many places before it was finally accepted. In my case, the problem came in the TV airing of a fight. Early in 1966, former champion Floyd Patterson was matched against George Chuvalo, the Canadian champion, in a closed-circuit bout at the Garden. Lester Malitz was the producer of the show, and asked me to be the blow-by-blow announcer. Ali was to be my color commentator. This was before Ali's new name was accepted in most places, and *Ring Magazine,* the "Bible of Boxing," was still calling him Cassius Clay. I avoided any difficulty by calling him "Champ," and we got along fine. He was an excellent analyst.

To me, Muhammad Ali has always been contradictory. He was a great fighter, no question about that. It was a delight to watch his graceful movements in the ring. But he was the only fighter I ever knew of who made fun of an opponent. To me, boxing is a serious business, and in this Ali was not very gallant. The "Ali shuffle" may have looked great to some people, but I thought it was uncalled for. He usually did it when he had an opponent in trouble and ready to fall, such as poor Cleveland Williams in their fight in Houston. When he fought Henry Cooper, the Britisher, in London, it was fairly even going into the fifth round. Ali and Cooper went into a clinch and banged heads together, and Cooper, a notorious bleeder, came out of the clinch streaming blood. Ali went into the Ali shuffle. It wasn't very gracious. After the fights, however, Ali was always very friendly with his opponents. He sometimes was like night and day in that respect.

Because of his cockiness, Ali was not a popular fighter in the early part of his career. What gave him his great popularity was his stand against the draft in the Vietnam War. Because of that he became a cult hero and his popularity zoomed. Ali came along at a time when boxing needed someone of his personality. He took the people's minds off their troubles and made them concentrate on him instead. He brought to boxing a legion of new fans who might never have been interested in the sport. His impact was great. I leave it to history to decide where he stands in the boxing firmament. For my own part, I'm glad I was around when he was.

Great Rounds

Earlier I mentioned that I have covered in the neighborhood of two thousand fights. If picking the greatest fights was a difficult assignment, how about picking the greatest rounds? Two thousand fights adds up to an awful lot of rounds. Some fights, the championship ones, were scheduled for fifteen rounds. Regular fights were usually scheduled for ten. Some ended early. If you strike an average—say seven or eight rounds per fight—you come up with something like fourteen thousand rounds I've done in over forty-five years. Trying to go back through that pile and pick out a few is daring if not foolhardy. But some do stand out, even over a long period of time, and I'll pass them along to you.

The ones I've chosen are from championship bouts, which is

natural. A title bout makes more impression than a non-title one, and is more easily recalled. Again I remind the experts and the fans that their thoughts on great rounds are as important as mine. So here goes with the ones that have impressed me the most.

Jack Dempsey–Luis Firpo
POLO GROUNDS, SEPTEMBER 14, 1923

In all the history of boxing championships, there has never been a round to compare with the first round of the fight between the Manassa Mauler, William Harrison Dempsey, better known as Jack, and the Wild Bull of the Pampas, the Argentinian Luis Angel Firpo. The bout was held at the Polo Grounds in New York City on Friday night, September 14, 1923, and it's a wonder the outer walls didn't collapse. Ninety thousand fans jammed their way into the old ballpark, paying an estimated $1,250,000, a fantastic amount for those ancient days, long before inflation. But it was worth every penny. The fans were treated to less than two rounds of unexampled dramatics, power, ring savagery, and plain raw courage. Those fortunate enough to be there that night never forgot it and cherished it as a moment never to be repeated in any of the fistic extravaganzas since.

Jack Dempsey won and retained the title, but what a fight it was. The first round is the one that in my estimation will always be listed number one in important rounds in championship boxing history. Yes, Dempsey won, but never before or after did he have to fight so desperately—not the first round in Toledo, where he slaughtered Jess Willard to take the crown, and not even in the famous long count when he had the champion, Gene Tunney, down in the seventh round of the title bout in Chicago in 1927. The long count, of course, aided Tunney in keeping the crown. In both of these fights, Dempsey was on his feet. In the Firpo bout, he found himself out of the ring, driven there by Firpo's huge fist.

I didn't see the fight, but I heard the broadcast by Major J. Andrew White. The exciting first round went roughly as follows:

The challenger landed the first punch of the fight after Dempsey missed a left-hand body punch. Firpo's right landed on the jaw, and to the crowd's amazement, Dempsey was driven to one knee. They went into a clinch. After being parted by referee Jimmy Gallagher, Dempsey beat Firpo to the punch and hooked a left to the jaw. Firpo went down and took a count of two. The champion attacked the midsection, and Firpo, taking a left to the body, went down for a count of three. (There was no mandatory eight-count in those days; that rule came many years later.) Another left to the body floored Firpo again, but the challenger was up immediately. At this point, no one would have given a dime for Firpo's chances, but that was to change. Three times more Dempsey floored Firpo, but the game Argentinian was up each time. (Here the announcer, Major White, was shouting, "He's up, he's down," but the listener wasn't sure who was up and who was down.) Suddenly it all changed. Firpo unloaded a right to the jaw that caught Dempsey flush. The blow was so powerful that it drove the champion through the ropes and out of the ring, into the press section. The scriveners, being patriotic Americans and not wanting to see the title go to South America, rushed to the aid of the stricken champion and helped him back into the ring. (There was much controversy about this, and there were those who maintained that Dempsey should have been disqualified for not getting back into the ring under his own power.) Dempsey was assisted back into the ring and resumed fighting. He was now in terrible shape. He had taken Firpo's best punch and he was hurt. Dempsey, an inviting target, stood against the ropes, tottering and seemingly ready to be taken. The championship was Firpo's for the asking. But the challenger, having been floored seven times, was weary and—worse, from his standpoint—overanxious. He fired three successive rights at Dempsey's jaw, but they were wild. Dempsey's hard training for the bout now served him well. Although still hurt, he was able to dance away. When Firpo caught up with him, they clinched and the bell rang, ending the round—and Firpo's hopes for the championship. It had been an unforgettable round.

The second round was anticlimactic. Both men were refreshed by the minute's rest, but apparently Dempsey benefited more. The spectators could tell by looking at the combatants that Dempsey was in charge again. Firpo no longer was the aggressor. Dempsey quickly was on top of him, hooking a left to the jaw, and Firpo was down again. It was the eighth time he had gone to the canvas in less than two full rounds, but he was still going. Up at two, he went down again from a series of body shots. Up at five, he went down again from a Dempsey flurry, and this ended the spectacle in fifty-seven seconds of the second round. The champion had proved his greatness, and the challenger had proved his incredible tenacity.

Firpo said he would be back. He fought a few more times, but never fought Dempsey and never fought anyone for the title again. This has always puzzled and mystified me. Why was there no rematch of this classic Dempsey–Firpo battle? If ever a fight had a built-in selling point, this was it. It was the most sensational heavyweight championship fight up to that time; the loser knocked the winner out of the ring and came within inches of winning the title. Tex Rickard, the great promoter, was still on the scene. He subsequently made other great matches. Why not this one? The lack of a return bout always bothered me. In later years, I asked people I knew who had been at the fight. I asked Dempsey. He said he didn't know. I asked my friend Sam Taub, the boxing writer and announcer. He didn't know. I asked Nat Fleischer, editor and publisher of *Ring Magazine*. He didn't know why, either. I got the feeling that nobody seemed to care whether or not these two great heavyweights ever fought again. Am I the only one who cares? As a matter of fact, Dempsey didn't fight again for three years. Then he lost the crown to Tunney in 1926. Firpo just disappeared.

Sugar Ray Robinson–Jake LaMotta
CHICAGO STADIUM, FEBRUARY 14, 1951

The thirteenth round. How many times in great fights has the thirteenth literally been the unlucky round? Joe Louis–Billy Conn, 1941: Louis comes from behind to kayo the young Pittsburgher in the thirteenth. Rocky Marciano–Jersey Joe Walcott, 1952: Marciano comes from behind to kayo the champion with the single most important and decisive punch I ever saw; it was a right hand to the jaw, and game Jersey Joe just seemed to disintegrate. Sugar Ray Leonard–Thomas Hearns, 1981: Leonard comes from behind in the thirteenth to beat Hearns so badly in that round that the fight is stopped in the fourteenth.

One of the all-time great rounds was a thirteenth, when Sugar Ray Robinson dethroned the middleweight champion, Jake La-Motta, at Chicago on February 14, 1951. It had been a bruising fight, close for a while, but then Sugar Ray pulled away. There has never been a gamer fighter than the Bronx Bull, LaMotta, or anyone who could take more punches and survive. That's the way it was in the thirteenth. Jake had never been floored, and one wondered what kept him on his feet in this round. Robinson scored with a long right to the head, nailing the champion as he was coming in. Jake's knees sagged and he grabbed Robinson. Robinson scored with four successive lefts to the nose. LaMotta was taking a terrible beating, but he wouldn't go down. He couldn't seem to get his hands up. Robinson landed a left to the head and a right to the midsection. LaMotta was showing his great courage. The champion backed to the ropes and just stood there helpless. Sugar Ray belted him with a series of punches, and LaMotta held on. Finally the referee stopped the fight and Sugar Ray Robinson was the new middleweight champion of the world.

But as Robert De Niro, playing LaMotta in the movie *Raging Bull*, would say at the end of that fight scene, "Ya couldn't knock me down."

Joe Louis–Tami Mauriello
YANKEE STADIUM, SEPTEMBER 18, 1946

After knocking out Billy Conn to retain the heavyweight championship on June 19, 1946, the Brown Bomber didn't wait long before putting the title up for grabs again. The date of the fight, at Yankee Stadium in New York, was September 18, and the opponent was a tough young man from the Bronx named Tami Mauriello. Mauriello had failed to win the light heavyweight title, and now was campaigning among the heavies. He was a hard hitter with either hand, and took a good punch. Louis was a prohibitive favorite to win, but those who gave Tami a chance pointed out that at 211 pounds, Louis was at his heaviest ever, and that in his recent bout, when he kayoed Conn in eight rounds, he had looked lackluster.

At the bell, Louis forced the action and Mauriello retreated toward the ropes. Louis landed a couple of punches, and then it was like a bully forcing a scared kid backward. But suddenly, like a desperate kid cornered, Mauriello lashed out with a right to the jaw. It caught Louis flush and he staggered; he was driven across the ring. The champion was in real trouble, but Mauriello, never fast going forward, seemingly took a long time to get across to Louis. When he got there, he was on top of Louis, firing both hands. But now the champion's head was beginning to clear. Mauriello came in wide open and took a solid right to the jaw. Louis followed with a left and a right to the jaw. Mauriello was hurt. After a left hook to the head, the challenger sank to the canvas in a neutral corner. He failed to beat the count of referee Arthur Donovan, and it was "Louis, the winner and still champion, after two minutes, nine seconds first round." When I interviewed Tami after the fight, he almost made the microphone shiver as he uttered these immortal words, "I got too goddamned careless." Mauriello had come awfully close with a great right-hand punch.

Joe Frazier–Jimmy Ellis
MADISON SQUARE GARDEN, FEBRUARY 16, 1970

In 1970, Muhammad Ali was still inactive because of his draft board problems, and Jimmy Ellis was recognized as champion by the World Boxing Association. However, Joe Frazier was recognized as the champ in New York and several other states. To clear up the confusion, Ellis and Frazier were matched to fight for the vacant title. The battle took place at Madison Square Garden on February 16, 1970.

Here's the way I described the fifth round:

"Frazier brings up a left hook to the mouth. He digs a left hook to the body, a left hook to the jaw. Ellis is hurt. There's another left hook to the head. Ellis goes down in his own corner. He's flat on his face. They're counting over him. Five. Six. He's trying to get up. Seven. He's on one knee. Eight. Ellis is up at the count of nine. Here's Frazier coming after him. The round is almost over. If Ellis can last a few more seconds. Ellis takes two left jabs to the head. Fights back with a left hook on the jaw. Frazier rips a right to the body, and Ellis is down again. Two, three, four, five, six. There's the bell."

The bell saved Jimmy Ellis, but the fight was stopped between rounds, and Joe Frazier from Philadelphia became the undisputed champion.

Muhammad Ali–Earnie Shavers
MADISON SQUARE GARDEN, SEPTEMBER 29, 1977

On September 29, 1977, Muhammad Ali defended the heavyweight championship against hard-hitting Earnie Shavers at Madison Square Garden. Despite Shavers's fine knockout record, the champion was a heavy favorite to win. The challenger had fought sixty times and had won fifty-four, with five losses and one draw. A solid puncher, Shavers had run up fifty-two knockouts in his sixty ring appearances. But he was vulnerable. The knockout artist had been stopped three times—in one round by Jerry Quarry, in five by Ron Stander, and in six by Ron Lyle. Fighters who feature the knockout punch often are kayoed themselves because they come in swinging, disdaining defense and leaving themselves wide open.

Muhammad Ali had been in fifty-six pro fights, winning fifty-four and losing two by decisions to Joe Frazier and Ken Norton. Of course, he had never been stopped. He had proved that he could take a good punch, and that he could rally after being hurt, which was probably why he was such a heavy favorite over Shavers.

No longer the lithe youngster who had won the title from Sonny Liston in 1964, Ali was now thirty-five years old and came in heavy at 225 pounds. He stood six feet three, three inches taller than Shavers, who was thirty-three years old and weighed 211¼.

Arthur Mercante was the referee of what turned out to be a surprisingly close and interesting bout that ended in a hotly disputed decision for Ali.

The bout went the fifteen-round limit, with many of the rounds so close that they could have been called either way. But the second round was the best and most exciting of the fight.

It started with Ali putting out a couple of jabs. Shavers countered with a hard right to the head. They battled evenly for a while, then, with less than a minute to go in the round, the challenger put on a strong rally. He drove a left hook to the head, followed by a right to the head. Muhammad went into the "Ali shuffle" at this point. He put a jab on Shavers's chin. This was typical of Ali. He always had been a great actor in the ring, and out of it as well. When you saw him take powerful punches and then go into his dance, you were never sure whether he was hurt or playing possum. This may have been a foil to impress the judges, which often it did. But quickly, Ali was rocked by a right hand. This time he *was* hurt. Shavers had him in trouble with about fifteen seconds left in the round. Now Ali was playing "rubber legs" in the center of the ring to show that he was not hurt. Shavers went after him, nailing him with a right hand to the jaw. Shavers unleashed a wild right at the bell.

There were no knockdowns in the hard-fought battle. At the end the two judges and the referee all voted 9–6 in rounds in favor of Ali, the winner and still champion. But there were many in the large crowd who disputed the verdict.

Floyd Patterson–Archie Moore
CHICAGO STADIUM, NOVEMBER 30, 1956

The legendary Rocky Marciano retired undefeated as heavyweight champion in 1956, and Floyd Patterson and Archie Moore were matched for the title in the Chicago Stadium on November 30, 1956. Floyd was five weeks short of being twenty-two years old, Archie was two weeks short of being forty-three. Patterson, with his terrifically fast hands, had a lead as the fight went into the fifth round.

Patterson took a short right, then a left hook to the head. Moore followed with a light jab to the chin. Patterson countered with a short right to the head. Moore was dug to the body by a left hand. Both landed left hooks to the body simultaneously. Moore was short with two left hands. Patterson hooked a left to the jaw and Moore went down flat on his face. At the count of four he was getting to his knees. At six he staggered to his feet. Patterson was on him quickly. A short right by Floyd, and Archie was down again. It was all over.

Floyd Patterson became the youngest man ever to win the heavyweight championship.

Ezzard Charles–Joe Louis
YANKEE STADIUM, SEPTEMBER 27, 1950

On March 1, 1949, Joe Louis retired as heavyweight champion. Since winning the title by a knockout from James J. Braddock in 1937, Louis had defended the crown a record twenty-five times. Ezzard Charles and Jersey Joe Walcott were the two best heavyweights around, and they battled for the vacant title in Chicago in June 1949 with Charles, who weighed only 181 pounds, winning a unanimous fifteen-round decision over Walcott who was 194½.

Louis's retirement was of short duration and he was matched to fight Charles for the title at the Yankee Stadium on September 27, 1950. Going into the fifteenth round, it was obvious that the ex-champ needed a knockout to win.

Charles started the round by missing a left hook, then hooking a hard left to Joe's head. That punch put Joe in trouble, but he came back with a right, high on the head. Charles scored with a right to the face, and another right drove Louis back. Time was running out on the fight and on Louis, too. He no longer was the dark destroyer of old. Charles worked the midsection, but Louis was able to tie him up. Louis brought up a right uppercut and jabbed a left to the nose.

To no one's surprise, Charles retained the title with a unanimous decision.

It was the Brown Bomber's last shot at the crown he had worn with such dignity for twelve years.

The Greatest Fighter

The most difficult part of writing this book has been to answer a question people have been asking me for years: Who would I nominate as the greatest fighter I saw in the years when I was in my prime as a radio and TV commentator of the nation's best fights? That would be the period between 1941, when I did the Joe Louis–Billy Conn heavyweight championship, and 1981, when I did the Sugar Ray Leonard–Thomas Hearns welterweight championship. That era was the heyday of hundreds of great fighters. Limiting myself to this era allows me to eliminate some titans of the ring who came before that, such as John L. Sullivan, Jack Johnson, Jack Dempsey, Gene Tunney, Mickey Walker, Benny Leonard, Henry Armstrong, Barney Ross, and many, many other greats of the squared circle. Also not included in my consideration are other fighters who hadn't achieved greatness by 1981 but who might now be considered. These would include Marvin Hagler, Sugar Ray Leonard, who had not yet fulfilled his great potential, Thomas Hearns, who has as much potential as anyone, and Mike Tyson, who, as I write this, shows the same possibilities of greatness that Joe Louis did at a comparable stage in his career. Certainly some of the earlier greats should be on an all-time list, and some of today's young battlers will end up there, too. But in making my call I have limited myself to those I broadcast and was able to concentrate on. This is only one man's opinion.

How do you go about picking the best of a list that includes Joe Louis, Rocky Marciano, Muhammad Ali, Larry Holmes, Sugar Ray Robinson, Willie Pep, Roberto Duran, Marcel Cerdan, Carlos Monzon, Tony Zale, Bob Foster, Billy Conn, Archie Moore, and so many others?

In trying to come up with the best, I find myself forced to evaluate several different factors. It's easy enough to go through the *Ring Magazine Record Book* and look for facts, and conclude, for instance, that Marciano was better than Joe Louis because in the one time they met, Rocky knocked Joe out. But it would be laughable to say that Trevor Berbick was better than Muhammad Ali because, in the Great One's last bout, Berbick outpointed him. I find myself thinking in terms of how good a man was in his prime. What were his outstanding qualities? How big was his fighting heart? On that basis, perhaps Marciano would have been a test for Louis, but Berbick was not even in the same league as Ali.

Also to be considered, if you keep looking at the record book, are those fighters who won titles in two divisions. There were many, of course, but the ones who stand out in my mind are Carmen Basilio, welterweight and middleweight, Emile Griffith, welterweight and middleweight, Dick Tiger, middleweight and light heavyweight, and Roberto Duran, lightweight and welterweight. These men were outstanding and should receive fistic badges of merit. So should some others who won more than one title. Please don't remind me that Robinson won two titles, because I'm going to get to him later.

In making my way toward the greatest, I think of two great

middleweights from foreign countries, Carlos Monzon from Argentina, and Marcel Cerdan from Algeria. Both of them had fantastic records and both were middleweight champions. Monzon fought 102 times, winning 89, with 61 knockouts. He lost three decisions, fought nine draws, and had one no-contest. To my knowledge, he fought only once in the United States, knocking out Tony Licata in ten at Madison Square Garden. Aside from that bout, I saw him only a couple of times on TV. Monzon certainly rates consideration as the all-time great, and maybe some future historian will rate him as such, but based on my limited exposure I can only give him honorable mention.

Marcel Cerdan's situation is similar, but I did several of his fights and saw him more often in person. The gallant Frenchman had a fantastic record, fighting 115 times, winning 111 of his fights, and scoring 66 knockouts. He lost once on a decision and twice on fouls. Cerdan won the middleweight championship by knocking out Tony Zale in twelve rounds, and then defended against Jake LaMotta. In this bout, he injured his shoulder in the second round and fought the next eight rounds with only one hand. He was finally stopped in the tenth. He was on his way back to this country for a return bout with the Bronx Bull when he was killed in a plane crash. I have nothing but admiration for Cerdan as a person and as a boxer. The sport should have more like him.

Another plane crash victim was Willie Pep, who was injured while at the height of his career. His legs were hurt in the crash, but he continued to fight, though he was slowed a little bit. He was a remarkable performer. I can't pick him as the greatest all-around fighter, but I can say that from a pure boxing standpoint, Willie Pep was the greatest I ever saw. It's too bad that his efforts were not preserved on TV. It was unbelievable what this will-o'-the-wisp from Hartford did in the ring.

Carmen Basilio didn't have the greatest record, but no one had a greater heart. After winning the welterweight title, Carmen outpointed the great Robinson at Yankee Stadium to win the middleweight championship. He lost it in a return bout in Chicago, with one eye closed early in the fight. His gameness was unparalleled as he fought the action against the great Sugar Ray. He lost in a split decision that saw the referee voting for him.

This brings my list of great fighters down to the final four: Joe Louis, Rocky Marciano, Muhammad Ali, and Sugar Ray Robinson. These fighters had similar qualities that made them stand out. Ali was probably the fastest heavyweight champion in history, and, as he himself would modestly admit, he was the prettiest as he "floated like a butterfly and stung like a bee." He had a fine jab and good combinations, but his power was questionable and so were some of the close decisions he received.

Louis, though not flashy like Ali, was a fine boxer and had the best left jab from a standpoint of power. He had great patience and his combinations were awesome. Although often roughed up by opponents, the Brown Bomber never retaliated in kind. Prior to Louis, it was customary for the heavyweight champion to defend once a year, although Jack Dempsey went three years without a fight between his bouts with Firpo and Tunney. Louis held the heavyweight title for twelve years and changed heavyweight title procedure by defending it a record twenty-five times. He left a great mark on the game.

No one ever accused Rocky Marciano of being a good boxer, but with his power, he didn't have to be. Early in his career, it was said he would take two to give one, but that changed under the expert tutelage of his little trainer, Charlie Goldman. In size and style, Rocky has been compared with Joe Frazier. But Joe, great fighter that he was, got by with the left hook (as Ali well remembers). Marciano, on the other hand, could fell you with either fist. And as he improved, he became more difficult to fight. He developed a "moving crouch," moving from side to side with both hands at the ready. The opponent had to be careful not to miss, for Rocky was a deadly counterpuncher. His record is unequaled in the heavy-weight division—forty-nine fights, forty-nine wins, forty-three of them by knockout. That's greatness.

And now we come to Sugar Ray Robinson, of whom many of the

experts have said, "Pound for pound he was the greatest." I'll confine my appraisal of Robinson to the years when I was broadcasting. We were contemporaries. He fought his first fight on October 4, 1940. I did my first network broadcast on June 18, 1941. Unusually tall for a lightweight at five-eleven, a scrawny kid at the time, he dazzled the fans and opponents with his speed, his footwork, and his good punch. As a nineteen-year-old, he won six bouts, five by kayo. At twenty years, he won twenty bouts with twelve knockouts. His was no padded record. Among his victims were good fighters of the time: George Zengaras, Jimmy Tigh, Joe Gnouly, Sammy Angott, Maxie Shapiro, Marty Servo, and Fritzie Zivic. Angott was the lightweight champion at the time, and Robinson beat him in a ten-round, over-the-weight match. Servo was a future welterweight champion, and Zivic was a former welterweight titleholder.

On July 2, 1941, I broadcast the Fritzie Zivic–Al "Bummy" Davis bout at the Yankee Stadium. That was the first time I saw Robinson fight. He dispatched one Pete Lello in four rounds, and you could tell he was headed for Olympian heights. The first Robinson fight I broadcast was on September 19, 1941, at the Garden. He kayoed a good fighter, Maxie Shapiro, in three rounds.

His bout with Zivic on October 31, 1941, was his first big test. There were those who felt that Zivic, who had fought the best, had too much experience for Robinson. It was a good close fight, and proved that Robinson had made the big time. He won a ten-round decision over the wily Pittsburgher. The bout was so fast that I had trouble keeping up with the punches in my blow-by-blow description. There is a cute story connected with that bout. Zivic was managed by Luke Carney, an old-time veteran of the fistic wars. Robinson was managed by Curt Hohrman, a scion of the Rubsam and Hohrman brewery people. Curt was not a real boxing man, and Carney used to belittle Robinson and Hohrman, calling them amateurs. When Robinson beat Zivic, Hohrman went up to Carney and said, "Hey, Luke, is it all right if we turn pro now?"

The return bout with Zivic a few months later attested to Robinson's greatness. In the ninth round of a close bout, Zivic caught Robinson coming in, with a powerful solar plexus punch. It landed flush in the midsection. I saw that Robinson was hurt. His mouth flew open and his mouthpiece went flying. But a split second later, Robinson landed a whipping right to Zivic's jaw. Zivic went down, face-first into the canvas. Before or since, I have never seen a fighter who went down face-first. Zivic staggered up, chalk-white from the rosin dust. Referee Arthur Donovan had to stop the fight temporarily. He took out his handkerchief and wiped off Zivic's face to keep the dust from getting into his eyes. The temporary respite was not enough for Zivic. Robinson now easily kayoed him. The Sugar Man had arrived.

Robinson continued his winning ways, taking his first forty bouts, twenty-nine of them by knockouts. He was meeting tough opposition, Angott and Servo again, Izzy Jannazzo, Maxie Berger, and Jake LaMotta, whom he defeated in ten. On February 5, 1943, as a welterweight, Robinson again took on the middleweight La Motta and lost his first bout, a ten-round nod. In all, he fought the rugged LaMotta five times and won four of them, the last by a kayo.

After the loss to LaMotta, it was over eight years and ninety-one bouts before he lost again. In that time he won the welterweight title and the middleweight crown. His streak ended when he was enjoying a trip to Europe and took on a British fighter, Randy Turpin, in London to help pay expenses. Turpin was a tough customer and took the middleweight title from Robinson by decision. That was July 10, 1951. In September at Yankee Stadium, Robinson took it back via a ten-round kayo.

It's clear that Robinson was good enough to win the lightweight title, but he never fought for it. He won the welterweight crown, and won and lost the middleweight title in bouts with Gene Fullmer, Carmen Basilio, and Paul Pender. And he was winning the light heavyweight title in a bout with Joey Maxim, the champion. The bout was fought in 106-degree heat and Robinson was so far ahead that had the fight gone the limit, he would have won easily. But a dehydrated Sugar Ray, outweighed by fifteen and a half pounds, couldn't answer the bell for the fourteenth and suffered a TKO. It was the only time he failed to go the distance in 201 bouts over a span of twenty-five years.

Louis, Marciano, Ali, and Robinson. They are my top four. They had a lot in common. Someone once said all fighters have courage, but some have more than others. These four had courage to the nth degree. They had the ability to respond to pressure, to come from behind when they had to.

Louis did it in the first fight with Billy Conn. He was a beaten man going into the thirteenth round. His title was about to take wing, but he came through with a knockout.

Marciano, challenging Jersey Joe Walcott for the title, took an incredible beating from an aroused champion in the eleventh and twelfth rounds. At the mike, I didn't think Rocky could make it. But a single right-hand punch in the thirteenth round devastated Walcott, and Rocky took the title. That was coming from behind. Defending the title against ex-champion Ezzard Charles, Rocky suffered a slashed nose in the seventh round. Between rounds, his handlers couldn't stop the bleeding. It was a mess. Reluctantly the officials let the bout go one more round. That was all Rocky needed. He kayoed Charles in the eighth.

Muhammad Ali, coming back from exile because of his stand on the draft in the Vietnam War, fought tough Oscar Bonavena at the Garden. A win would put Ali into the big-money title match with Joe Frazier, but Ali was losing the bout in the fifteenth round. He needed a knockout to win. He got it. He kayoed Bonavena.

Robinson lost the middleweight crown to Randy Turpin in London, then fought a return at the Yankee Stadium. Sugar Ray was winning the fight, but he suffered a badly cut eye in the ninth round. He was in jeopardy as the officials were ready to stop the bout. They let it go another round and Robinson came through and kayoed Turpin in the tenth.

Louis, Marciano, Ali, Robinson. It's tough to pick one out of that four. They were all great. I knew them all, admired them, and saw them at their best. With the exception of Marciano, they all suffered losses, but these losses usually came at the end of a great career, when Louis, Ali, and Robinson had retired and tried ill-advised comebacks.

Louis, Marciano, and Ali were, to me, the best of the heavyweights. But Robinson was unquestionably the best of three divisions—lightweight, welterweight, and middleweight—and he was winning the light heavyweight title when the 106-degree heat did him in. I agree with those who say Sugar Ray Robinson was the greatest. He's my choice for Number One.

Terrible Fights

Many times a fight is so good and so glamorous that it calls for a return bout. That happened after three heavyweight championship bouts: Louis–Conn, 1941; Marciano–Walcott, 1952; and Ali–Spinks, 1978. They were all great fights. Unfortunately, the return bouts were not.

After Conn's great but losing effort in 1941, there was so much interest that promoter Mike Jacobs did something almost unimaginable for their return match in 1946. He charged $100 for ringside seats. This had never been done before, but Mike was a great promoter, and knew what he was doing. And he knew what he was not doing. The return match was set for June 19, 1946, five years and a day from their historic first meeting. Conn and Louis had been in the service from 1943 to 1945 and had seen no ring action.

Many experts went to Jacobs and said it would be good if Louis and Conn had tune-up bouts before their rematch. "No way," said Jacobs. He was afraid they had left their skills in the service. A bad tune-up bout might kill the gate at the rematch. Jacobs was right. The return go was a dog, as Louis and Conn lumbered through eight rounds, Joe finally ending it with a knockout.

The second Marciano–Walcott bout was even worse. Their first fight had been one of the all-time greats, but in the return bout, less than a year later, Walcott went down from a Marciano charge and was counted out in 2:25 of the first round. You can't blame Rocky. He did what he was paid to do.

In February 1978, Leon Spinks, with practically no ring record at all, surprised the boxing world by outfighting Muhammad Ali and winning the title by decision. Promoter Bob Arum rematched them in September of that year. The return bout, a dreary affair, proved one or both of two things: either Ali had been woefully out of shape in the first fight or hadn't taken Spinks seriously. Anyway, Ali took the title back, and Leon Spinks was never again in contention.

Gosh, in thinking of important fights that were terrible, I almost forgot the Joe Louis–Lou Nova bout for the heavyweight title at the Polo Grounds, September 29, 1941. This is understandable. It was an easy fight to forget. In fact, it was a real bomb.

After the smashing success of the Louis–Conn fight, which achieved a record 56.4 listener rating, those of us connected with the new fight series found our enthusiasm running high. It ran even higher when we learned that the great Louis was putting the title on the line again, against so formidable an opponent as Lou Nova.

Prior to the Conn fight, there were those who said that Nova should have been the opponent of Louis in the June bout. And Nova himself insisted that he should have been. After Conn's great showing in the Louis bout, Nova's stock reached a new high. After all, he was a legitimate heavy, while Conn was only a light heavyweight. Nova was about the same weight and height as Louis, and he had a heavyweight's punch.

In those days before television, it was usual for a movie company to film an entire prizefight and show it in theaters around the world. This was done with the Louis–Conn fight, and it was a real moneymaker. So a deal was made to film the Louis–Nova go. A couple of days before the fight, General John Reed Kilpatrick, the president of Madison Square Garden, called me to his office, told me about the screening of the fight, and agreed to pay me a nice sum if on occasion during my blow-by-blow description I would say something like "That punch will look good in the movies of the fight." I wasn't to overdo it, just a few times during the fight. I agreed, and looked forward to the scrap.

The fight was terrible, and it wasn't easy to sneak in an occasional mention of the movie. Nova had come into the fight claiming he had a "cosmic punch" with which he would knock out Louis. Joe referred to it as a "comic punch." Actually, it was neither. Nova's punching was nonexistent and the champion knocked him out at 2:59 of the sixth round of a dreary affair.

The day after the fight, General Kilpatrick again called me to his office and told me that the fight was so bad that the movie company wouldn't show it anywhere. However, the general said, it wasn't my fault, and he gave me a check for what he had promised me.

Some time after that, I was at the bar in Toots Shor's when Nova walked in with Tom Gallery, at the time a West Coast promoter. They came up to me and Nova said, "Tom, I want you to meet the guy who made me look good against Joe Louis."

We all had a hearty laugh over that.

Rewriting History:
The Archie Moore Incident

On October 3, 1985, I was at ringside at the Riviera Hotel parking lot in Las Vegas for the radio broadcast of the Larry Holmes–Michael Spinks heavyweight championship bout. With me on the broadcast for Don King's promotion were Lou Boda, Art Rust, and Sam Nova. John Chanin was the producer of the show. It was a historic bout by boxing standards, and there were some interesting circumstances surrounding it.

Michael Spinks was the light heavyweight champion at the time. No light heavyweight champion had ever won the heavyweight title. Some had come close, notably Billy Conn, who led champion Joe Louis on points going into the thirteenth round, an unlucky round for Billy, who was kayoed.

Rocky Marciano was the only former heavyweight champion to

have retired "undefeated and untied," as they say in football. Hard-hitting Rocky had won all his forty-nine bouts, forty-three of them by knockouts, and stepped down undefeated in 1956. In his last bout in 1955 at Yankee Stadium, he knocked out light heavyweight champion Archie Moore in nine.

Which brings us to Larry Holmes. Holmes was undefeated after forty-eight bouts. He was a big favorite to beat Spinks, and if he had, he would have tied Rocky's mark of forty-nine in a row without a defeat. In all probability he would then have won his next bout and set a new heavyweight championship record of fifty in a row without a defeat.

I remember saying on the air before the bout that my list of great heavyweight champions had Joe Louis, Rocky Marciano, Muhammad Ali, and Larry Holmes at the top, not necessarily in that order. But, I added, should Holmes lose to Spinks or subsequently, I would have to drop him down on the list. At the time that didn't seem a likelihood.

Rocky's record was definitely on Holmes's mind in the days before the fight. He mentioned it several times in press conferences. I began to wonder whether Larry was fighting Spinks or Rocky's ghost. But there seemed little chance that Holmes would lose to a light heavyweight who had suddenly put on twenty-five pounds and weighed just under two hundred pounds at the weigh-in.

Now Archie Moore enters the picture. Archie, a great, smart fighter in his day, joined the Holmes camp as an adviser for the Michael Spinks fight. Archie has always been very voluble and was great copy for the sportswriters. He gave them many, many interesting stories.

Much of the pre-fight preparations and publicity from Holmes and his handlers referred to Marciano's record. It was mentioned constantly in the press conferences, and it was all over the newspapers, radio, and television. Not to be outdone, Archie Moore joined in, but his approach was different. In his own words, we heard for the first time that Archie, who had floored Marciano in the second round of their 1955 bout, had been kept from winning by the referee, Harry Kessler, who got in Moore's way after the knockdown, kept him from following through on the offensive, and allowed Marciano precious seconds to recover. It reminded one of the famous Dempsey–Tunney "long count" in Chicago of 1927.

These statements by Moore came as quite a surprise to a lot of people, as they heard them during Art Rust's prefight interview, which was taped earlier:

MOORE: In the second round he came out after me, he came right after me swinging punches and he missed one and he started another one—overhand right. It was then I picked him off with the right uppercut counter. He dropped to both knees and one elbow in a tripod landing so I swung around and stationed myself in the nearest corner to him. Marciano took the count of two. Then he arose at two and walked to the ropes near me and placed his both forearms on the rope as though in an appeal to the audience and a benign smile on his face as if apologizing for being knocked down. . . . And I said, now I'm gonna have to fight these sixty-one thousand people here in Yankee Stadium. He was out of it. And, uh, referee Kessler took that opportunity to jump in between us and seize Marciano's gloves. And he wiped 'em. . . . In the meantime there was supposed to be no mandatory count. . . . See, now Marciano has been up on his feet now at least five seconds and then he looked back at me and he said, "Go to the corner over there," and I didn't go. . . . He continued to wipe Marciano's gloves like that . . . and then he sent me to the corner. . . . I knew what he was doing, he knew what he was doing [unintelligible]. . . .

RUST: You still feel you should have won the fight?

MOORE: I should have won the fight in the second round. That was the only chance I had, the only opportunity I had. When I knocked him down. I blew that and I was still fighting.

RUST: All right now, we both were at ringside in September 1955. . . . The third man in the ring that night was the St. Louis metallurgist, one Harry Kessler. What's your response to what Archie said about that, Don?

DUNPHY: Well, I'm, I'm disappointed in Archie Moore. I thought he could be a little more gracious. He's rewriting history, thirty

years later. I've never heard this before. I never read about it. I
was an avid reader of all the papers before the fight. I was at the
fight. It was a flash knockdown. Rocky bounced right up, and from
then on, it was all Rocky until he knocked out Moore in the ninth
round. I think he's castigating the referee unfairly. We ought to get
the films of the fight. But I'm really surprised at Archie. I always
thought he was a great gentleman. Frankly, I'm disappointed.

RUST: You're saying it's balderdash or poppycock, huh?

DUNPHY: Well, at least one of them.

At this point Lou Boda, the anchorman of the broadcast and a
fine sports announcer, entered the conversation.

BODA: I think, Art, before you go on here, the case that Don
makes that we ought to, say, look at the documentation, that one
of the writers in New York did look at films and says there's nothing
like that that happened.

I'd like to repeat what I've always said, that Archie Moore is one
of the all-time great light heavyweights. I thought it was a pity that
he brought this matter up for the first time after so many years.
Maybe all the hoopla around the idea of Holmes beating Rocky's
record brought a wished-for history to life in Moore's memory. Both
Holmes and Moore wanted to have beaten the Rock from Brock,
but there's no shame in their having come as close as they did and
failed.

Eddie Eagan

Eddie Eagan was one of the finest men I ever met. He was indeed a true Olympian.

A great athlete, Eddie had the unique distinction of being an Olympic champion in two far-from-related sports, sixteen years apart. He was the heavyweight boxing champion in the 1920 Olympic Games in Brussels, Belgium, and a member of the four-man championship bobsled team in the 1936 Olympics at Garmisch.

An outstanding lawyer, he was chairman of the New York State Athletic Commission for many years. This is the body that regulates boxing in the Empire State. In the 1950s, in recognition of his great abilities and contributions to human betterment, President Eisenhower appointed Eagan chairman of the important People to People

Committee. To no one's surprise, Eddie did a superb job in this post.

I had long admired Eddie Eagan, and it was a real thrill for me when I found myself sitting next to him on the dais of the Buffalo AC dinner in 1951. We talked of many things: of the difficulties of administering boxing in a great state like New York, about how the sport seemed constantly under siege. I complimented him on his recent reference to boxing as "the last outpost of the underprivileged," which it most certainly is. And of course I mentioned his Olympic exploits.

As a kid growing up in New York City, I had of course been a rabid sports fan. That wasn't unusual; every kid was in those days. I knew batting averages and football statistics, I knew about Man o' War and Sir Barton, and was up on all the other sports information of the day.

Somewhere in the back of my mind I remembered that at that time there were those who thought that Eagan was good enough to fight and possibly beat Dempsey for the world title. Now, as I was sitting beside him, that thought occurred to me again. I asked if he'd ever thought of fighting Dempsey and if he thought he could have beaten him.

"Don," he answered, "we did fight and I'll tell you about it. At this time, shortly after the end of World War I, a committee for refugee relief was formed and it happened that the chairman of the committee was a rabid boxing fan and a good friend and rooter of mine. He cooked up the idea of having Dempsey, the world champion, box me, the Olympic champion, in an exhibition. The idea caught on and a great crowd turned out for the charity affair.

"The bout started quietly enough, with both Jack and I landing some light, meaningless blows. I must say at this point," Eddie continued, "that I too had heard the talk that possibly I could beat Dempsey and I must confess that at times I was intrigued by the idea. As we sparred around the ring, I suddenly got the idea that now was the time to find out. Jack seemed careless, so I waited for an opening. Suddenly, there it was. Quick as I could, I crashed home my Sunday punch, a solid right hand to the jaw. All of a sudden the place was in darkness. My knees were crumbling, bright lights were flashing through my head. But I didn't go down. Two huge arms were around me, holding me up, and a calm voice was whispering in my ear. 'Now, kid,' it said, 'if we take it easy and don't do anything foolish, we'll have a good time finishing out the bout and these people will enjoy themselves.'

"Needless to say, I took the hint and the three-round bout went the limit. That's how much I could have beaten Jack Dempsey!"

Unusual Fights

Fritzie Zivic–Al "Bummy" Davis

When Joe Louis fought Billy Conn at the Polo Grounds in New York in June 1941, the ring announcer, Harry Balogh, introduced the principals of a bout scheduled to be presented at the Polo Grounds a couple of weeks later. Let's listen to Harry:

"Ladies and gentlemen, with your kind permission, please. Again thanking you. Mike Jacobs presents his next all-star boxing show in this ballpark Tuesday evening, July the first. In the feature attraction of twelve rounds duration, a return match that all the boxing fans are waiting for, bringing together the current welterweight champion of the world, Fritzie Zivic. [Loud cheers] Come here,

Fritz. And may I respectfully ask if I may, in view of the fact, his opponent, a soldier in the U.S. Army, doing his humble share for the safety and democracy of America. Let's give him an ovation, Private Albert Davidoff, better known to us as Al Davis."

Davis was generally known as "Bummy" Davis. Zivic had won the welterweight crown by outpointing the great Henry Armstrong on October 4, 1940, at the Garden. A few weeks after that, in November, he had fought an over-the-weight bout at the Garden against Davis. It was one of the zaniest fights I ever saw. Right or wrong, Zivic had a reputation as a dirty fighter who, on occasion, would thumb his opponent's eyes. There were those who said this was a bout between "Bummy" and "Thumby." I must say that I saw Zivic in action many times and never saw him commit an infraction. Davis was a rough fighter with a powerful left hand. He apparently believed the rumors about Zivic and felt that Fritzie either was thumbing or was trying to.

In the second round, all hell broke loose. Davis began to retaliate. A southpaw, he suddenly became like a submarine pitcher in base-ball, throwing underhand punches—below the belt, if you will. The punches, as I remember them, actually swept the ring floor as they made their way to Zivic's groin. Fritzie tried to defend what the legendary Jimmy Johnston used to call "the family jewels" by using his gloves to stop them, and by leaping a foot high every time an underhander arrived. But Davis wouldn't be denied. He trailed the fleeing Zivic around the ring, pouring in one low blow after another, shaking off the referee's attempts to stop him. The Garden was in bedlam; the thousands of fans were on their feet, half of them booing Davis, the other half cheering him on. I remember Boxing Com-missioner John Phelan shaking his hands and running around the ring, yelling something like, "This is awful. This is awful." It sure was. Finally his handlers and the referee were able to grab Davis and stop the one-man riot. Order was restored and Davis was dis-qualified. He was hauled before the Boxing Commission and sus-pended for life. For life? Well, you know boxing. Seven months later, at the Louis–Conn fight, here was Harry Balogh announcing the

Davis–Zivic rematch. He made a nice figure in his army uniform. Too bad he couldn't wear it in the return bout. Zivic, an active fighter, caught Davis woefully out of shape as a boxer after his time in the service, and punished him unmercifully. He floored Davis in the first round to show him who was boss, then battered him round after round and finally knocked him out in the tenth. The bout could have been called "Fritzie's Revenge" or "Davis's Demise."

Jimmy Carter–Tommy Collins

One of the most bizarre and almost tragic of boxing bouts occurred in the Boston Garden when lightweight champion Jimmy Carter defended his title against Boston's Tommy Collins, a challenger who seemed capable enough on paper. The date was April 24, 1953, and about twelve thousand were in attendance. The bout was covered nationally by both television and radio, and I called the blow-by-blow on radio.

In 1951, Carter had won the title with an upset kayo of the great Ike Williams in the fourteenth round at Madison Square Garden. He lost the title on a fifteen-round decision to Lauro Salas in Los Angeles on May 14, 1952, and won it back from Salas on a fifteen-round decision in Chicago on October 15 of that year. After a few other matches, he defended against Tommy Collins.

On this occasion, boxing, the "manly art of self-defense," took a long step back into the dark ages. The bout referred to in newspaper headlines as "the new Boston Massacre" was one of the worst in boxing history. It was the worst I ever broadcast. After two uneventful rounds, the whole thing exploded unbelievably. In the third, Carter floored Collins. Then he floored him again. Then a third time. They didn't have the three-knockdown rule in Boston, or the bout would have ended there in a kayo by Carter. Collins kept getting up, and Carter kept knocking him down. Four times, five times. Outmatched and outgunned through no fault of his own, Collins was all heart, and kept coming back for more. He got it,

too. Seven knockdowns in one round. Collins showed courage un-
surpassed in the annals of fistiana. The referee was brave, too.

In fact, he was one of the bravest referees I ever saw, as he
permitted the carnage to continue. An ex-fighter himself, he was
most culpable in permitting a fighter under his jurisdiction to be
floored again and again. He stood by and counted seven different
times over Collins in the third round and three more times in the
fourth. All this while, the twelve thousand Collins rooters booed
and begged that the fight be stopped. Finally, after the tenth knockdown, while the referee was counting, Collins's handlers got the idea
and jumped in the ring to end the fight. It should have been done
a lot sooner. The referee alone wasn't to blame for this sickening
action. The Commission doctor sat idly by through all this and made
no move. He was sitting behind me, and I turned around to him, almost pleading after the third round. But he made no move. He
didn't even bother to examine Collins between the third and fourth
rounds, and was immobile through the three knockdowns of the fourth.

And where were the Massachusetts boxing commissioners while
the mayhem was going on? No one seemed to know. No move was
made to stop it. Finally they put in an appearance the next day and
absolved the referee of all blame.

Boxing has been, is, and always will be a target for reformers. If
it is to survive as a sport, it must be kept clean and regulated within
itself. Unfortunately, the Boston Massacre was a black eye to the
innocent as well as to the guilty.

All this happened about thirty-four years ago. I have deliberately
not mentioned the names of the referee or the doctor. I see no point
in embarrassing them after so many years, but the story needs to
be remembered as a warning.

Jack Sharkey–Max Schmeling

In June, 1932, Ted Husing aired the heavyweight championship
bout between champion Max Schmeling and Jack Sharkey at the

Madison Square Garden Bowl in Long Island City. A brief history of the heavyweight championship up to that time might be in order at this point. Gene Tunney took the title from Jack Dempsey in 1926, successfully defended against Jack in 1927 and Tom Heeney in 1928, and then retired undefeated as a heavyweight, although he had lost an earlier light heavy bout to Harry Greb. The title was vacant from the summer of 1928 until July of 1930, when Jack Sharkey, recognized as the number-one heavyweight, was matched with Max Schmeling of Germany for the crown. The bout, held at Yankee Stadium June 12, 1930, drew a crowd of 79,222, paying a gate of $749,935.

In those days a fighter could win a bout on a foul, and many had. Some, it was claimed, were hit on the belt line, then grasped at their groin seemingly in pain as they headed for the canvas. It worked more often than not, and if you go back through old ring records, you will see notations like "WF4," which means, "won on a foul in the fourth."

In the fourth round of this fight, Schmeling went down from a punch to the midsection. Was it fair or foul? Schmeling lay there supposedly in pain. Films show referee Jimmy Crowley racing from one side of the ring to the other. According to Frank Menke's *New Encyclopedia of Sports*, the blow landed after two minutes and fifty-five seconds of the round. Crowley and one judge, Charles Matheson, did not see the blow. Harold Barnes, the other judge, declared he saw it, and on his word, Crowley disqualified Sharkey. The bout ended in wild disorder.

A week later the New York Commission, by a two-to-one vote, appointed Schmeling as champion. On the Commission, Jim Farley and John Phelan favored the German as champion, but Commissioner Bill Muldoon voted against it, on the grounds that winning on a foul did not prove that Schmeling was a worthy champion. Shortly after this, the rule was changed so that a fighter couldn't win a bout on a foul.

Gus Lesnevich–Billy Fox

I'm sure you've heard of the "trap play" in football, but have you ever heard of one in boxing? I saw one in a light heavyweight championship bout at Madison Square Garden on March 5, 1948. Gus Lesnevich was the champion at the time. Gus, from Cliffside Park, New Jersey, had been at the top or near the top of the division for years. In 1939 and again in 1940 he had fought the then title holder, Billy Conn, for the crown, each time losing a close fifteen-round bout. In 1941 he had defeated Anton Christoforidis for the NBA light heavyweight title. This was the bout in which I took the audition to become announcer for the Garden bouts. That year Billy Conn gave up the title to campaign as a heavyweight and Gus fought Tami Mauriello and beat him in fifteen rounds for the vacant world title. Gus again beat Mauriello in a return bout later that year, then was inactive for a couple of years because of the war. In 1946 he went to London to defend against Freddie Mills and kayoed the Englishman in ten.

In 1947, "Black Jack" Billy Fox, a young phenomenon from Philadelphia, amassed a terrifically impressive record and challenged Gus for the title at Madison Square Garden. It was a tough fight, but Lesnevich's greater experience carried him to victory over the youngster, whom he finally kayoed in ten rounds. But it was a tough and grueling fight for the champion.

They were rematched at the Garden on March 4, 1948. On November 14, 1947, Fox had stopped indestructible Jake LaMotta in what became known as "the tainted bout." Now it was felt that Fox had the experience necessary to beat Lesnevich for the crown. He had given a good account of himself against Lesnevich in the first bout, and many thought he could unseat the champion, who had by then been fighting for fifteen years.

I don't know what Lesnevich's thoughts were on the subject, but that night he introduced the trap play into boxing.

At the bell, the champion and the challenger advanced cautiously toward each other. Lesnevich was known as a very slow starter, so

I'm sure Fox wasn't surprised when Lesnevich grabbed him in a quick clinch. The referee broke them, and Gus quickly grabbed Billy a second time. They separated and Gus clinched again. You could see by the look on Billy's face that he was surprised at the clinching tactics of the champion. After the third clinch, Lesnevich moved toward Fox as though he would clinch again. Not to be outdone, Fox dropped his guard so he could get a better grip on Lesnevich. But, *wham!*—it was no clinch. Gus fired a right-hand shot to Fox's unprotected jaw. It landed with terrific force right on the button and Fox went down and out in round one. Lesnevich was the winner and still champion, because of a well-executed trap play.

Truth or Consequences

Back in the forties, "Truth or Consequences" was a fine and popular radio program. Hosted by Ralph Edwards, it was on the top rung of the ratings. Remember how it went? The contestant would have to answer Edwards's question correctly or take the consequences. Rarely was the question answered, and some of the consequences were hilarious.

One night the consequence was that the contestant would have to fight the "Australian champ." Now, the contestant didn't know it, but the "Australian champ" was a kangaroo lodged in Stillman's Gym, a few blocks across town from the NBC studios. Bill Corum and I were at ringside in Stillman's, ready to report the boxing epic. The contestant, having missed and being forced to take the consequence—of which he was not yet aware—was rushed to an elevator, stripped and adorned with boxing trunks and gloves, then rushed into a cab and across town to Stillman's and up the grimy stairs to his fate.

The kangaroo was ready. He was wearing boxing gloves, and the fight got under way. As bad as the contestant was, the kangaroo was worse. While Bill and I struggled valiantly to make a show of it, it wasn't much. Even a bad fight might have been fun on TV, but this was radio. Why do I remember this ignominious moment? Because I'll never forget Lou Stillman's immortal words. The kangaroo had been in his gym for a couple of days, and it really stank. Stillman was firm. Taking one last sniff, he said, "I'll never allow a kangaroo in this place again."

Harold Johnson–Julio Mederos

I considered Harold Johnson one of the finest boxers among the big men of the forties, fifties, and sixties. A superb boxer with a good punch, he was good enough to win the light heavyweight title. Among the heavies, he was good enough to beat the likes of Jimmy Bivins, Nino Valdes, Ezzard Charles, and Eddie Machen. He was kayoed in three rounds by future champion Jersey Joe Walcott.

At the start of his career he ran up twenty-four straight wins, including fifteen knockouts. There was a time when I felt that Johnson would have had a good chance of beating Floyd Patterson, when the latter was the heavyweight title holder. He had a continuing series with Archie Moore. In late 1951 and early 1952 they fought three ten-rounders to decisions, with Moore winning two of the bouts. Later that year, Moore took the light heavyweight crown from Joey Maxim. Johnson, on another winning streak, was matched with the Old Mongoose for the crown on August 11, 1954, in New York. Johnson was apparently on his way to a victory when Moore, a truly great light heavyweight, nailed him in round fourteen and knocked him out.

This apparently disheartened Johnson, for later in 1954 he was kayoed by "Boardwalk Billy" Smith in two rounds. Johnson then righted himself, for he won decisions from Julio Mederos and Marty Marshall and kayoed Paul Andrews in six.

Which brings us up to May 6, 1955, and a rematch with Mederos at Philadelphia. During the preliminaries, I was chatting with Ralph Grossman of United Press International, who remarked to me that he had talked to Harold Johnson in the dressing room and that he didn't look well. I kept that in mind as Johnson and Mederos squared off for round one.

Johnson seemed to fight in a listless manner and did very little in the first round. Even though he didn't appear to have been hit hard in that round, he wobbled back to his corner after the bell. I remarked on the air that he looked as though he had been drugged. The bell sounded for round two. Johnson came out and Mederos kayoed him quickly. I read in the papers the next day that someone had come into Johnson's dressing room before the fight and given him an orange to suck on. 'Nuf said.

Years later Johnson went on to win the light heavyweight crown.

Benny Leonard

One night in the early spring of 1947, I was watching the bouts at the St. Nick's Arena, when Billy Stevens came over and sat with me. Billy was a very fine boxing writer who knew the game inside out. He covered the sport for a variety of publications and was widely read. Usually he was very warm and ebullient, but this night he seemed troubled. "What's wrong, Billy?" I asked.

"I'm bothered," he said, "by the fact that there is only one referee assigned to these bouts. He starts at 8:00 P.M. for the first bout, and he's still in there alone when the last bout ends near eleven. Many of these officials aren't that young, and even if they were, it's too much for one man to be on his feet for three hours or so. Walking around the fighters, breaking up clinches, watching to see that no one is badly hurt, and then standing in a corner during the one-minute rest between rounds. You mark my words, some night some-one is going to pass out." I had never thought about it before, but he was right. While two or more referees were assigned by the Boxing Commission to the Garden bouts, the smaller clubs, such as the St. Nick's, the Broadway Arena, and the Ridgewood Grove usually got only one. I don't know why, maybe it was to save expenses. How much could they save by having only one referee?

I told Billy I agreed with him and hoped something would be done about it. A short time later, on April 18 of that year, Bill Corum and I were doing a Friday-night fight at the St. Nick's. The Garden was occupied by some other event, so our network fight that evening came from the St. Nick's.

Benny Leonard was the referee that night, and he was the only referee for the entire card. Benny had been the lightweight champion of the world from 1917 to 1924, when he retired undefeated. Ray Arcel, the famous trainer, always maintained that Leonard was the greatest lightweight champion of all time, and Ray had worked with Barney Ross and Roberto Duran, both of whom would be legitimate contenders for that title. I never saw Leonard fight, but respected the words of a veteran of the game, like Arcel.

Benny Leonard always entered the ring with a fine pompadour, and the chances were that at the end of a bout his hair would remain unruffled. Not only did he have great natural ability, but he was exceptionally smart. One night against a fine contender, Lew Tendler from Philadelphia, Leonard saved the title by his quick thinking. Tendler was a southpaw and early in the bout nailed Leonard with his best punch, a straight left-hand shot to the jaw. Leonard was badly hurt, but he didn't go down. He thought quickly, smiled at Tendler, and said, "Come on, Lew, you can hit harder than that." This puzzled Tendler, who was baffled for a moment. He hesitated, thinking Leonard might counterpunch him. That hesitation was all the champ needed. Leonard, in superb condition, recovered quickly and went on to win a fifteen-round decision. Later, Benny admitted that his quick thinking had saved the title. Without that pause, Tendler could have knocked him out.

Like so many great champions, Leonard essayed a comeback as a welterweight in 1931. He won eighteen of nineteen bouts, scoring nine knockouts and fighting one draw. Unfortunately, in 1932, at the age of thirty-six, he faced Jimmy McLarnin at Madison Square Garden. Baby Face, as the Irishman was called, was then at the peak of his career and he easily kayoed the ex-great in six rounds to end the comeback.

Now it's April of 1947 and we're at the St. Nick's with Leonard as the referee. It was hot in the old fight club that night, and under the ring lights it had to be worse. Between the ninth and tenth rounds of the feature bout, I looked at Leonard as he stood in a neutral corner. I remember we smiled at each other. Now the main bout was over, but there was still another four-round bout. This was what was usually called a "fire department bout" or a "walkout bout," whose purpose was to keep the whole crowd from leaving at once, jamming the exits. Corum and I were still on the air, and Benny was the referee for this final contest. I looked at him again. Now, apparently feeling the heat, he had taken off his tie. The extra bout got under way, and Leonard circled the fighters. Suddenly he seemed to slip, and went down. The remaining crowd laughed at the spectacle of a referee on the canvas. It was the same type of laughter that greets an umpire at a baseball game when he is hit by a foul ball, as if the spectators think it didn't hurt. We all waited for Benny Leonard to get up, but he didn't. Now the crowd, sensing something unusual, became very quiet. The fighters stopped fighting and went to Leonard, who just lay there. Dr. Vincent Nardiello of the Boxing Commission staff quickly jumped into the ring and ministered to the fallen referee. After a few moments the doctor looked over at Bill Corum and me, shook his head, and said, "I'm afraid he's out." It was a sad moment. Benny Leonard, born Benjamin Leiner on April 7, 1896, had passed away in the ring. His hair was still unmussed. This greatest of lightweight champions was elected to the Boxing Hall of Fame in 1955.

I remembered what Billy Stevens had said to me. From then on, at least two referees were assigned to an evening's boxing card.

The Madison Square Garden Bowl

The Madison Square Garden setup for boxing had a capacity of about 18,000. This was more than enough for an ordinary fight, and even for championship events. But the Garden occasionally promoted extraordinary bouts that would draw from 50,000 to 90,000. These included such blockbusters as Dempsey–Firpo and Louis–Conn at the Polo Grounds and Louis–Carnera and Louis–Schmeling at the Yankee Stadium. Naturally the Garden had to pay rent to the ballparks for these events, and sometimes the rental, usually on a percentage basis, ran to an awful lot of money. Checking the *Ring Magazine Record Book*, I notice that some bouts promoted by the Garden went over the million-dollar mark. For instance, Dempsey–Firpo drew 82,000 spectators, paying $1,188,603; Dempsey–Sharkey drew 75,000, with a gate of over a million; Joe Louis–Max Baer brought in 85,000 and over a million; the Louis–Schmeling second bout drew 70,000 and over a million. I don't know what percentage the ballparks took, but it could have been anywhere from $100,000 to $250,000 on a million-dollar gate. I imagine the Garden directors winced when they saw these figures, for around 1930 they came up with the idea of building their own outdoor arena. It went up on Northern Boulevard in Long Island City, New York, not far from Queens Plaza, which made it accessible to both the subway and the bus lines. The Arena was not far from Calvary Cemetery, which was fitting, since it was the graveyard of many a champion's hopes.

Between 1932 and 1936, six boxing title holders defended their crowns there, and all lost. No champion ever successfully defended in the Bowl. Three heavyweight champions passed the crown to challengers. In 1932, Max Schmeling lost to Jack Sharkey; in 1933, Sharkey lost to Primo Carnera; and in 1934, Carnera lost to Max Baer. Meanwhile, there was also a lot of losing going on there with the welterweight title. In May 1934, "Baby Face" Jimmy McLarnin lost to Barney Ross. In September of that year, Ross lost it back to McLarnin. After regaining the title at the Polo Grounds, Ross defended against "Hammerin' " Henry Armstrong at the Garden Bowl in 1938. Sure enough, Ross lost, making it six for six in the lost column for the title holders defending at the Madison Square Garden Bowl. Somewhere along the line a wrestling champion, Hans Steinke, managed to be unseated there as well.

Not only were the title holders doing poorly in Long Island City, but the Garden wasn't doing well either. Soon it closed and was turned into a huge post office building. The Madison Square Garden Bowl passed into history, aptly dubbed by the sportswriters "the Madison Square Garden Hole."

PART THREE

PART THREE

The Way It Was

In 1974, Gerry Gross, a television sports producer, called from Hollywood and asked me if I would appear from time to time on a program to be called "The Way It Was." The program would feature great classics from the American sports scene, showing actual films of these wonderful events, newly described and commented on in the studio by the sports announcer who had done the original broadcast. The host of the show would be Curt Gowdy. My performance would be a reprise of my announcing of the classic fights to be shown. Gerry told me that the series would be shown on public television and that Herb Schmertz, who was head of public affairs for Mobil Oil, was very enthusiastic about the idea and wanted Mobil to give the series as a grant to the Public Broadcasting System. I was enthusiastic, too, when I heard of some of the fights Gerry was hoping to use. For starters, he would have the middleweight championship match between Sugar Ray Robinson and Rocky Graziano. Also, he hoped to get Louis–Conn, Zale–Graziano, Pep–Saddler, Robinson–LaMotta, and several others.

Among other top sports events to be included in the program was the famous home-run hit in 1951 at the Polo Grounds by Bobby Thompson of the New York Giants off Ralph Branca of the Brooklyn Dodgers. That one had won the pennant for the Giants. Gerry said he had lined up, besides Thompson and Branca, manager Leo Durocher, Willie Mays of the Giants, and Duke Snider and Clem Labine of the Dodgers. Also scheduled for later appearances were Joe DiMaggio and Tommy Henrich of the Yankees and Cookie Lavagetto of the Dodgers. Bill Bevens of the Yankees would be there too. It was he who almost had the first no-hitter in the World Series in 1947 until Lavagetto broke it, and the game, with a two-out double in the ninth inning. Also on film from that series would be Al Gionfriddo's amazing catch of a drive by DiMaggio.

Among the sports spielers scheduled were Red Barber, Mel Allen, and Dizzy Dean from baseball, and Bob Neal from football.

Naturally, my greatest interest in the series was the boxing sequences. The first one I did was the Robinson–Graziano championship match. At the taping of the program, Robinson and Graziano, though clearly older than when they had fought in 1952, nevertheless looked in good shape and talked well. Ray, as usual, was quiet and reserved; Rocky, ever the blithe spirit, was his usual outgoing self. I was being made up for the program when Rocky passed behind me. "Gee, Don," he said, "why don't you get your hair touched up? You're getting gray." So I was.

It was interesting to note the fighters' reactions as they watched the film of their confrontation twenty-two years earlier. They were looking at the films, trying to remember their thoughts on that long-ago night, while I was doing the blow-by-blow in my staccato style. History didn't change, and the pictures told the story. It was all Robinson in the first two rounds, but in the third Rocky fired one of his wild right hands. It pounded the champion's head and he went down for a second. It was a knockdown and as close as Rocky came to winning the fight. Watching the TV, Rocky looked on intently, giving a little body English as he did. Robinson was calm. They both knew the ending. I knew the ending too, but I had to describe it from the film as though it were just happening. It was an exciting evening at the PBS station in Los Angeles, but the nicest thing about it was when Ray and Rocky left arm in arm for the post-broadcast reception.

The former great heavyweight champion, Joe Louis, was on the program three times with challengers he had beaten: Billy Conn, Jersey Joe Walcott, and Tony Galento. The films were most interesting and so were the fighters—all were good speakers and added a lot to the program. The night before he appeared, Billy and I had a couple of drinks and a lot of conversation about the old days. He was still disappointed about losing to Louis after he seemingly had the fight won going into the thirteenth round.

Walcott still felt he had gotten a bad decision in his first fight with Louis, and a lot of people agreed with him. The pictures showed the champion down after good right hands by Jersey Joe. On the show, Walcott suddenly turned to me and asked who I thought had won the fight. I tried to be diplomatic and skirt the subject, but he persisted. Finally, I had to admit I thought he had deserved the decision. It had been a bad break for Walcott, and he was knocked out by Louis in a return bout. But things righted themselves for him when he knocked out Ezzard Charles to win the title.

Pep–Saddler was a doozey. They had fought three times before this bout, with Saddler scoring two knockouts and Pep, in a dazzling display of boxing skill, winning back the featherweight title. The fight we did on the program was a real brawl, with tactics by both fighters that beggared description. At one point the going got so rough that both fighters went down and took the referee, Ray Miller, down with them. The manly art of self-defense it was not. I was glad when that was over. But like all bitter contestants in boxing, these two were now the best of friends.

Tony Zale and Rocky Graziano were the stars of another show. They fought three times in all for the middleweight championship.

The first two scraps were among the great fights of all time. In the first, at Yankee Stadium in 1946, Zale came from behind in the sixth round to kayo Rocky and successfully defend the title. A year later, in Chicago, Rocky reversed things and took the crown with a six-round kayo of Tony. Unfortunately, there were no films taken of their first two fights, and there was no TV, either. There were no films because the managers of the fighters got into a heated argument over who would control the picture rights. The argument raged and raged, and finally promoter Mike Jacobs threw up his hands in disgust and said there would be no films at all. Through the years, you may have seen the third Graziano–Zale fight on TV and wondered why you never saw either of the first two. Now you know. It's too bad, because, in the long run, pictures of the first two Zale–Graziano fights would have brought the fighters a lot of money. The third fight, in 1948 at Newark, was sort of anticlimactic. Rocky tried hard, but Tony overwhelmed him and knocked him out in three. Having earlier been knocked out by Robinson on the show, Rocky was 0 for 2 on "The Way It Was." Mrs. Zale, Tony's wife, was at the studio as I broadcast the fight. She was always protective of Tony, and came up after the show and bawled the daylights out of me for not saying nicer things about "her Tony." I protested that I had tried to be fair. It didn't seem to impress her, and I could understand her position. There was no question in her mind that Zale was the better fighter, but Rocky was getting rich with his TV commercials and personal appearances. It reminded me of that saying about the Civil War: "Lee was the better general, but they paid off on Grant."

One segment featured films of the Louis–Galento bout for the heavyweight championship on June 28, 1939. Not many had taken the fight seriously beforehand, because Louis was at his peak then, and "Two-Ton Tony," as he was called, had had a checkered career, winning some and losing some. But Galento was not among those who took the bout lightly. The colorful tavern owner from New Jersey had two things going for him. First, he could hit, particularly with a winging left hook, and second, he was fearless. Day after day in the training sessions for the bout, he would taunt the champion with such expressions as "I'll moida da bum." Outwardly, Louis didn't seem to mind, but inwardly it must have gotten under his skin. As Curt Gowdy, Louis, Galento, and I looked at and commented on the fight film, we were reminded again that Galento had been no pushover for the title holder, and that he had carried the fight to Louis, rocking him in the first round and flooring him in the third. But Louis had remained calm and knocked out Tony in the fourth.

As we talked during the screening, I asked Louis, "Joe, were you ever really mad at an opponent? Weren't you really mad at Max Schmeling when you knocked him out in one round in 1938?" Remember, the 1938 fight against the German had come on the eve of World War II; that Schmeling had scored the only win over Louis when he knocked him out in 1936; that Louis was black and that Adolf Hitler was holding up Schmeling as an example of Aryan supremacy. I was trying to get Joe to express his real feelings, and his answer surprised me. First he laughed, then he said, "That's not so. I wasn't mad at Schmeling. That was all newspaper stuff. Schmeling and I were good friends." Now he laughed again and pointed at Galento. "But that little fellow," he said, "he really got me mad. All those mean things he said about me while training for our fight. He got me mad, all right. So I decided to carry him for a while in the fight and punish him for those nasty things. But when he knocked me down in the third round, I decided I better not fool around. He hit too hard. So I knocked him out as quickly as I could."

Our "The Way It Was" program on the Sugar Ray Robinson–Jake LaMotta middleweight championship was most interesting. In that fight LaMotta had been defending the crown. The match took place on February 14, 1951, in Chicago and is often referred to as "the second Valentine's Day Massacre." Ray and Jake watched the film of the fight intently while I described it. It had been a fairly even fight for the first seven or eight rounds, with Robinson then pulling away and finally annihilating LaMotta in the thirteenth before the referee stopped it. But Jake, the Bronx Bull, had somehow preserved his record of never having been knocked off his feet.

Robinson was gracious and generous to LaMotta in the interview following the showing of the film. Then I turned to LaMotta with the logical question, "What happened, Jake?" Jake startled me with his reply.

"I was six and a half pounds overweight the day before the fight with Robinson, and had to spend a lot of time in a Turkish bath to get down to the 160-pound weight limit."

That was hard to swallow. I said to him, "Jake, that's hard to believe. I'm incredulous. Here you are, fighting Ray Robinson, who already is a great fighter. You have beaten him once, but he has beaten you four times. You know he's good. You're an intelligent person. You had a lot of time to train for the fight. How could you let it happen that you were that much overweight the day before the fight?"

Jake was vague with his answer and we let it go at that.

Not only for boxing but for baseball, for football, and for basketball, "The Way It Was" was a program for all seasons and for all sports. It brought you back, for a brief time, the great moments, the great athletic stars, the great announcers of an earlier time. I don't know what happened, but this great show suddenly went off the air in 1978 and hasn't come back since. Gerry Gross was a great producer of a great program. He owes it to everyone interested in sports to bring it back.

The Missing Heir

I never knew my father, Frank Bradley Dunphy. He died when I was only a year old. My mother went back to her parents, Patrick and Ellen Donlan, and they raised me while my mother worked. I didn't know much about my father. I was told he had been a good athlete and had had fine manners. I knew he came from Brookline, Massachusetts, and that his father was a sea captain. Somewhere along the line, I saw a letter from the captain to my mother, also named Ellen, but called Elsie so she wouldn't be confused with my grandmother. Everyone called her Elsie, including me. My grandparents with whom I lived were Mama and Poppa.

The captain's letter, which I recall seeing so many years ago, was written in a strong style, with flowing letters. I remember he said he was eighty-five at the time and was beginning to suffer from arteriosclerosis. He remarked that he hoped my mother and I were getting along well and that I would grow up strong and sturdy and be a good person. He died the following year. My mother received a copy of his will, which she showed me. In it he left me seven hundred dollars. He also left seven hundred dollars to a William Dunphy. It never occurred to me to ask who that was.

I also learned that I had several aunts who still lived in Brookline. I remember one of them coming to our home on 103rd Street in Manhattan one day. As she was leaving, I was playing on the stoop of the house. Since I was only about four years old at the time, I hardly remember her.

I had no other connection with my father's family until one day in early 1941 when a newscaster at WINS whose name, unfortunately, I have forgotten, told me he had met a cousin of mine, an older man, who had known my father. I found this very interesting because I didn't know I had any paternal cousins. But the newscaster assured me he had met a Captain Dunphy at the Maritime Exchange Building in New York, and that the captain was indeed a distant cousin of mine. My skepticism evaporated as I remembered that my paternal grandfather had been a sea captain. I called the Maritime Exchange, which was down near the Battery in Manhattan, and asked to speak to Captain Dunphy. After a few words of greeting, I made an appointment to see him the following day.

Captain Dunphy was a tall, distinguished-looking man with white hair, a mustache, and a goatee. He looked every inch a retired sea captain. He had a very firm grip as we shook hands and said hello. After a few pleasantries, he said he would like to show me something. He took me over to a large glass case that contained the logbooks of many, many old sailing vessels. He removed one, from a ship called the *Willie Rosenfeld*, and pointed to a notation that showed that a Frank Bradley Dunphy had been born on the *Willie Rosenfeld* in San Francisco harbor to Captain William Dunphy and Elizabeth Dunphy *née* Bradley. This was something I had not known, and it was certainly most interesting. Captain Dunphy told me many things I had not known about my father's side of the family. For instance, he told me that my grandfather, Captain William Dunphy, was the number-one captain for the Rosenfeld family, which had a fleet of sailing vessels, and that my father had four sisters. The oldest, Grace, had married Henry, a son of the Rosenfelds. They lived in San Francisco. This encounter with the veteran of the sea and the story of my father's birth on the *Willie Rosenfeld* proved important years later. Captain Dunphy, who must have been about my father's age, was most interesting, and repeated the story my mother had told me about my father being a fine athlete. In 1942, when I married Muriel, the captain was a guest at our wedding, and gave us a beautiful ship's clock that we still cherish. He died in 1943.

Perhaps it was because of pride that my mother rarely, if ever, brought up the subject of my Brookline relatives. Never having known them, I wasn't very curious, but intermittently they would come back into my life. In 1947, when I was doing the fights on a national basis, I got quite a surprise one day. In the mail was a letter from a Boston lawyer, Michael Fahey, who said he had been listening to the fights the previous Friday and heard the name Don Dunphy mentioned. He wondered if I was the Donald Dunphy whom he had been seeking for years. If I was, he wrote, I was a "missing heir"—he used the Latin term for this. Now I remembered a few things: the letter from my grandfather, and his will in which I was remembered; the old sea captain, a cousin who knew my father; and most important, the log book of the *Willie Rosenfeld*, and the notation of my father's birth on the ship. These things raced through my mind as I read Mr. Fahey's letter. I was sure that the lawyer's search for Donald Dunphy was over. I immediately called him in Boston and told him I was convinced I was the one he was looking for. He was pleasant in our conversation, but, being a lawyer, was very skeptical. When I told him, however, of the logbook of the *Willie Rosenfeld*, his skepticism seemed to vanish. He said he had to go over to Dedham, Massachusetts, to check something, but that he would be back to me. Before he hung up, he startled me by saying, "By the way, what do you do on those fights? Are you the referee?" I can use a Latin phrase, too: *Sic transit gloria mundi*.

In about two days, Mr. Fahey got back to me and said I was

indeed the missing heir, the Donald Dunphy for whom he had been searching. This chain of events had been triggered by the death of an Elizabeth McCarthy, a cousin of my father's, who had remembered me in her will. She had died about ten years earlier and left a bank book in my name. Time passed and no one claimed the inheritance. A petition was entered and printed in newspapers that Donald A. Dunphy be declared legally dead. It was signed by the Reverend William Dunphy. Now, for the first time, I found out who the William Dunphy was who had been mentioned in my paternal grandfather's will, and who, like me, had been left seven hundred dollars. He was my half brother! I learned that my father had been married and divorced before he married my mother. For all those years I had assumed I was an only child! I didn't blame the Reverend Dunphy for signing the petition. I'm sure he had tried to locate me, but I no longer lived at 103rd Street. My maternal grandparents had died. My mother lived in Jackson Heights, as did my wife and I. Apparently he had called a Boston station that carried the fights and inquired about me. He was told I was about fifty years old (wrong by eighteen), that I had gone to Fordham University (also wrong, I went to Manhattan College). I received the bankbook of Aunt Lizzie McCarthy, as I later learned she was called. The balance it showed was $1,900. Not a fortune, but it was awfully nice of the lady to remember someone she had never met. Besides, the money wasn't exciting. What was exciting was that my life now entered a new and most interesting phase.

Not only did I discover a half brother, whom I would meet later, but I also found two living aunts—Julia Dunphy, who lived in Brookline, Massachusetts, and Grace Dunphy Rosenfeld, who lived at the St. Francis Hotel in San Francisco. Two other aunts, Marguerite and Elizabeth, had died. Elizabeth was the one who had visited and chatted with me on the stoop so many years before. It was ironic that she had lived at the Plaza Hotel on Fifth Avenue and 58th Street, and had died there in 1938. During that time, I worked at WINS at 58th Street and Park Avenue. Apparently we spent years one block apart and never knew it.

In the midst of all this excitement, I received a letter from a firm called Skip Tracers. They had seen the petition and realized I was the missing person. They wanted to handle the case for me, and would try to get me on a program called "The Court of Missing Heirs." I thanked them but declined the invitation, feeling that the book should be closed on the missing-heir business.

Early in 1948 I was scheduled to broadcast a Holy Cross–Harvard basketball game at the Boston Garden and I felt that this would be a good time to meet my Aunt Julia, who lived on Beacon Street. Mr. Fahey had given me her phone number (I still remember the exchange as Aspinwall), so I called her to set up a meeting. She was delightful to talk to on the phone, and her Boston accent was pleasant to hear. I told her I would drop over the afternoon of the game.

My first impression of Julia was that of a slim, attractive lady in her early seventies. She had never married but apparently was very well off financially. Her apartment was small but tastefully furnished with priceless antiques. She was most enthusiastic in welcoming me, and I felt that she was a very warm person who was genuinely happy to have found a long-lost nephew with a wife and two sons. On her piano was a picture of a priest, and Julia told me that was Father Dunphy, my half brother. I naturally assumed he was a Catholic priest until she mentioned his wife, Helen. She told me that he was a high Anglican priest, had been educated at Harvard, and was an intellectual and an authority on Russia. Most interesting was the fact that he was the pastor of the Wanamaker Church in Philadelphia, which is just around the corner from the Warwick Hotel. This was most ironic, because I had done many broadcasts in Philadelphia and usually stayed at the Warwick. Here were two brothers who for years were within a block of each other and didn't know it. Had he been a sports enthusiast rather than an intellectual, I am sure he would have heard me on the air and would have made the connection. He told me later that he had never seen a fight or listened to me.

I was very interested in finding out about my Aunt Grace, who lived in San Francisco. She had been married to an industrialist out there named Henry Rosenfeld, who had died some time ago. She now lived at the St. Francis Hotel with one Carrie Nicholson, a lifelong companion. Julia told me that Grace also was very happy that I had appeared on the scene.

Father Dunphy, unable to be present that afternoon at Julia's, had asked that I make a date to bring my family to Philadelphia. The following month he met us at the railroad station there. My half brother, William, was a slender man of medium height, about eight years my senior. He had regular features and a most pleasant manner. He greeted all of us warmly, as did his wife, Helen. When we arrived at the rectory we met his mother, Phyllis Dunphy. She was an effusive, warm-hearted person who was most enthusiastic in her meeting with me. Apparently after the divorce she and my father had remained friends. I'm sure she bore my mother and me no resentment. As a matter of fact, she told me she now listened whenever I did a fight. About a week after our visit to Philadelphia, we received a beautiful gift from my Aunt Grace: a complete set of eighteen place settings of her sterling silver. It was an extraordinary gift! When we called to thank her, she said she would be visiting New York, staying at the Waldorf, and looked forward to seeing us there.

When we first met Grace, it was Kentucky Derby Day in 1951. I remember listening to the broadcast of the race as we drove to the city. It was won by a long shot, Count Turf, ridden by Conn McCreary, who was near retirement, and handled by a venerable trainer, Slim Sulley, a friend of mine. Unlike her sister, Julia, Grace was a tiny, round woman, eighty years old. Her hair was snow white, and with her chubby face and elegant manner she reminded me of Queen Victoria. She was delighted to see us, embraced Muriel, and gave her a beautifully wrapped gift of a pearl necklace. From that time until Grace died, Muriel always thought of her as a fairy godmother. Her companion, Miss Carrie Nicholson, was a very pretty, tall, slim woman, also about eighty. Molly, an Irish maid who had been with Grace for many years, was most pleasant. After that first meeting, she followed the sports and radio columns religiously and reported to Grace as soon as it was announced that there would be a fight broadcast from San Francisco. The phone would ring in our Manhasset home, and Grace would be on the other end, asking when I would arrive. In those years there were many fight broadcasts originating from the West Coast, and Muriel and, whenever possible, our boys, Don and Bob—accompanied me. Grace would be at the airport with Van, her chauffeur, to pick us up. She insisted we stay at the St. Francis, and we always had the same suite. Each trip was memorable. During the time we were there—usually a week—Grace would arrange dinner parties and secure tickets for the theater, and if the boys were with us, they would be in the care of Molly and Van. We made several trips with her, including one to Pebble Beach, and we knew San Francisco's best restaurants because we had lunch and dinner at all of them. Our suite always had fresh flowers, fruit, and candy. Her husband, Henry, and she had selected their apartment at the St. Francis just after it was built, following the earthquake of 1906. In those days they had also maintained a home in Piedmont. Years later, when the hotel was in financial trouble, Henry had helped to save it. Consequently, even after her husband's death, when her suite was in great demand because of its prime location, she was never asked to move to a different one, and she remained there until her death, in 1962. Since her husband had been a board member of many companies and banks, including Wells Fargo, she still had many, many friends among the elite of the city. These people were most gracious to us whenever we visited.

Grace and Julia told me many interesting things about my father and my paternal grandfather. Grace told me that when my father, Frank, was a young man, attending Santa Clara University, she, her friend Carrie, and he were walking down a street in San Francisco one day when they passed a curio shop. The girls so admired a vase in the window that Frank said he would get it for them. The price on the vase was fifty dollars. They laughed at him, since they knew he didn't have any money, let alone fifty dollars for a vase. But he insisted that he would get it. Sure enough, in a couple of days Frank showed up at Grace's home and had the vase. He also had two black eyes and a swollen jaw. Alarmed, they asked him what had happened. What happened was how he got the vase.

In those early days of the twentieth century, itinerant boxers used to travel from town to town and city to city, giving exhibitions. Usually a feature of their performance would be to offer fifty dollars to anyone in the audience who would last three rounds with them. And that's what Frank did. He accepted the offer, got in the ring, had the gloves put on, and lasted the three rounds. He took a bad beating, but he lasted, got the fifty dollars, and bought the vase for Grace.

She told me another interesting story about Frank. He was a close friend of the future great author, Arthur Somers Roche. One year on summer vacation, Frank got both of them jobs as deckhands on a tramp steamer going to Europe. Frank showed up for work wearing patent leather shoes. The sight of them sent the seamen into hysterics. One of them, a big, burly guy, carried the hysterics to extremes, made fun of Frank, and started to push him around. Frank stood it for a bit, then turned on his tormentor, giving him a boxing lesson and cutting him to ribbons. The result was that he and Roche were left alone for the rest of the trip. When I heard stories like these, it made me realize how sad it must have been when Frank, then a newspaper reporter, died at the age of thirty-one. It made me more sad that I never knew him.

Julia told me many stories about her father, William, my grandfather. He had sailed around Cape Horn many, many times, and rediscovered Pitcairn Island, later made famous in *Mutiny on the Bounty*. He had put down mutinies himself, and during raging storms had himself lashed to the mast so he could direct his crew. One story about him was poignant:

Upon completing a long sea journey, Captain Dunphy took the *Willie Rosenfeld* into Boston Harbor. He noticed that the flags of many of the ships were at halfmast and inquired about it. He was told they were at half mast because of the death of a sea captain's wife. When he landed, he learned that it was his own wife who had passed away.

Grace died in 1962 in her suite at the St. Francis Hotel, a suite she had occupied since 1907. Julia died in 1966, and my half brother,

Bill, died in 1985, the last of the relatives on my father's side.

I've thought many times about fate and wondered about the often surprising highways and byways of life. In my early years I hardly ever gave the Boston Dunphys a thought, and I'm sure they rarely thought of me except for a brief question in 1941 when my name became prominent on the fights. The answer they probably got from a Boston station apparently didn't come close to identifying me as Frank's son and they forgot about it.

And then all of a sudden in 1947 my life took a joyful turn when a Boston lawyer listening to a prizefight heard the name Don Dunphy and discovered that I was the one he had been searching for for some time.

Grace brought a lot of joy to me and my family, but I think we brought a lot of sunshine to her in her late years. She particularly loved the boys and they her. And she introduced us to a great city, San Francisco. We'll always cherish those times.

Kickapoo Juice

When the Friday-night fights were put on a regular basis, with fifty-two a year, the majority of them came from Madison Square Garden in New York. Naturally, there were many Fridays when the Garden was occupied by other events, such as the circus, the rodeo, and ice shows. On many of these occasions the Friday fights would be taken out of town or to the St. Nicholas Arena at West 66th Street and Columbus Avenue in New York City.

The north side of 66th Street between Columbus Avenue and Central Park West had a riding academy on the park end, and the St. Nicholas Arena on the Columbus Avenue end. Years later, when the American Broadcasting Company was spun off from NBC, its offices and studios were located in the building that had been the

riding academy. Whenever I did a program there, I could still smell
the horses. The old St. Nicholas Arena is also part of the vast ABC
complex. Whenever I visit, I am reminded of the nights we did
fights there. But even my sensitive nostrils can't pick up those old-
time smells.

Dubbed the "Bucket of Blood" by its aficionados, the St. Nicholas
Arena was almost devoid of fresh air. It was a real old-time fight
club, dating back to the turn of the century, with a capacity of about
four thousand. The front of the center balconies projected almost
to the sides of the ring; this made it easy for a disgruntled fan to drop
a chair on those below. Fortunately, I only saw this happen once.

It was bad enough that the St. Nicholas Arena was almost airless.
To make matters worse, most fight fans smoked, and most smoked
cigars. I was doing radio blow-by-blow, and after a couple of fast-
paced rounds one night, I noticed my voice beginning to crack. At
the time I was a patient of Dr. Samuel Farrar Kelly, a well-known
throat specialist. He also treated Kate Smith and Morton Downey.
I don't know if Kate or Morton ever sang at the St. Nick's, so they
must have gone to Dr. Kelly for other reasons. I told him I was
having throat problems in that heat and smoke, and Dr. Kelly
recommended I make up a solution of honey, lemon, and glycerin
in equal parts, put it in a small bottle, and take it with me whenever
I did a fight broadcast. If I felt my throat getting raw, I was to take
a swig of it between rounds. This proved so effective that no matter
where I was doing a fight broadcast, I would carry it along. Muriel
would make the potion for me. Our producer, Ed Wilhelm, dubbed
it "kickapoo juice."

Some interesting experiences followed. Ed Sullivan, columnist for
the *Daily News* in New York, was watching a fight one night, and
the next day asked in his column, "Who was the sportscaster at
ringside sipping the cup that cheers between rounds?"

Doing a fight in Chicago, I was sitting next to Spike McAdam,
one of the judges. Naturally, I used my kickapoo juice. Spike asked
me about it, and I explained how to make it. The next time I did
a fight in the Windy City, Spike came over and said he had mentioned this to Senator Paul Douglas of Illinois. The senator, he told

me, now took the juice with him on his many speaking engagements.

In 1955 we were doing the Rocky Marciano–Don Cockell heavy-weight championship fight at Kezar Stadium in San Francisco. Since Muriel and our sons were accompanying me, she had done the packing and unfortunately had put the kickapoo juice in a compartment with her traveling iron. We arrived at the St. Francis Hotel, on Union Square, in early afternoon, and since the fight was scheduled for 7:00 P.M. (which was the usual 10:00 P.M. New York time) I lay down for a nap. The boys went to visit my aunt Grace, who lived on the third floor of the hotel. Muriel decided to press a dress, and when she opened her traveling case, she was startled to discover that the bottle of kickapoo juice had broken. The contents were all over the iron. Quietly and quickly, she did a clean-up job. Shortly after, however, when she plugged the iron into a socket, there was a burst of smoke and an odor like burning newspapers. There was no fire, the smoke quickly disappeared, and I lay down again. But soon there was a knock on the door, and a housekeeper asked if there was a fire in the room. We assured her there was no problem. Again I tried to resume my nap. But a few minutes later I heard a siren, then more sirens. I thought, "Oh no!" The sounds of sirens were approaching the hotel. Most of the time sirens get louder, reach a peak, and then recede into the distance. I hoped that would happen now. But the sirens reached a peak and *stopped*. I realized what had happened—an alarm had been turned in. Quickly I looked out the window. Union Square was packed with fire engines, chiefs' cars, police vehicles, and, it seemed, a thousand people, all looking up at our hotel. Moments later there were several knocks on the door. Three firemen were outside, in full firefighting regalia, asking what had happened. If you had been one of the firemen, would you have believed my wife's explanation, that her husband was a fight announcer, that he was doing the Marciano fight that night, that she made up this concoction in New York and brought it to San Francisco, etc., etc., etc.? I don't think I would have. They shook their heads in smiling disbelief, saw there was no evidence of a fire, and left. I don't know how much Dr. Kelly's kickapoo juice cost the lovely city of San Francisco that afternoon.

I used kickapoo juice with great success for many years. Recently a friend asked me about its ingredients. When I mentioned the glycerin, he was shocked. "That's a poison! You shouldn't drink that!" Now, in case you're thinking of being an announcer and just filed the "kickapoo juice" recipe away for future reference, I'll pass my friend's warning on to you. I don't know if it has hidden dangers, but I do know it does wonders for a scratchy throat.

Movies and
Golf Tournaments

My so-called movie career spanned
eleven years, from 1970 to 1980, and included six pictures: *Bananas,
The Greatest: The Story of Muhammad Ali, Matilda, Raging Bull, The
Marciano Story,* and *Final Countdown.* It was a most interesting de-
velopment for me, and lent a new kind of excitement to my career
about thirty years after my first big effort, the broadcast of the Joe
Louis–Billy Conn heavyweight championship bout in 1941. With
the exception of *Bananas,* all of these pictures were either about
boxing or had a boxing sequence. As a sports announcer, I was
fortunate that I had a unique style of describing action, which lent
itself to these pictures.

Bananas, the Woody Allen picture, which was shot partially in
San Juan, Puerto Rico, had no boxing in it, but Woody thought I

fit into the proceedings very well. I opened the picture as a reporter on ABC's "Wide World of Sports"—so it wasn't too wide a stretch for me. I was the first one on camera, standing in the center of a plaza in a banana republic, announcing that the president of the republic was shortly to be assassinated and that we had set up our cameras to film the event, complete with videotape replay. If you saw the picture, you will remember some exciting scenes as the president was brought down, Howard Cosell's microphone capturing his dying words.

Besides Woody Allen, I met a very interesting personality who had a vital part in the picture. He was Carlos Montalban, the brother of movie star Ricardo Montalban. Carlos was a TV personality himself as the famous "El Exigente," who was so demanding in those famous coffee commercials. Carlos and I had many conversations between takes of the picture, and I found him very knowledgeable in world affairs.

The next picture I was in was *The Greatest*, a 1976 film that told the story of Muhammad Ali's career up to that time. Ali, of course, was in the picture as himself. Dina Merrill also starred, as did Ernest Borgnine playing the trainer Angelo Dundee. But the real stars were the films of Ali's fights, which were very exciting. Naturally, I did the blow-by-blow descriptions of his fights as they were shown on the screen in the theater we worked in. Believe me, it was hard keeping up with the movements of the champ, he was so fast in those days.

Matilda, made in 1977, was no great box-office hit, but it was the picture I enjoyed being in the most, partly because of its unusual theme and partly because of meeting the swell people connected with it. It was shot in Reno, starred Elliott Gould, Robert Mitchum, Harry Guardino, and Karen Carlson, and was directed by Danny Mann.

Matilda was a famous boxing kangaroo brought to this country to fight for the heavyweight title. He almost won it. The ending was unforgettable and very touching as the thousands in the audience sang and the band played "Waltzing Matilda." I'll never forget those scenes, nor will Muriel, who was an extra. When she accom-

panied me to Reno, she had no intention of being in the picture.
But the first day, a stage manager saw her with me and asked her
if she would like to sit near me. She was glad to, and he put her
right behind me in the first row ringside. They started shooting the
picture and she became part of the scene. Now she was trapped.
She had to sit in the same seat and wear the same dress for seven
days in a row. She had mixed feelings about the whole thing. Besides
the stars, I mentioned, I remember well Al Ruddy, the producer of
the picture, and Jimmy Lennon, the great ring announcer whose
introductions lent such authenticity to *Matilda*'s fight scenes.

Raging Bull, starring Robert De Niro as middleweight boxer
Jake LaMotta, was filmed in 1979. I had an important part in that
one as I described the rise and fall of LaMotta, who won and then
lost the middleweight title. The film, directed by Martin Scorsese,
also featured Cathy Moriarty as Jake's wife, Vicki. I was supposed
to go to Los Angeles and stay there for two weeks for my part in
the picture. But De Niro, who won an Oscar for his acting in the
picture, went all out in every boxing sequence. In one of them he
may have overdone it as he rushed one of his opponents into the
ropes. The fellow got rope burns and was out of action for a spell.
This caused a revision of the shooting schedule, and my wife and
I ended up staying in L.A. for six weeks instead of two. We spent
the weekends visiting friends in Santa Barbara and San Diego, and
it was a very enjoyable time.

I no sooner got home from the making of *Raging Bull* than I
got a call from another Hollywood casting director. They wanted
me as the ringside blow-by-blow announcer for *I'll Get By*, the life
story of former heavyweight champion Rocky Marciano. The stars
were Tony LoBianca as Rocky, Belinda Montgomery as his wife,
and Paul Picerni as the ring announcer. It was a good picture, but
I don't have too many remembrances of it since my part was finished
in two days.

The last part I had in a picture was the shortest and easiest of
them all. It was *Final Countdown*, starring Kirk Douglas. In the film,
an aircraft carrier commanded by Douglas is patrolling the Pacific
a few years ago when the radio man, just twisting the dials, is amazed

to hear 1941 music coming out of his set. He turns the dial and to his amazement he hears a blow-by-blow broadcast of the Louis–Conn fight of 1941. He is startled at this, because it is not a recording but a live description of the earlier time. He is hearing this in the late seventies. He reports to the commander, and it turns out that they are now in a time warp that takes them back to the days just before the Japanese attack on Pearl Harbor. Now they're back in December 1941, and they know what is going to happen. The question is, should they report it and try to reverse history?

As I said, this was an easy assignment for me. When I got the casting call I was in Santa Barbara for a charitable golf tournament sponsored by St. Francis Hospital. It was an easy matter to get to Hollywood, and my description of the fight didn't take more than a few minutes.

Charity golf tournaments became a big part of my life from the 1960s to the 1980s. There weren't as many of them twenty-five years ago, and they've kept getting bigger and better and more and more. I guess the two best known through the years have been the Bob Hope tournament at Palm Springs, and the Bing Crosby at Pebble Beach, California. I never made it to those biggies, but I sure played a lot of others. I wouldn't say that I was a good golfer, but I was adequate, and since these tournaments were all played on a handicap basis, I think I held my own.

Through those years I imagine I have played in about sixty-five tournaments—not sixty-five different tournaments; very often I would play in an event four or five years in a row. In all of these fundraising tournaments, the players pay a fee and play with a pro or a celebrity or both.

My baptism by fire was at the Huntington Crescent Club at Huntington, Long Island. In 1961 the Gillette fights were on ABC, and its sports information director, Bill Brendle, thought it would be good publicity if he got me a spot in this charity event. Through my two years there, I played with the great Tony Lema and with Billy Farrell, the pro son of the former champion Johnny Farrell. The next year I played in a foursome that included all-time ladies' champion Kathy Whitworth and TV personality Jinx Falkenburg. I was now hooked on this type of golf play, and looked forward to it every spring.

One of the most interesting of them all was the one at Sun Valley. Paul Picerni is probably best known as Lee, the assistant to Eliot Ness in the famous TV series "The Untouchables." I met him for the first time on the set of the Marciano picture, and we became good friends. We had a long time to talk between takes of the picture, and the conversation got around to golf. I mentioned to him that I enjoyed playing in charitable events and he said, "Listen, how would you like to play in a great tournament at Sun Valley?"

I said, "Wow, would I."

Sure enough, shortly after I got home, I received an invitation to the Danny Thompson Memorial Tournament at Sun Valley, Idaho, in 1979. The invitation was signed by Harmon Killebrew and Ralph Harding. Killebrew, of course, was the Hall of Fame home-run hitter of the Minnesota Twins of the American League, and Harding was a former congressman. They were partners in a business venture in Boise, Idaho. Danny Thompson, while a star teammate of Killebrew on the Twins, developed leukemia. Killebrew and Harding came up with the idea of running this charity tournament in his memory.

It caught on from the beginning. Killebrew was able to get innumerable sports stars, while Harding brought in the political figures and show business personalities. At that first tournament I met ex-President Ford and Speaker of the House Tip O'Neill, besides Clint Eastwood, who I found was a great boxing fan. Telly Savalas, an old friend from earlier TV days, was there, as were a galaxy of sports and entertainment personalities. My wife and I had the honor of sitting with Danny Thompson's parents at the closing dinner.

Sun Valley, I think, is one of the most beautiful spots in the world, and the golf courses are among the best. The outdoor skating rink, with a diaphanous covering to hold off the sun's rays, was always peopled by skating stars preparing for the 1980 Olympic Games. I played in this tournament five years, and the wonderful times we had will always be a happy memory. Another great tournament was the one that Julie Wintraub ran for the Dunes Hotel in Las Vegas. This one was loaded with celebrities.

I got a tremendous amount of enjoyment from all these charitable pro-am and pro-celebrity golf tournaments. Muriel and I went to many nice places and met some wonderful people. I feel that I will always owe a great deal for the fun I had. But I also feel that I have contributed something worthwhile.

In 1973 and 1974, St. Francis Hospital in Roslyn, Long Island, invited me to play in a golf tournament it ran at the Plandome Country Club on Long Island. This gave me an idea. Prior to this time, all the pro-am events that I had been in or had heard about were all-male affairs. I thought, why not a ladies' pro-am or pro-celebrity golf meeting? Over lunch I broached the idea to Mike Quane from the community relations department of the hospital. He liked the idea and introduced me to Anne McSweeney and Nancy DeMatteis, who did much volunteer work for the hospital. They too thought it was worth trying. It was something that had never to our knowledge been tried—a golf tournament with ladies paying to play with a pro or a celebrity. We knew it wouldn't be easy. From the community relations department we got Ella Cavaliere and Lorraine Henrich to work with us, and Frank Regnante, head of the department, pitched in. With yeomen's efforts by all, and a lot of sweat, we finally came up with a full field of women.

Meanwhile I was working on the celebrities. It was difficult to get them for a late-August meet, which this was, but I finally came up with a representative field. Two baseball Hall of Famers topped the list, Whitey Ford and Ralph Kiner. Kyle Rote, the football Hall of Famer, was there, and so was Jim Bouton, who'd pitched for the Yankees in the World Series. Others participating were Jerry Hart, for the New York Islanders hockey team, Dave Anderson, Pulitzer Prize–winning sports columnist of *The New York Times*, who is a very fine golfer, and Bill Gallo, sports cartoonist of the *Daily News*. From the field of entertainment were bandleader Sammy Kaye and famous announcer Ed Herlihy. Also present was Lynn Burke Hedeman, who won two gold medals for swimming in the 1960 Olympics.

The day of the tournament dawned dark and foreboding. It looked

as though the heavens would open up at any moment. I stood outside
the North Hempstead Country Club as the 9:30 A.M. tee-off time
approached, and wondered if anyone would show up. Who do you
think was the first celeb to show? Another All-American, the great
basketball player Bob Cousy. He drove down from Worcester, Massachusetts, at that hour of the morning. Finally, everyone was there
and play began. The day remained sullen but it never rained and
we got through safely.

Two earlier tournaments that St. Francis had run, with male
participants, had netted about $8,000 apiece, which was considered
pretty good in those days. The ladies' venture netted $18,000 and
everyone was ecstatic. The tournament has grown unbelievably and
now includes men as well as women. From its humble beginnings,
netting less than $20,000, it has become a $300,000 affair played
over three golf courses and with a Gala Fiesta at Wheatley Hills
Club. The St. Francis Tournament is recognized as one of the finest
of its kind.

Finis

For some time I've been wondering how I would bring this story to a close. Now I know.

As I look back to the opening chapter, "Early Times," I'm reminded that sometimes writing it was easy and sometimes difficult, and sometimes I said to myself, "What are you doing this for, at your age? You should be taking it easy." But I put those thoughts out of my mind and I'm glad I didn't quit. I feel that I have accomplished something, and maybe in some small way, with this history as I have known it, I have repaid boxing and all sports for what they have done for me. But I could never repay my mother, my wife, my sons, and the rest of my family for their patience and their confidence in me. Nor could I ever repay the host of friends

I made on the sports beat. And finally I'm indebted to the many, many listeners and viewers who encouraged me along the way. And not to be forgotten are the many who asked me, "Why don't you write a book?" So now I have. A thousand thanks to all of you.

Don Dunphy

Index

277